LEADERSHIP THROUGH STORY

Diverse Voices in Dialogue

Sarah J. Noonan
with
Thomas L. Fish

Rowman & Littlefield Education
Lanham, Maryland • Toronto • Plymouth, UK
2007

Published in the United States of America
by Rowman & Littlefield Education
A Division of Rowman & Littlefield Publishers, Inc.
A wholly owned subsidary of The Rowman & Littlefield Publishing Group,
Inc.
4501 Forbes Boulevard, Suite 200, Lanham, Maryland 20706
www.rowmaneducation.com

Estover Road
Plymouth PL6 7PY
United Kingdom

British Library Cataloguing in Publication Information Available

Library of Congress Cataloging-in-Publication Data

Noonan, Sarah J., 1949–
  Leadership through story : diverse voices in dialogue / Sarah J. Noonan with
Thomas L. Fish.
      p. cm.
  Includes bibliographical references and index.
  ISBN-13: 978-1-57886-642-7 (hardcover : alk. paper)
  ISBN-10: 1-57886-642-1 (hardcover : alk. paper)
  ISBN-13: 978-1-57886-643-4 (pbk. : alk. paper)
  ISBN-10: 1-57886-643-X (pbk. : alk. paper)
  1. Educational leadership. 2. School management and organization. I. Fish,
Thomas L. II. Title.
  LB2831.6.N66 2007
  371.2–dc22
                                                           2007017245

⊗™ The paper used in this publication meets the minimum requirements of
American National Standard for Information Sciences—Permanence of Paper
for Printed Library Materials, ANSI/NISO Z39.48-1992.
Manufactured in the United States of America.

CONTENTS

Acknowledgments   vii

Preface   xi

1   Leadership Through Story: An Invitation to Dialogue   1
Invitation to Dialogue   4
Story—A Catalyst and a Vehicle for Change   6

2   Story Elements: Metaphor, Meaning, Myth, and Memory   10
Metaphors in Leadership   11
Meaning: Making Sense of Life Experience   15
Finding Meaning in Auschwitz   17
Myth: Mysteries and Heroic Tales   19
The Star Trek Myth: To Boldly Go   21
Autobiographical to Social Memory   23
Human and Cultural Worlds   25
The Meaning of Diversity   30

3   Telling Stories, Changing Lives: Turning Points in Dialogue   33
The Purpose and Moral of the Story   34
The Interactive and Transformational Nature of Story   37

Lance Armstrong's Victories   39
Drinking in All This Democracy   42

4 Personal and Cultural Stories: Sources of Authenticity
       in Leadership   47
Elizabeth's Story of Personal Transformation   49
Identity and Authenticity   53

5 The Quest Narrative and the Call to Adventure:
       Defining Moments, Reflections, and Epiphanies   56
Big Grace   60
The Leader of the Band   61
The Life Walk   67
The Gift From a Stranger   75

6 "I Am Another You": Leadership as a Moral Endeavor   77
The Pursuit of Goodness and Loving Actions   79
Forming a Moral Character   82
Jody Williams, Nobel Prize Winner   85
A Moment of Madness: Leading in Dangerous Times   87
John Gardner's Resignation   90
Seeds of Moral Courage and Cultural Change   94
A Special Bond Between Doctor and Patient   96

7 Official Stories, Cover Stories, and Deceptions: Truth, Lies,
       and Everything in Between   98
The Case of the Broken Water Main   101
Cover Stories   105
Jayson Blair at The New York Times   108
Jack Kelley: A Star Reporter Resigns   112

8 Foolish Mistakes, Poor Decisions, and Reckless Conduct:
       Avoiding Traps and Acts of Self-Betrayal   115
Commander Scott Waddle   117
Fallacies and Self-Deceptions   120
Traps and Self-Betrayal   122
Exercise Caution: Hospital Zone   124
"Time Out" and "Knock It Off": Overcoming
       Human Elements   130

The Last Flight to McMurdo Station, Antarctica   133
Failure and Accountability   138

9 It's *Never* Too Late to Learn: The Importance of Learning
    in Leadership   140
Jacques Demers Tells His Secret   143
Learning Organizations   144
Jet "Black and Blue": A Valentine's Day Horror Story   145
Dialogue and Appreciative Inquiry   148

10 Change as a Metaphor for Life: Transitions and Innovations   151
Table Creep   152
Disruptive Events and Lives in Transition   155
Change Myths   158
The Border–Hennepin Union   162
The Accidental Founding of Medtronic, Inc.   164
Rewarding Success and Folly   167

11 Wounds, Illness, Loss, and Suffering: The Therapeutic
    Nature of Story   169
Going Into the Fire   170
Life Changes in an Instant   172
The Stages of Grief and the Nature of Courage   175
The Cedar Strip Canoe   177
The Gift of a Loving Response   179
Johanna's Story: The Kindness and Terror of Strangers   181
Fighting Against Loss   184
Baby, Baby, We Are Going to War   187
Remembrance   190
Sites of Mourning and Memory   192

12 Stories of Moral Courage: Seeing Injustice, Hearing the
    Call, Taking Action   195
The Story of John Howard Griffin   196
The Psychology of Hate   201
Women Working in America   204
Katrina Stories   205
The Matthew Shepard Story   209
Unpopular Causes and Dangerous Stands   211

Protest at the Lake Street Bridge   214
Nelson Mandela   218

13   Wolf and Wolf's Brother Speak: Listening to Diverse Voices   221
     Groupthink, Mental Traps, and Avoidance Strategies   226
     José Finds His Voice   228
     Becoming a Voice for Others: The Silent Agreement   230
     Dialogue Failure and Breakdowns   235

14   Cultural Identity and Survivance: The Power and Gift
        of Cultural Story   237
     Survivance   238
     Seeing Humanity in the Stranger   241
     Fleeing Ethiopia: Gorse's Story   245
     An African Tale   250

References   253

Index   267

About the Authors   281

ACKNOWLEDGMENTS

We gratefully acknowledge the contributions of the storytellers who appear in the pages of this book. We made a conscious decision to tell the stories of ordinary people as well as the dramatic and larger-than-life stories of famous people to illustrate the many different kinds of stories that have the power to change us. Many people, particularly our students at the University of St. Thomas in Minneapolis, Minnesota, generously contributed personal stories, often describing significant and life-changing moments that caused deep personal change. Colleagues, friends, and family members shared their stories, sometimes reluctantly and at other times with pleasure. Thanks to all who offered the gift of your story and trusted us to get it right.

We often found stories in newspapers, books, and online digital sources to illustrate many different aspects of leadership. Unless a contributor requested confidentiality, we identified the contributor or provided an appropriate citation from copyrighted material throughout the book.

The book project grew from our professional collaboration and personal friendship. As professors of leadership at the University of St. Thomas, we teach a doctoral class together, "Leadership Narratives Seminar," and we used what we learned from teaching and our interaction with students to begin this book about leadership and story. We offer thanks to Dr. Robert Brown, Professor Emeritus at the University of St. Thomas, who encouraged us to submit a proposal, and to Thomas Koerner, vice president and editorial director of Rowman & Littlefield Education, who reviewed and accepted the proposal for publication.

We wish to acknowledge and celebrate our collaboration and its unique expression of our individual and shared knowledge and creativity. Sarah Noonan served as the primary author and researcher of the book, providing the overall vision, structure, and manuscript for publication. Thomas Fish contributed to the book as an associate author by locating and analyzing stories and collaborating in the discussion of leadership theory throughout the text.

We really appreciated the work of Bonnie Jungels, a doctoral student and graduate assistant, who edited the entire manuscript through several successive drafts. Sister Clara Teul also served as a graduate assistant during the early phases of our research, locating cultural stories and folktales for our consideration. Thanks for your help and enthusiasm. We also thank our colleagues at the University of St. Thomas, including the members of the Leadership, Policy, and Administration Department, who offered encouragement and support.

Finally, we wish to express our individual thanks to family, friends, and colleagues.

Thomas Fish thanks his children, Scott, Heidi, Lindsey, and Kellen, who give his life meaning and also serve as the source of his greatest stories. Heartfelt thanks go to Deborah Nicholas for her love and encouragement throughout the entire process. Special thanks go to Dr. Donald Weaver, Professor Emeritus, Western Michigan University, who awakened my interest in leadership thirty-five years ago and still serves as a wonderful mentor and storyteller.

Sarah Noonan thanks Rob Hawkinson for his love, patience, support, and editorial assistance. He did it the old-fashioned way, using his considerable intelligence and a sharp red pencil to improve the manuscript. Mary Jo Carlson, who listened to my stories and added a few of her own during our thirty years of morning talks on the telephone, deserves my appreciation. Thanks to the members of my family, Jessica and son-in-law Lenny, Libby, and Johanna, who fill my life with their stories. My mother, Mary Noonan, deserves my thanks as well. She often helped me keep my head above water and encouraged me throughout my entire professional career. Thanks go to the members of my new family, the Hawkinsons, for their stories and willingness to let me talk nonstop during family visits.

I belong to a family of storytellers. We love a good story. Although we all tell stories, my sister Merijean Stensby earns the top prize for storytelling because she can ring a laugh out of even the most taciturn member of our family. She understands the funny thing about telling a humorous story— if you don't do it right, it can make people cry. We rarely do. I acknowledge the family legacy and pass it on to the readers of this book.

PREFACE

Stories, ancient as life itself and deeply embedded within family and cultural traditions, transmit knowledge and shared meaning, linking people together in a human chain of history and memory. Drawing from human experience, cultural knowledge, traditions, beliefs, values, and history, leaders and members use story to facilitate the work of leadership within diverse communities.

Creating meaning together, members form relationships and expand their collective knowledge through the exchange of cultural stories in dialogue. In dialogue leaders and members affirm identities, gain multiple perspectives, and experience social unity not by insisting on sameness in thought and action, but rather by appreciating differences in people and possible approaches to leadership. Turning points in dialogue—places where we are influenced and changed by others—inspire our moral imagination as well as commitment to finding a different way to be together. In this way dialogue serves as a foundation for personal and social change as well as cultural survivance (the struggle of marginalized people to preserve their cultural identities and traditions) in human communities.

Story, shaped by the metaphors in use, interpreted through an analysis of its meaning, passed on as myth, and committed to social memory as a result of the important purposes served, connects our past and present experience to future action. Revealing underlying assumptions, values, and beliefs, cultural stories influence the way we know and experience the world. To support participation in leadership within diverse communities, leaders use stories to help people locate and experience their individual and cultural identities, articulate life purposes, and realize the rights and obligations of membership. Serving as a bridge to connect people and engage them in meaning-making activities through shared experience and culture, story inspires us to act.

As an intentional act of leadership, leaders select and tell stories to realize the possibilities for future action. Communicating a point of view, leaders promote the exchange of stories to encourage self-discovery and authorship as well as influence people to take concerted action to achieve worthy goals. Critical to individual and cultural survival, the exchange of stories helps leaders and members acquire and share knowledge as well as transmit individual and collective history and wisdom to the next generation.

Many stories offer lessons and strategies for leadership. To utilize stories to their fullest, leaders must be aware of how story helps people identify the purpose of their individual or collective leadership. When shared with others or examined as a self-story, identity, empowerment, wounding, and/or transformational stories help us order life experience, interpret meaning, and discover future purposes and goals. Leaders and members tell stories to highlight the various aspects of leadership contained within the story, such as experiencing change, listening to others, or promoting social justice.

For example, in chapter 13, "Wolf and Wolf's Brother Speak: Listening to Diverse Voices," a Native American story illustrates how refusing to hear the voice of Wolf and Wolf's brother threatens the tribe. A flawed decision-making process endangers their survival and provides an important leadership lesson. Effective leaders listen to diverse voices, establish participatory and inclusive groups, avoid mental traps, and support the listening process. Leadership and story merge in this process.

In chapter 9, "It's *Never* Too Late to Learn: The Importance of Learning in Leadership," several stories about the painful and often hidden costs of illiteracy illustrate what happens when individuals or organizations fail to learn. A discussion of various types of literacies follows, including theories related to individual and organizational learning. Weaving in and out of story and leadership theory, the connection between the two occurs as a result of an integrated discussion of leadership and story throughout the book.

Each chapter features one or more themes related to leadership such as learning, listening, justice, or change and includes a discussion of related leadership theory as well as stories to illustrate key concepts. These themes relate to general aspects of leadership, often incorporating several related themes. It's difficult to imagine how leaders might preserve culture without forming relationships or adapt to change without listening to others. A rich spectrum of purposes and expressions of leadership reveal its complexity and connection to community.

Leadership Through Story: Diverse Voices in Dialogue offers a way to see the connection between leadership and cultural stories as well as to examine and experience the way story serves leaders and leadership. For example, how might a story about change help people adjust to the chaotic experiences associated with change? The interactive and transformational aspects of story show how telling stories changes lives.

Several assumptions guide the approach to leadership throughout the book. Emphasizing culturally sensitive and morally responsible leadership, stories from diverse populations with alternative viewpoints reveal both the moral and cultural dimensions of democratic leadership. Using story to affirm diversity, establish trust in interpersonal relationships, and create belonging within communities, particularly where differences divide rather than draw us together, democratic leaders engage us in story to accomplish moral action.

Viewing leadership as a moral endeavor, valuing people; preserving human rights and dignity; and exercising responsible stewardship of human, capital, and natural resources appear as important themes throughout the book. Leadership as both an individual and collective activity engages leaders and members in the exchange of personal, community, and global stories to support leadership within their families, organizations, communities, and the transglobal world.

Story serves as a tool, building material, and foundation for community building. "The members of a good community deal with one another humanely, respect individual differences and value the integrity of each person. . . . There is a sense of belonging and identity, a spirit of mutual responsibility" (Gardner, 2003, p. 184). Good communities serve as hosts for engaging people in democratic leadership.

A world famous storyteller, Garrison Keillor, describes the culture of his hometown, St. Paul, Minnesota, illustrating the power of story and possibility of dialogue with a perfect stranger:

> You could be waiting for the Grand Avenue bus with a man you've seen around the neighborhood over the years, at the dry cleaners and Kowalski's and Tom the Tailor's and La Cucaracha and ask him how he's doing and he'll tell you about the death of his father the night before and you will listen to his spontaneous monologue and ease his loneliness a little. An utterly common occurrence in a society that isn't hung up on social status—people turning to each other and dishing up a story of astonishing frankness and intimacy. (2004, p. 6)

In Keillor's story Midwestern culture serves as a metaphor for the loving embrace of community. The authors live in Minnesota, where an appreciation for honest work and community participation produces genuine people with an aversion for artifice and a passionate love of company and dialogue.

By candle or firelight, we read and listen to stories to learn about each other, reaching across boundaries and creating openings for others to enter into our lives. A central thesis of the book—that stories exchanged with others have the possibility of producing the changes we seek within us—offers a reason to turn the page and begin exploring how story may help one continue one's transformation as a leader and member of many communities.

Take a chair by the fire, rest awhile, experience the power of story, and reflect on its meaning. Call others to the circle, engage in dialogue, and discover how story serves as a vehicle and catalyst for leaders and members to experience and authentically collaborate in democratic leadership. Your journey begins now.

1

LEADERSHIP THROUGH STORY: AN INVITATION TO DIALOGUE

It has been said that all societies need drummers, warriors and sto-rytellers. Drummers unite people behind a cause. Warriors fight for the cause. Storytellers interpret the cause and create history.

—Daft & Lengel, 1998, p. 144

The Ute Indians selected their tribal leaders based on their ability to share their collective values and decisions with the outside world (Daft & Lengel, 1998). During meetings, members talked for long hours, listening, speaking, and exchanging stories. Collective views emerged after stories were shared and interpreted, revealing important knowledge about tribal identity, values, and decisions. The exchange of stories helped them find wisdom, preserve their communities, and develop new strategies to meet the immediate challenges in their environment. Holding on to sacred cultural values and traditions as well as identifying ways to survive in the present environment, the Ute Indians storytellers used story "to interpret the cause and create history" (Daft & Lengel, 1998, p. 144). Storytelling, a universal practice often associated with cultural preservation and survival, engages people in sharing their culture and ways of adapting to their environment in human communities.

and frames our experi-
d survive. "Some people
insist that organizations
). Learned, transmitted,
neet our physical needs,
ty and also experience a
ommunities (Samovar &
sess a deep and intimate
ltural stories, which not
fluence us as we are be-

comfort, reassurance, di-
n & Deal, 2003, p. 257).

Like breathing, culture is automatic, vital to survival, and in constant
motion, fueled by exchanges of people, technologies, and cultural adaptations. Culture resides in human and cultural worlds, continuously
changing due to the constant interactions between and among people
and environments. Unlike the sterile environment of a scientific laboratory, in which control of influential variables occurs, cultural encounters
and clashes, adaptations, and innovations take place in a dynamic environment.

We interpret our own experience as well as the experiences of others
through story, discovering our mutuality and humanity in the process.
Stories convey what nothing else can: who we are, what we know, how
we feel, the way change affects us, and our thoughts about what we
should do next. Emphasizing the intimate and critical connection between leadership and story, leaders and members (followers) share stories to accomplish many aspects of leadership. *The mutual exchange of
stories and the meaning created from this exchange promote the changes
we seek within and among us.* No matter what the leadership purpose—
managing change, achieving goals, influencing others, building relationships, or promoting the greater good—stories help us accomplish leadership.

A story about managing change alerts us to the challenges associated
with it. As a kind of preparation for the experience of change, the si-
multaneous act of listening and interacting with the storyteller and the
content of the story changes perspectives, leading to a clearer under-

standing of the current reality and the adoption of a new viewpoint. During the process of receiving, interpreting, and reacting to the story, the exchange of meaning causes the consideration of new possibilities. Reflecting on experience and using knowledge to enlighten us, we retrieve stories from personal and social memory to make sense of past life and present reality. Leading us to identify purpose, establish goals, and realize future dreams, leadership is accomplished when we share experiences through story. Story's integral relationship to leadership becomes evident once the process is closely inspected.

Leaders tell stories about struggle and accomplishment to motivate members to achieve ambitious goals despite the difficulties encountered. When shared, stories about how others have solved intractable problems, used alternative approaches, or warned against a truly bad decision offer strategies for leadership. Shedding light on the process and the effort needed to achieve a goal, stories help us embark on a tough course, sustain efforts during the process, and assess the results. Looking back on the results, stories help to interpret the experience and mark the changes that have occurred. Stories explain not only who we are but also what we are willing to do. Our unique capacities, enduring values, and life experiences affect what we bring to leadership and how we participate in it.

Community stories help form social identities and move us from family to community membership, preparing us to participate in leadership beyond our extended family system as members of communities. Story serves as a foundation, building material, and a tool for community building. Because leadership takes place in community, an understanding of "good communities" provides a framework for locating how stories serve the actions of leaders seeking to support participatory, democratic communities. Gardner offers the following criteria:

Good community

The members of a good community deal with one another humanely, respect individual differences and value the integrity of each person. A good community fosters an atmosphere of cooperation and connectedness. There is recognition and thanks for hard work, and awareness by the members that they need one another. There is a sense of belonging and identity, a spirit of mutual responsibility. (2003, p. 184)

Stories that support community perform four important functions: "(1) honoring diversity, (2) holding [managing] conflict, (3) engaging in dialogue, and (4) speaking for self and deep listening [claiming power, authenticity, speaking truths without judging others]" (Moxley, 2000, p. 196). Leaders value caring, trust, and teamwork to support participation in community (Gardner, 2003):

> [The] first necessary step is to give all subgroups and individuals reason to believe that they are fully accepted. . . . Another step—equally crucial— is to institutionalize arrangements for dispute resolution. . . . The third step is based on shared tasks. . . . Finally, a healthy community creates a considerable variety of bonding experience. (pp. 184–85)

Cultural stories contain central messages about identity and appropriate adaptations to the environment, establishing bonds through their exchange. They also provide answers to life's central questions about the nature and meaning of existence; the origins of core beliefs; and the importance of cultural practices, rituals, and traditions.

Kegan describes the two greatest yearnings in human experience: (1) "the yearning to be independent or autonomous, to experience one's distinctness, the self-chosenness of one's direction, one's individual integrity" and (2) " the yearning to be included, to be part of, close to, joined with, to be held, admitted, accompanied" (1982, p. 107). These yearnings reveal the tensions of individual expression and social unity. We need both, although the temporary sacrifice of one or the other goal may be necessary.

Though not the same as individual stories, cultural stories coexist within us, sometimes in harmony while at other times in conflict with the dominant story. Tensions often exist between individual, family, or ethnic cultures and the cultural values and traditions found within the larger community. Many different cultural stories forge bonds and reduce barriers between and among cultural groups and social identities.

INVITATION TO DIALOGUE

Leaders invite diverse voices to dialogue, gaining multiple perspectives and inviting collective action in the world through the power of story:

Dialogue is based on the premise that there is meaning outside any particular individual, and that this meaning is accessible if, for example, partners in the activity of leadership suspend their assumptions and "think together." In dialogue, individuals don't come together with objective truth in hand, they gather with a commitment to search for another truth or a new truth not already known or obvious. (Moxley 2000, p. 163)

Relationships form the central aspects of dialogue: "[I]t is not something we *do* or *use*; it is a relation we *enter into*" (Burbules, 1993, p. xii). The "dialogical relation with others involves forming emotional bonds, such as respect, trust, and concern; as well as the expression of character traits or virtues such as patience, the ability to listen, a tolerance for disagreement, and so on" (p. xii). Listening to diverse voices and incorporating *cultural* stories support dialogical relationships.

All stories are cultural stories because they require cultural knowledge to interpret them. If we can't access the story because we lack cultural knowledge or aren't included in the meaning-making process, we are unable to participate. If we're not part of the story or others fail to hear our story, we are simply unwilling to participate in leadership. Both conditions limit the opportunities for leadership within diverse communities.

While some stories serve us well, others exclude or limit us by leaving us out of the story, making us invisible. The social costs of invisibility, paid by all in the form of cultural clashes, conflict, and the loss of valuable contributions by all members, cannot be overestimated. Democratic, culturally sensitive leaders promote the exchange of cultural stories to ensure the widest possible participation in the process. A more inclusive, democratic, and collaborative form of leadership develops in communities in which the mutual exchange of cultural stories occurs.

Cultural stories create a secure holding environment, establishing boundaries and structure to help us live with others in communities. Recognizing the importance of traditional stories to transmit important cultural knowledge and preserve communities, cultural leaders as storytellers also value and invite the discussion and interpretation of present experience as an evolving story, helping members to successfully adapt and change. Using story to examine underlying assumptions and biases, express and examine conflicts, and identify core values, leaders engage members in discovering viable solutions and taking action through the exchange of stories.

STORY—A CATALYST AND A VEHICLE FOR CHANGE

Here's the BIG idea: *A powerful story, when shared with others, serves as both a catalyst and a vehicle to accomplish the purpose or life lesson embedded within the story.*

Stories stressing the importance of achieving goals, being compassionate, carrying through with efforts to bring about change, and promoting social justice excite and inspire action. Recognizing the worthiness of the goal fuels desire but does not always reveal a strategy for accomplishing the goal. Stories about how others accomplished goals in similar circumstances or in related fields stir imagination and open possibilities for action. In circular fashion, leaders use story to clarify the purpose and goals of leadership, inspire commitment from members, and examine the possibilities for taking action. Engaging in sense-making and problem-solving activities, leaders and members use stories to access the collective intelligence and imagination of the group.

People develop ownership of goals when they agree on their worthiness and see possibilities to accomplish them using the available resources in their environment. To accomplish a "big, hairy, audacious goal" (BHAG) (Collins, 2003, p. 3), leaders often tell "gladiator" tales to gain ownership of the goals. Through stories, leaders describe how others have surmounted the odds despite the barriers, to encourage participation. Famous "industry" stories illustrate how a variety of approaches helped others achieve worthy goals.

Collins's *Good to Great: Why Some Companies Make the Leap . . . And Others Don't* (2001a) offers many examples of success stories, which not only illustrate wonderful accomplishments but also describe the specific strategies and approaches used to achieve goals. The book may be successful in part because it galvanizes people to action through inspirational stories and also offers specific strategies to potentially "replicate" winning strategies employed by top firms. Examining the practices of the most consistently successful companies in the United States over a fifteen-year period, Collins introduces leaders and their corporate success through engaging stories.

Each story features a "defining moment": (1) company fortunes fall on hard times, (2) a pivotal decision made by a courageous chief executive officer (CEO) causes a dramatic change in direction, and (3) leaders adopt winning strategies and produce spectacular results. Story moves people to action (as catalysts) and also helps them examine possible approaches (as vehicles) to accomplishing the work.

Many winning stories shared in Collins's book describe how the personal qualities or humble wisdom of the CEO caused a shift in thinking, leading to dramatic change. For example, the CEO of Kimberly-Clark, Darwin Smith, made a potentially dangerous decision to sell the paper mills owned by the company, including the original mill located in the same town as its headquarters.

Smith made the decision to change the direction of the company from a paper production company to a consumer products marketing company, a bold and risky move. Smith believed this move offered the greatest potential for future growth. During this same period Smith was diagnosed with cancer. Although doctors predicted he had less than a year to live, he continued to work during his treatment and informed the board "that he was not dead yet and had no plans to die anytime soon" (Collins, 2001a, p. 18). Smith recommended the change in corporate strategy while receiving radiation and battling cancer.

Overwhelmed by fatigue during this tumultuous period, Smith later shared a story about his decision to sell the mills, relating it to battling a deadly illness:

> Coming home from work during this particularly difficult period, a wearied Smith said to his wife, "It's really tough. But if you have a cancer in your arm, then you've got to have the guts to cut off your arm." (Collins, 2001b, p. 6)

Smith survived another twenty-five years, beating cancer and becoming a living legend and corporate symbol of risk taking, perseverance, and courage. Despite his accomplishments, Smith refused to boast and summed up this tenure as CEO by saying, "I never stopped trying to become qualified for the job" (p. 6). Like *The Little Engine That Could* (Piper, 1976), Kimberly-Clark went up against industry giants like Scott Paper and eventually acquired the company, boldly selling the mills, a mediocre business according to Smith, to compete and "win," while facing a formidable challenge (Collins, 2001a). Smith's qualities, humble wisdom, and decisive action inspired others.

Smith established credibility through his personal character and qualities as well as through the corporate track record of success. The story also contains winning strategies, implying that if an "ordinary" person like Smith can do it, we can too by using similar approaches. Emphasizing the importance of continuously exploring alternative approaches, Smith's story encourages others to pursue excellence, serving as both a catalyst and a vehicle for change. The story endures beyond the company because of its usefulness in present-day circumstances. Collins uses industry comparisons to prove his case, eliminating other factors such as a unique product or unusual market conditions. He identifies leadership and the application of winning strategies as key factors in the success of great companies.

Empowerment stories encourage people to grab the brass ring despite the views and negative reactions of others. As a motivational tool, stories sell us on ourselves, encouraging us to see the potential within us and accomplish more, while maintaining balance and perspective in our lives. Many themes in Smith's personal and Kimberly-Clark's corporate story relate to the purposes and goals of leadership, including making changes, exhibiting courage, overcoming obstacles, and thinking futuristically. Each theme embedded in the story contains a "moral" or lesson.

Memorable stories containing important narrative themes have the possibility of producing the effects described in the stories themselves. To utilize stories to their fullest, leaders need to be aware of how the exchange of powerful stories, containing a moral or purpose, helps members to discover identity, become empowered, accomplish transformation, and recover from wounds (to name a few). An awareness of how to compose, tell, and share stories can assist leaders and members in accomplishing the work of leadership through the exchange of stories—an inherently collaborative process.

Gardner (2004) describes the challenges of drawing people into the story as an aspect of leadership. "Short of walking nude through Trafalgar Square or streaking around the Washington monument," he asked, "[H]ow can one gain and hold the attention of a diverse audience?" (p. 82). His answer is simple: create "a compelling story, embodying that story in one's own life, and present[ing] the story in many different formats so that it can eventually topple the counterstories in one's culture" (p. 82).

Deconstructing Gardner's answer, several important factors regarding leadership and story emerge. Leaders tell "compelling stories" to draw members into the story, inviting their participation. Storytellers must "embody" or serve as examples of the story's content. Immoral people cannot tell moral stories and expect to be believed. Leaders present stories in "many different formats" to include and influence the widest possible audience. Telling stories that incorporate the diversity of the audience and their life experiences, leaders compose many "different stories" with the same underlying theme or moral. Finally, leaders "topple the counterstories" to overcome barriers associated with rigid adherence to cultural traditions and values. Presenting, comparing, and contrasting the "new" story to the story that no longer serves the members, leaders persuade and influence action. The story should serve our "deep desire for autonomy and self-reliance combined with an equally deep conviction that life has no meaning unless shared with others in the context of community" (Bellah, 1985, p. 150).

In the next chapter, an analysis of story elements reveals how metaphor, meaning, myth, and memory influence the way we participate in story and support the goals of leadership.

Handwritten note at top of page:

Leadership is like a
volleyball —
to work well, you need to be inflated
- most of the time in the air
I can
be served,
be blocked or
spiked

2

STORY ELEMENTS: METAPHOR, MEANING, MYTH, AND MEMORY

> We merge our myths with our facts according to our feelings, we tell
> ourselves our own story. . . . All "truths" are only our truths, because
> we bring to the "facts" our feelings, our experiences, our wishes.
> Thus, storytelling—from wherever it comes—forms a layer in the
> foundation of the world; and glinting in it we see the trace elements
> of every tribe on earth.
>
> —Delaney (2005, p. 1)

Story, shaped by metaphors used, interpreted through an analysis of its meaning, passed on as myth, and committed to social memory as a result of the important purposes served, connects our past and present experience to future action. The exchange and interpretation of stories conducted within cultural contexts "frames" situations (Bolman & Deal, 2003), shapes our perspective, and points the way to authentic action.

Composers and tellers of stories understand how context, setting, themes, use of language and symbols, and storyline influence how others access, experience, interpret, and relate to the story.

Story elements such as metaphor, meaning, myth, and memory influence the way stories are composed, retrieved, accessed, and interpreted. Because leaders often express their ideas in metaphor, its importance to how leadership is framed, experienced, and expressed in their stories draws our attention.

METAPHORS IN LEADERSHIP

Metaphors provide structure to a story and allow us to experience something without actually being there. "Metaphors, as *linguistic, image-generating devices,* help us think about what is not yet known or understood" (Noonan & Fish, 2005, p. 53). When a colleague describes his or her first year in business as a rollercoaster ride, we instantly know how to interpret the story. Framed in an "experience" metaphor, the story invites others to share some of their own ups and downs regarding the thrilling or terrifying moments in their careers.

One of our students described her workplace as a "shark tank" and shared her devious strategies for avoiding her colleagues, the predator "fish." As the subtext of the story, metaphors reveal the way we view power and our role in the story. For example, the shark tank traps innocent prey in a hostile environment with a fierce predator, locked in a battle for the prey's life. Only cunning, resourcefulness, and perhaps luck protect the prey from its demise. The opening frame, "my workplace is a shark tank," sets the stage for her story about how she survives in a highly competitive technology firm.

The "experience" metaphor allows others to understand what happened to her even though they have never directly experienced it. If she had described her workplace as a garden or playground, our thoughts would have moved in another direction. The metaphor allows understanding of an experience without being part of it as well as serving as a kind of shorthand in storytelling. A few words captured her life at work.

Metaphors embedded within our stories help to describe and make sense of leadership experiences. Using "role" metaphors, when leaders are described as "kings, captains, commanders, or evangelists" (Noonan & Fish, 2005, p. 56), members become subjects, sailors, soldiers, or servants of God. "The metaphor calls forth a mental schema that defines roles, relationships, norms, values, assumptions, activities, and so forth. Highly influential metaphors are embedded in our personal and cultural memories and widely shared" (p. 56). An understanding of leadership shaped by metaphors influences what we do with and for others as participants in leadership.

The "vocational" metaphor establishes expectations about the rights and responsibilities of the parties. Two vocational metaphors found in the popular press—how to lead like a firefighter (Salka, 2004) or Santa Claus (Harvey, Cottrell, & Lucia, 2003)—illustrate how the metaphor works to guide thinking about leadership. Firefighters follow the smoke, recognizing that the source of the smoke deserves their undivided attention (Salka, 2004, p. xi). The premise reminds leaders to pay attention to what's going on around them. Of course, Santa Claus keeps a list of who is naughty and nice and rewards appropriately. "Make sure they avoid being naughty, help them stay nice and work with them to get even nicer" (Harvey, Cottrell, & Lucia, 2003, p. 63). Portraying employees as children in need of punishment or reward frames the Santa leader's actions in coercive terms, promoting the avoidance of punishment and the promise of external rewards as major considerations in employee performance. In this case the metaphor fails to serve.

While a bit of practical advice might be found in books like these (although some provide just the opposite), many vocational metaphors disappoint because of the limited role and horizons implied by the metaphor. Instead of helping leaders gain perspective and wisdom from empowering metaphorical devices, limited vocational metaphors reduce leadership to a "job" of one sort or another, ignoring the participation of members in leadership along with the various perspectives hidden by the organizing metaphor.

Because communication is a critical ingredient of leadership, expressing ourselves in metaphor allows others to access ideas and assess the way leadership is envisioned. Metaphors build a "collective" consciousness by inviting members to see themselves in the story, carrying out the roles implied by the metaphor through its repeated use. If members are supposed to "get on board" or take up positions as soldiers in battle, both the power of language and the metaphor influence perceptions and actions.

In *The Argument Culture: Moving From Debate to Dialogue*, Tannen (1998) illustrates the power of language and the often insidious nature of metaphor, particularly those metaphors that work against collaboration and peaceful resolution of differences. Discussing her concern about the predominance of military metaphors in everyday talk, Tannen stresses the importance of language and metaphor in public discourse:

> [W]ords matter. When we think we are using language, language is using us. As linguist Dwight Bolinger put it (employing a military metaphor), language is like a loaded gun: It can be fired intentionally, but it can wound or kill just as surely when fired accidentally. The terms in which we talk about something shape the way we think about it—and even what we see. (Tannen, 1998, p. 14)

Describing the argument culture, Tannen examines how aggressive language and metaphors inspire uncivil behavior toward others. The metaphor establishes winners and losers who emerge from battle. Instead of seeing the enemy as a potential ally, combatants hold fixed positions while maintaining rigid boundaries in their viewpoints. The metaphor tells us how to think and what to do.

Stories framed in metaphors serve as a reference point for organizing and understanding their content. The metaphor employed must draw on the resources of listeners. For example, while serving as superintendent of public instruction in Wyoming, Diana Ohman offered the following comment about leadership during an official visit to Jackson, Wyoming. Drawing on the Western theme of fierce independence and the pioneer spirit, Ohman said, "You're either making dust or eating it" (personal communication, 1994). Portraying leadership as decisive and trail blazing, she encouraged innovation from her constituents. Her message was clear: Saddle up and get going before the others get there first. Transporting us to the Wild West, Ohman's statement makes a complete story.

The harsh, competitive environment requires leaders to act decisively and swiftly. Those who fail to successfully compete will be left behind in disgrace. This "cultural" story evokes images of pioneers, trails, the range, trail bosses, and wagon trains—meaningful images in rural, Western culture, but less meaningful in urban environments. In many ways, the metaphor becomes the story because it establishes an orientation, implying something about the characters, actions, or circumstances, causing us to experience "something like it" in the new story:

> Metaphors compress complicated issues into understandable images, influencing our attitudes, evaluations, and actions. A university head who

views the institution as a factory establishes different policies than one who conceives of it as a craft guild or a shopping center. Consultants who see themselves as physicians are likely to differ from those who see themselves as salespeople or rain dancers. (Bolman & Deal, 2003, p. 268)

Metaphors include or exclude others based on who is in the story and what knowledge is required to access its meaning. Cultural metaphors, when widely shared and embedded in personal stories, help others access and meaningfully interpret their use in story. The selection of the organizing metaphor plays a crucial role in story meaning and suitability for the audience.

Those with little interest in professional or collegiate sports rarely appreciate the incorporation of sports metaphors in stories. Lacking knowledge of or even interest in the game, some are inspired by sports stories while others are uninterested because of unfamiliar or unfriendly territory. If someone resents the excessive financial investment in professional sports, why describe a coach who makes several million dollars a year as a hero? On the other hand, a wonderful sports story told to a team during half time to motivate them or perhaps a dramatic story told to booster club members may be quite inspiring.

The same reasoning applies to "war" and "privilege" stories. A battle story falls on deaf ears to a pacifist, and an exotic vacation adventure story offends those who lack the resources to support their family. The point seems obvious, yet examples of this practice abound. "Human interest" or "good Samaritan" stories describe how ordinary people do extraordinary things, inspiring others, particularly during distressing times. Know the audience, including the multiple worldviews and values found among the members. Culturally sensitive leaders compose and share stories incorporating accessible metaphors to encourage meaning-making and participation by the widest possible audience:

As a general rule, when one is addressing a diverse or heterogeneous audience the story must be simple, easy to identify with, emotionally resonant, and evocative of positive experiences. . . . In addition to its conscious appeal, a story must also capture an audience at a deeper, more visceral level. (Gardner, 2004, pp. 82–83)

Explaining life experience to others through story, leaders employ rich metaphors to draw people affectively and cognitively in, influencing how situations are understood and interpreted. Effective leaders guard against the overuse of dominant and limiting metaphors that distract people from considering other interpretations and possibilities. Avoiding the trivializing effect of poorly selected metaphors, leaders inspect their metaphors to see if they serve the goals of collective action and resonate with members. Effective stories invite others to access their "imaginative powers" (Gardner, 2004, p. 83). Metaphors frame experience, encapsulate a complex idea into a simplified form, and stimulate thinking, inviting members to exchange ideas as well as participate in a meaning-making process.

MEANING: MAKING SENSE OF LIFE EXPERIENCE

The meaning-meaning process engages individuals and groups in making sense of life experience to "organize action" (Robinson & Hawpe, 1986, p. 122). Stories trace the path of development, providing a map of life experience and its meaning. As both a process and an ideal (Carlsen, 1988), meaning-making engages us in ordering and interpreting life experience (process) with the goal (ideal) of understanding these events and their effects.

After sequentially arranging the disconnected experiences and happenstance events in life, the reflective person interprets experience and its meaning. The fruits of this reflection help the meaning-maker to compose a coherent life story, bringing others up-to-date on his or her current status. The story proceeds in narrative form, as if the teller says, "Here's what happened to me, this is how I've changed, this is who I am now, and this is what I intend to do now and why."

Becoming more self-aware causes changes in identity and purposes. As a result, personal transformation occurs and serves as a new "reference point for purpose and intent" (Carlsen, 1988, p. 5). New goals emerge or existing ones are affirmed once the effects on identity are known. When new experiences are incorporated into the current version of a life story, the story gets revised and sets off a chain reaction: Lives are ordered and interpreted, meaning (learning) occurs through reflection, identity is reimagined, and purposes and goals extracted from the reflective process fuel the future direction. Meaning-making engages us in the search for a "unifying purpose that justifies the things

[we] they do day in, day out—a goal that like a magnetic field attracts [our] their psychic energy, a goal upon which all lesser goals depend" (Csikszentmihalyi, 1990, p. 218). Having a sense of purpose gives life meaning.

Imagine an alter ego, a second self, who constantly detects and evaluates what's going on moment to moment, making sense of our activities and guiding us in the process. Vital to our success, the alter ego evaluates actions to ensure the accomplishment of goals and locates the changes that have occurred and how they have affected us. Finding meaning, engaging in meaning-making, and making sense of the meaning of our experience relate to the important content and action of our lives. Meaning-making helps us devise a strategic plan for living. "We create narrative descriptions for ourselves and for others about our own past actions, and we develop storied accounts that give sense to the behavior of others" (Polkinghorne, 1988, p. 14).

"[P]eople develop their concept of who they are, and of what they want to achieve in life, according to a sequence of steps" (Csikszentmihalyi, 1990, p. 221). Moving in a progression of survival to actualization and finally integration within the larger society, individuals display a zigzag pattern of accomplishing individual goals and then adopting community roles and goals. As maturing adults, higher levels of development may lead members to become more "other" directed and less self-serving in their interests and actions.

The following stages illustrate the developmental progression. Beginning with individual needs, we act to ensure our "survival, comfort, and pleasure" (Csikszentmihalyi, 1990, p. 221). We then go outward "to embrace the values of a community," usually requiring conformity to the norms and standards of the community (p. 221). Returning to our individual goals, we turn inward through "reflective individualism," finding value in self, developing an "autonomous conscience" seeking "growth, improvement and the actualization of potential" (p. 221). Finally, moving outward again we integrate our goals with other people, adopt universal values, and merge our individual interests with the larger whole (p. 222).

The above progression closely approximates what may happen when members participate in leadership. Meaning-making helps people negotiate the competing interests for time, energy, and resources as well as assess goals in light of "purposes." If the purpose is worthy enough, people may set aside their individual goals, merging their interests with the community goals ahead of the "normal" maturation schedule Csikszentmihalyi describes. This happens more often when group survival is threatened, disrupting their natural progression as a result of the changes in the environment. During these times, existential questions about the meaning of life emerge as a driving force to get people through difficult moments and learn from them.

FINDING MEANING IN AUSCHWITZ

Victor Frankl, a Jewish psychiatrist imprisoned at Auschwitz during WWII, described his search for meaning amid horrifying circumstances. He addressed the following question in a book about his experience: "How was the everyday life in a concentration camp reflected in the mind of the average prisoner?" (Frankl, 1984, p. 17). According to Frankl, the breakdown of the will to live due to severe and threatening circumstances occurred in three periods: "the period following admission; the period when he is well entrenched in camp routine; and the period following his release and liberation" (p. 22). The first period begins with shock, then the "delusion of reprieve" (an unrealistic hope that one will be saved at the last minute); a "striking out of a former life"; thoughts of suicide; the experience of raging emotions including grief, loss, and longing; and making adjustments to an "abnormal life" (pp. 25–35).

During phase two, the prisoners experienced a loss of emotion, no longer averting their eyes from horrid sights, and became desensitized to daily beatings. Apathy, obsessive preoccupation with food and survival, struggle with daily living, and a deepening of spiritual life occurred (Frankl, 1984, pp. 35–47). The significant deprivation of all physical life-giving resources caused prisoners to retreat within themselves for sustenance. They found meaning by focusing on future goals because nothing in their present experience contributed to the will to live.

Frankl pictured himself surviving the concentration camp and lecturing to an audience about his experience, clearly focusing on a future goal. He maintained his will to live by seeing value in his past life and recalling it, discovering his ability to experience love through the recall of his wife's image, and in that love, truth:

> I saw the truth as it is set into song by so many poets, proclaimed as the final wisdom by so many thinkers. The truth—that love is the ultimate and the highest goal to which one man can aspire. Then I grasped the meaning of the greatest secret that human poetry and thought and belief have to impart: *The salvation of man is through love and in love*. I understood how a man who has nothing left in this world may know bliss, be it only for a brief moment, in the contemplation of his beloved. (1984, pp. 48–49)

A rich inner life allowed him to escape his present circumstances, retrieving them from "nostalgic" memory (p. 50).

After Frankl left the concentration camp (phase three), he experienced a period of liberation and adjustment, and eventually reclaimed his humanity. Frankl later developed "Logotherapy," a theory of psychoanalysis, which engages patients in using their life experiences (including tragedies and disappointments) to create meaning and then propel them toward finding fulfillment in their future. Using his experience to heal himself and others, he learned the importance of finding meaning through life purpose:

> [T]he meaning of life differs from man to man, from day to day, and from hour to hour. What matters, therefore, is not the meaning of life in general but rather the specific meaning of a person's life at a given moment. . . . Everyone has his own specific vocation or mission in life to carry out a concrete assignment which demands fulfillment . . . . Ultimately, man should not ask what the meaning of his life is, but rather he must recognize that it is *he* who is asked. In a word, each man is questioned by life; and he can only answer to life by answering for his own life; to life he can only respond by being responsible. (1984, pp. 112–113)

A comparison between a state of meaning and a state of meaninglessness illustrates why the search for meaning is vital. A state of meaningless occurs "when we have nothing to live for: nothing which provides a sense of purpose, dignity or self-respect; nothing which orders the myriad variables of everyday experience in a meaningful whole" (Carlsen, 1988, p. 24).

During the darkest days in Auschwitz, the exercise of finding meaning and relating activities to future goals sustained the survivors. Escaping the "time of meaninglessness comes when we are unable to answer the larger questions of life: 'Who am I? What am I created for? What is it that I can contribute to life?' " (Carlsen, 1988, p. 24). Meaning-making serves as a wellspring for action and, in some cases, offers hope during life's most dire moments. The meaning-making process organized in story form provides answers to questions about life purpose and goals.

While some stories are quite painful to hear, they serve as valuable reminders of how the unimaginable happens. Walter Halloran served as a combat photographer with the U.S. Army during World War II. Halloran entered Buchenwald camp in April 1945 and captured the haunting images of the Holocaust in horrifying and memorable photographs (Kersten, 2007, pp. B1, B3). Describing the impact of this experience, Halloran said, "We were hardened by years of combat, but nothing, nothing prepared us for the brutality—the sights, the sounds, and the smells we found there" (p. B3). Like many who experienced the horror of the Holocaust, Halloran put the experience behind him and didn't share his experiences with others.

> But in recent years, he has reconsidered. His generation is passing on, he says, and the younger generation needs to grasp the inhumanity that man can visit on man. "It happened in Germany and Japan then; it's happening in the Sudan today. It's the real world. I'm not wise enough to explain why." (p. B3)

Halloran recognizes the importance of the Holocaust story despite his inability to figure out exactly what causes this situation to continue. He knows its importance and ends his silence. The most enduring stories are accessed by successive generations, earning a valued place in social memory because of their ability to teach us something about ourselves.

MYTH: MYSTERIES AND HEROIC TALES

"Myths are like the beams in a house: not exposed to outside view, they are the structure which holds the house together so people can live in it"

(May, 1991, p. 15). Stored, retrieved, and shared through oral and written traditions, myths preserve the important human and cultural material needed to interpret events, examine options, and make choices. "Myths, widely told through 'hallowed stories,' transmit important information about cultural values and roles (Kottak & Kozaitis, 2003, p. 2).

According to Campbell (1988), myth serves four functions in human communities. The first function relates to the "dimension of mystery," giving us a way to understand and explain the larger questions of life that are as yet unanswered (p. 31). Myths help us to realize "what the wonder of the universe is and what a wonder you [we] are and experience[ing] awe before this mystery" (p. 31). The next function of myth addresses the need to understand the universe, including its shape and form, based on both scientific and mystical ways of knowing and experiencing it. The last two functions of myth address the social order and the prescribed ways of daily living (Campbell, 1988).

Heroic stories tell us about the right way to do things as well as the roles and responsibilities of members. The vehicle for transmission of myth is story. Myths address "the maturation of the individual, from dependency through adulthood, through maturity, and then to the exit; and then how to relate to this society and how to relate this society to the world of nature and the cosmos" (Campbell, 1988, p. 32).

The Thanksgiving story illustrates how myth is carried out and accomplishes the functions described previously. The Thanksgiving story celebrates cultural diversity and survival through the symbolic consumption of the harvest. Giving thanks for the fruits of cultural collaboration, European settlers and American Indians eat at a common table. The myth promotes social order and peaceful coexistence between American Indians and European settlers through the basic theme of cooperative living. Hard work and cooperation produce a bountiful harvest, enjoyment, and human survival.

This view, not widely shared by Native Americans, runs counter to the experience of American Indians who suffered due to theft of their lands, denial of Indian culture, and deaths resulting from conflict with Europeans. The story endured as a dominant myth because it promoted a favorable view of European settlers and portrayed American Indians as passively compliant with the encroachment on their lands. However, Native Americans have challenged the Thanksgiving myth because it falsely portrays a benevolent and cooperative picture of cultural sharing between American Indians and European settlers. The myth no longer serves as an enduring example of cooperation despite its prominence as a national holiday.

The "thanksgiving" in the Thanksgiving holiday now largely refers to the importance of family and the good life. Elementary children are more likely to see the Thanksgiving story examined more critically, reading about the story from several viewpoints. Tearing apart the Thanksgiving myth, some prefer to promote cooperation in a modern myth, *Star Trek*. In this television series, people cooperate, creatively incorporating their diversity to reduce evil and promote peace in the universe. No shameful legacy interferes with the story as myth.

THE STAR TREK MYTH: TO BOLDLY GO

In contrast, modern-day myths can serve as an "expansion of horizon" (Kottak & Kozaitis, 2003, p. xviii) as revealed in the *Star Trek* television series and films. The *Star Trek* stories stress the importance of teamwork, diversity, adventure, and the "subordination of individual differences within a smoothly functioning multiethnic team" (p. 5). Those on board the *Enterprise* symbolically represent the diversity of the American people and the "unity" of their culture. A close inspection of the "unity" myth would quickly reveal that this view is more likely fiction than fact. However, the myth carries out its intended purpose: to promote the values of some aspects of cultural assimilation, a founding value in a democratic society, while at the same time allowing for individual differences.

> *Star Trek* places in the future what the Thanksgiving story locates in the past—the myth of the assimilationist, incorporating, melting-pot story. The myths says that America is distinctive not just because of its assimilationist, but because the nation is founded on unity in diversity . . . . Thanksgiving and *Star Trek* illustrate the credo that unity through diversity is essential for survival, whether of a harsh winter or of the perils of outer space. (Kottak & Kozaitis, 2003, p. 3)

The highly diverse crew of the *Enterprise* manage their individual differences by participating in a civil and professional culture (society) and living and working together on board the ship. They achieve their mission, "to boldly go," under the command of "American values," represented by Captain Kirk. The crew contributes to the mission's success through teamwork. Kirk's decisions, informed by reason (Dr. Spock) and emotion and conscience (Dr. McCoy) are achieved through a democratic process (Walker, n.d.). While displaying a "command" style of leadership, Kirk leads by purpose as a transformational figure who appreciates the diversity and contributions of the crew.

As a cultural hero and icon, Captain Kirk represents the best of American life, serving as a symbol and embodiment of a new American hero, one who takes charge without overpowering others, seeing the value and beauty in his diverse crew and skillfully including the team in his command. Although the popularity of *Star Trek* may be due to its characters, plot, and imaginative technologies, certainly some of its biggest fans are also enthralled by the myths explored in the series. *Star Trek* envisions a more promising future than the vision offered by contemporary leaders lacking in moral imagination and action.

The myth of a future world absent of evil and guided by global values of love and international cooperation offers plenty of appeal. On a societal and individual level, mythical stories hold people together, freeing them to lead healthy lives and express their creativity (May, 1991). The *Star Trek* myth and its popularity may exist because the story offers hope and also a strategy for leadership, showing us how leaders capitalize on the diversity of the team and achieve the mission. Campbell entices us with a view of an earth that might be seen if we were on board the *Enterprise*, cruising past the moon into the next century:

> When you see the earth from the moon, you don't see any divisions there of nations or states. This might be the symbol, really, for the new mythology to come. That is the country that we are going to be celebrating. And those are the people that we are one with. (1988, p. 32)

Although individual differences are affirmed, the mission (peace, love, adventure, survival) takes precedence over individual differences and goals. A visit to www.startrek.com shows the enduring success of the *Star Trek* story.

To ensure healthy communities, we continuously expand and revise our myths to adapt to the environment. "A myth is a way of making sense in a senseless world. Myths are narrative patterns that give significance to our existence" (May, 1991, p. 15). A world of caution here: When "myths no longer serve their function of making sense of existence, the citizens of our day are left without direction or purpose in life, and people are at a loss to control their anxiety and excessive guilt feeling" (p. 16). Myths, preserved in memory, provide knowledge about our cultural identity and also contain wisdom regarding cultural values and ways to adapt to changing conditions. Each generation reimagines and reinterprets these stories as it adapts to its environment (Kottak & Kozaitis, 2003).

Myths, captured in traditional and futuristic stories, become part of individual and public memory as long as they continue to serve their primary functions: giving us identity based on an evolving cultural story and providing answers regarding future actions. The enduring power of myth comes from its underlying meaning and value to the next generation. May (1991) summarizes its importance to daily existence as well as its spiritual contribution to our lives:

> [I]n the moments when eternity breaks into time, there we find myth. Myth partakes of both dimensions: it is of the earth in our day-to-day experience, and is a reaching beyond our mundane existence. It gives us the capacity to live in the spirit. (p. 297)

Myths incorporated into cultural stories form a connective tissue, linking the memory of the immediate and distant past to future action.

AUTOBIOGRAPHICAL TO SOCIAL MEMORY

The landscape of story ranges from our personal history, retrieved through autobiographical memory (Nelson & Fivush, 2004), to the collective history of our social communities, accessed through social memory (Zerubavel, 2003). Stories stored and retrieved from memory shape our understanding of who we are; what our purpose in life is; what directions, goals, and actions to take; the likely effects of our actions; and finally, what it all means.

"An autobiographical memory is defined here as an explicit memory of an event that occurred in a specific time and place in one's personal past" (Nelson & Fivush, 2004, p. 486). "Personally significant" events filled with "personal meaning emerge[s] from emotions, motivations, and goals that are constructed in interaction with others in the world" (p. 488). Children develop their capacity for "autobiographical memory" when parents talk to them during an experience by explaining what is going on and then later reminisce with them about the experience, helping them form an autobiographical memory (Nelson & Fivush, 2004, p. 486). As a result of social interaction and cognitive development, children first listen to stories about what happened and later participate in the recall of these events.

Parents' talk about events and experiences aids in their recall and meaning, helping individuals

> gain a sense of who they are in relation to others, both locally, within their family and community, and more globally, within their culture. Through the creation of a shared past, we attain a shared perspective on how to interpret and evaluate experience, which leads to a shared moral perspective. In a very real sense, the achievement of an autobiographical memory sets the stage for intergenerational transmission of family and cultural history, which is the bedroom of human culture. (Nelson & Fivush, 2004, p. 506)

The presence of an autobiographical memory allows individuals to participate in their culture as an aspect of their cultural identity. The link begins with family and extends to community. The lack of an autobiographical memory threatens physical and emotional survival. Imagine what might happen if you woke up one morning and found yourself a victim of amnesia, lacking a sense of your identity and a memory of your past life.

Jeff Ingram lost his memory sometime after he left Lacey, Washington, on September 6, 2006, and before he "woke" up in Denver, Colorado, four days later, on September 10. Lost and unaware of his identity, Ingram asked strangers to help him and finally ended up at the Denver Health Medical Center. Ingram, a victim of "dissociative fugue," experienced "a rare type of amnesia that can be triggered by stress" (Associated Press, 2006a, p. 6). The police asked the media for help when they failed to locate Ingram in a database using his fingerprints. Ingram's family and friends recognized him, much to the relief of his fiancée, Penny Hansen.

Ingram, now reunited with his family and future spouse, looks through photo albums in an attempt to restore his memory. Ingram said, "I just keep trying everything, hoping something will click and just open it up [his memory]. In the meantime, he said, 'I go through my intuition because I don't have any memories coming back' " (Associated Press, 2006c, p. 15). He "remains hopeful that the jumbled pieces of his memory will fall into place someday" (p. 14). Lacking a memory, Ingram's resources for daily living are his native intelligence, instincts, and limited knowledge of his previous personal life. This limits what he can do; he's starting over in survival mode with only a cultural framework to guide his actions. His recall of language and routines helps him survive, but it tells him little about his life purpose and future direction. His personal story matters along with his access to the cultural story.

Comparing amnesia to other memory disorders, Alzheimer's victims suffer from declining memory, going from confusion to a complete inability to function. Problems with memory challenge stroke victims, who may suffer from a total loss of one or more functions, making them vulnerable to dangers in the environment due to their inability to remember, for example, how to use appliances or speak. Memory protects us from the dangers in our environment as well as serves as the wellspring from which we determine our future goals. When Ingram experienced amnesia, he lacked a sense of his life story, making it difficult for him to know himself and his life purpose, reducing him to survival mode. We instinctively understand the importance of personal and cultural memory because, like Ingram, we'd be lost without it. Because we have a past, stored in memory and easily retrieved, we possess the knowledge needed to move into the future.

HUMAN AND CULTURAL WORLDS

Leadership takes place in human and cultural worlds. Those who ignore this fact often miscalculate the human influence on leadership, instead offering mechanized views and solutions to obvious human dilemmas.

An amusing film, *Kitchen Stories* (Hamer, Bergmark, & Hamer, 2003), illustrates the folly of ignoring the human element in scientific work. A film reviewer summarizes the plot:

> Set in the late 1940s, the plot is propelled by the nearly oppressive presence of the pseudo-scientific Home Research Institute, a post-war branch of Swedish inspiration designed to study the household habits of the common Scandinavian housewife. Boasting to have revolutionized kitchen space so that the average Nordic hausfrau need no longer walk to the Congo in a year of cooking (just to northern Italy), the Institute has turned its eye to studying the kitchen behaviors of the Norwegian bachelor. (Borey, n.d., p. 2)

Bjørvik, an aging Norwegian bachelor farmer, participates in a scientific experiment designed to study efficient home management techniques in the 1950s. The scientific experiment takes place in Bjørvik's kitchen. Nilsson, a Swedish government observer, enters Bjørvik's home each day, proceeds to the kitchen, and climbs up the stairs to a lifeguard-like platform installed in the corner of the room. Nilsson sits down, opens his notebook, and begins his daily observation of Bjørvik. Avoiding eye contact and conversation, Nilsson abides by strict rules forbidding human contact, recording every one of Bjørvik's kitchen activities in his notebook.

Initially Bjørvik avoids the kitchen, uncomfortable with the observer's presence and lack of interaction. His behavior changes from avoidance to passive aggression. "Nilsson initially finds himself the victim of a dozen instances of passive defiance when the older Isak [Bjørvik] attempts to obstruct his researcher gaze by barring entrance into the house, by turning off the lights, and by stringing laundry across his visual pathway. He even goes so far as to drill a hole into the floor so that he can spy on the researcher below" (Borey, n.d., p. 4).

Days go by and finally, overcome by boredom, each man upsets the scientific process in his own way. Inspired mischief causes Bjørvik to peer through a hole in the ceiling right above Nilsson's head to observe his observer. Reading Nilsson's notes, Bjørvik amuses himself by deliberately changing his routines. Nilsson excitedly records the changes, believing he is making real scientific progress. The subject now controls the experiment.

One day Nilsson runs out of cigarettes and Bjørvik, noticing his distress, offers him one from his pack. Reluctantly accepting the cigarette from his subject, Nilsson crosses the invisible boundary between subject and observer. They smoke a cigarette together. Nilsson learns that he must come down from his chair to learn about Bjørvik.

Their communication changes from infrequent eye contact to head nods and finally to talk. Although Nilsson lives in constant fear of discovery by his supervisor for violating the scientific procedures prescribed by the study, he risks it, recognizing the ridiculousness of his situation. The men share stories, drink together, celebrate a birthday, and eventually become friends, achieving a higher level of "knowing" than what might be accomplished through mere observation alone.

Two men, one Swedish and the other Norwegian, one a farmer and the other a researcher, and both lonely bachelors living in the 1950s, bring their cultural selves and worlds into the kitchen of Bjørvik's home. These factors change the activity and goals of the project. *Kitchen Stories* illustrates the futility of ignoring the powerful human element in our work lives. Humanity must be accounted for at every turn. Real people interact in their human and social environments, disturbing the "scientific" view of the universe that is devoid of identity, culture, and experience. The change begins with the mutual recognition of the other's identity and the exchange of stories.

The experience of the men in *Kitchen Stories* mirrors our own as we engage in the human activity of leadership. Participating in leadership as cultural beings, we bring ourselves, along with our individual and collective stories and cultures, to leadership. Stories help us interpret the meaning of life, not in the abstract, but in the lived experience. We gain meaning from both the subjective analysis of the lived experience as well as the examination of what's going on in our historical and cultural worlds that intersect with it.

How can we understand *Kitchen Stories* without locating it in its social and cultural context? The main characters live in the 1950s during a time when objectivity and scientific analysis were highly prized and the human element ignored. Women, serving as "household engineers," would surely benefit from the advice of efficient males to streamline their work. Offering women an enlightened way to reduce the repetitive nature of household work, the goal of the experiment was to apply "male" strategies to female work. This frame works in a 1950s setting but not today, for obvious reasons.

We examine a life both in its subjective experience as well as the "objective" reality that exists outside our individual lives, influencing our lives and shaping the interpretation of our experience. Both the content of our subjective experience and the objective examination within the environment cause us to reflect on the particular experience and the general social conditions—a kind of weaving in and out to find meaning in the personal experience as well as to assess the impact of our experience related to the social and cultural world. Because it is a human activity, the leadership process is "more tribal than scientific, more a weaving of relationships than an amassing of information" (DePree, 1989, p. 3). Leadership takes place in social and cultural worlds, filled with exchanges of story.

Culture changes moment to moment, often creating dramatically different experiences for each new generation and sometimes causing a schism between generations. Culture, a gift passed on through "living bond of generations" (Halbwachs, 1950/1980, p. 63), leaves an imprint:

> Our grandparents leave their stamp on our parents. We were not aware of it in the past because we were much more sensitive then to what distinguished generations. Our parents marched in front of us and guided us into the future. The moment comes when they stop and we pass them by. Then we must turn back to see them, and now they seem in the grip of the past and woven into the shadows of bygone times. (p. 67)

Passing through various life stages, sharp distinctions between two generations cause us to notice the tug of cultural change, alienating us from our culture:

> A time will come when I will understand, as I have sometimes uneasily, that new generations have pushed ahead of my own, that society whose aspirations and customers are quite foreign to me has taken the place of the one to which I was most intimately attached. (p. 68)

The flow of culture from one generation to the next runs in a continuous stream of history, moving with us and then passing us by. Many cultures pass on stories about how to live in the form of proverbs, or *dichos* in Spanish. Passing on tried and true advice, *dichos* offer practical wisdom as well as warn of trouble. Consider the wisdom of the following expressions in Spanish and English:

El trabajo es virtud. Work is a virtue.
La diligencia es madre de la industria. Diligence is the mother of industry.
Pereza, llave de probreza. Laziness: key to poverty.
Los premios del trabajo justo son honra, provecho y gusto. Rewards for honest labor are honor, good health, and joy.
Arrear que vienen arreando. Keep things moving.
Sólo Dios sabe para quién trabajas. Only God knows for whom you work.
(Nava, 2000, p. 77)

These sayings show cultural attitudes toward work and its reward. However, the following sayings advise members to be on guard and maintain independence and self-respect:

En el modo de cortar el queso se conoce al que es tendero. How the cheese is sliced tells you who the shopkeeper is.
Tejado de un rato, labor parap todo el ano. A temporary roof means year-round work.
Al que le ven caballo, le ofrecen silla. Whoever looks like a horse will be offered a saddle.
(Nava, 2000, p. 78)

The wisdom in this last proverb inspires people in all cultures: "*Amor primero, amor postrero.* Love, first and last" (Nava, 2000, p. 293).

Cultural knowledge, constructed in social communities and communicated through story, influences the way we understand the past and frame the future. Cultural "presuppositions" (assumptions about others) and "self-perceptions" (identity stories), passed on from one generation to the next, influence our thoughts and actions (Jensen, 2006, p. 4).

Helping us locate our cultural particularities as well as our commonalities, leaders invite us to see ourselves in stories both as culturally complex individuals holding membership in diverse social groups and as members of the human tribe. Without the exchange of story, our very survival is at stake. Like a home, culture gives us a place to live while we develop and evolve. We hold many cultural identities (some in the near or distant past). The idea of only possessing one identity ignores who we are: increasingly diverse people with multiple identities.

THE MEANING OF DIVERSITY

Because we lack words or traditions to manage the accelerated complexity of our identities and status as a nation of immigrants, the term "diversity" broadly represents the cultural opportunities and challenges of the changing faces of the American people. Noonan (2007) offers a definition of the meaning of *diversity*, describing both cultural difference and pluralism:

> *Difference* includes "individual variations in physical and psychological make-up and 'particular' (Featherstone, 1992, p. vii) cultural adaptations and responses of individuals and groups to their physical and social environments" (p. x). *Pluralism* refers to a "condition of society in which numerous distinct ethnic, religious, or cultural groups coexist within one nation" (Pickett, 2000, p. 1351); pluralists "holds more than one office much like we 'hold' more than one identity, creating individual and societal value from our multiple identities." (Featherstone, 1992, p. x)

We are distinctly different, individually and collectively; multiethnic and culturally complex; members of many valuable family, tribal, and social communities; and citizens in a richly diverse world. Although we share membership in many "tribes," we also possess a personal culture. We interpret our experience and share it with others through story, identifying the distinctive features of our multiple identities that best explain our unique responses to others and the environment.

Stories help us construct our individual and cultural identities. The National Museum of American Indians (2004) offers a view of Native identity that universally applies to all cultures:

> For Native people, identity—who you are, how you dress, what you think, where you fit in, and how you see yourself in the world—has been shaped

[handwritten margin note: multiple values from ... identifies]

by language, place, community membership, social and political consciousness, and customs and beliefs. (p. 2)

Story, an important vehicle for conveying these key elements, helps us
acquire a collective identity. How else would we claim membership in a
group, know our place in the world, and figure out how to lead our lives?
Story making, telling, and sharing serve as the primary process and tool
to discover and express our individual and collective identities.
"Through telling, writing, reading, and listening to life stories—one's
own and others—those engaged in this work [educational practice] can
penetrate cultural barriers, discover the power of self and the integrity
of the other, and deepen their understanding of their respective histories and possibilities" (Witherell & Noddings, 1991, p. 4).

As a relationship between and among members, leadership emanates
from the members. People participate in leadership when they feel valued as individuals and experience belonging as group members. The human element tells us something different, something else that must be
considered. We matter.

What most people define as leadership generally gets carried out with
others and thus, by definition, would be considered *collaborative* and
relational. "Leadership is a reciprocal relationship between those who
choose to lead and those who decide to follow (Kouzes & Posner, 1993,
p. 1). For leadership to work, a relationship must exist between leaders
and members or followers. Burns "define[s] leadership as not merely a
property or activity of leaders but as relationship between leaders and a
multitude of followers of many types" (1978, p. 30).

Members actively participate in leadership. As participants in a reciprocal relationship, everyone shares responsibility for maintaining the relationship and accomplishing goals. Followers, co-participants in leadership, shape leadership and cause it to happen. "Follower is not a term of
weakness, but the condition that permits leadership to exist and give it
strength" (Chaleff, 2003, p. 19). Willingness to work together to explore
root causes and alternatives causes us to examine alternatives and future
actions in a problem-solving mode. Story serves as a vehicle to form and
sustain relationships.

Sharing individual as well as cultural stories encourages individual visibility and collective consciousness, paving the way for participation in

leadership. Global or species stories reveal how people connect across cultures and time. The collective story is not a "mere aggregate of the personal recollections of its various members, a community's collective memory includes only those shared by its members as a group. As such, it invokes a common past that they all seem to recall" (Jensen, 1996, p. 4).

We are socialized in different "mnemonic traditions" that cause us "to better remember facts that fit certain (unmistakably cultural) mental schemata." These schemata are enfolded in "highly formulaic plot structures" (Zerubavel, 2003, p. 4). The teller who composes a community story must be familiar with the story's rhythm (the way people expect to hear the story told and performed) and its meaning (being aware of various ways in which the story might be perceived by others).

We "co-reminisce" when we share stories that reveal the past and create "official" stories of our experience, making meaning of it in an acceptable narrative form. This aspect of story and membership allows us "to experience things that happened to the groups to which we belong long before we ever joined them as if they were part of our own personal past" (Zerubavel, 2003, p. 3).

Drawing on the power of individual and community stories, leaders and members exchange stories to establish core beliefs and take authentic action in the world. All levels of story, ranging from personal to community to transglobal, help to establish identity, forge relationships, and facilitate the exchange of wisdom through mutual sharing and dialogue. The interactive and transformational nature of story described in the next chapter explains how telling stories changes lives.

3

TELLING STORIES, CHANGING LIVES: TURNING POINTS IN DIALOGUE

> *To change minds effectively, leaders make particular use of two tools: the stories that they tell and the lives that they lead.*
>
> —Gardner (2004, p. 69)

A quick tour of motivational speakers available for hire on the Premiere Speakers Bureau website (http://premierespeakers.com) shows just what kind of story seems most valuable. Simply select speakers by highest price per speaking engagement ($40,000+) and click the search button. You can hire an astronaut, musician, or coach to tell his or her story for $600 or more a minute. Because their stories are often available to us through multiple media outlets and their own published work, why pay the money? We listen to motivational speakers because we want to hear their stories directly from them and participate in the meaning-making process, allowing us to extract the larger lesson, claim it ourselves, and thus find meaning in our lives.

Newscasters and political commentators also appear to be popular. Speaking about our times and culture, they serve as storytellers in the tradition of the Ute Indians, sharing stories to interpret the significant events of our times and forecasting how these changes affect us now and in the future. Peggy Noonan (unfortunately not related to the author by

name or speaking fee) commands more than $40,000 per speech and re-
quires two first-class airline tickets to travel to a place of business. A former news correspondent and Washington insider, Noonan wrote Reagan's speeches and published political commentary in some of the
world's best newspapers and magazines. She tells an insider's story about
one of the greatest communicators in presidential history, Ronald Reagan. Because she wrote many of his speeches and served as the chief ar-
chitect of his message, we assume the audiences who clamor to hear her
want to know about the universal appeal of Reagan's message and experience it or perhaps even replicate it.

Stories draw us together. Whether sitting around a campfire or taking
our seats in a large civic center, we listen to stories to decipher most of
life's meaning. To earn $40,000 or more per speaking engagement re-
quires more than just a fascinating story; the story must also contain an
important moral or life lesson and be well told by a credible and engaging speaker. Wonderful actors don't necessarily make great motivational
speakers; however, great storytellers who possess both oratorical skill
and a powerful story never struggle for an audience. Popular speakers
help audiences create meaning through the exchange and interpretation
of their stories, making their performances almost "priceless." The key
to their success relates to the purpose and moral of the stories and our
experience listening to and making meaning from them.

THE PURPOSE AND MORAL OF THE STORY

Tucked inside the storylines, leaders share stories about history, culture,
and experience to communicate important values and share wisdom.
The "story within the story" contains a message about what is important
and implies a theory of action to guide us. The story alerts members
about what to do and also shares ideas about how the work gets accomplished. Although the "who and what" details of the story may initially
appear important (providing background and context), the real value of
the story involves the "why and how": What challenge is presented, what
motivates us to participate, and how it is accomplished. All worthy stories offer some kind of life lesson, exhorting us to "learn from my experience, do or do not do what I did, follow my lead, watch our for the dangers when you try to do something this way." The same "story logic"

applies to the leadership goals of empowering others, managing loss, promoting healing, seeking justice, and encouraging imagination.

A story isn't a story without a point. Gornick (2001) describes the importance of the moral or purpose of the story:

> Every work of literature [oral or written] has both a situation and a story. The situation is the context or circumstance, sometimes the plot; the story is the emotional experience that preoccupies the writer; the insight, the wisdom, the thing one has come to say. (p. 13)

Embedded within our stories, leadership narrative themes ("the thing one has come to say") draw us to the important work of leadership. A narrative theme refers to the subject or main point of the story that gives it meaning (Armstrong, 1992) and includes the related story matter in support of the main idea (for example, the images or metaphors used, characters, events or happenings, the order and flow of the story, etc.). The cover story describes the "situation," while the real story or "the story within the story" becomes known in the telling and interpretation of its meaning.

Change leaders use story to alert people to the challenges associated with change, as preparation for the experience. Their stories warn of loss, struggle, and chaos likely to occur when the implementation of a new plan or process creates a shift in direction or the manner in which work is accomplished. Members hear change stories and react to them. Using story as a way to manage their inner turmoil and conflict, members may share their experiences with change to get control over their emotions and minimize its disruptive effects. Members adapt to the change through the exchange of stories. When knowledge is applied to the unknown and fear-based responses are replaced with intelligent action, the loss of control associated with change diminishes.

Survival stories contain advice regarding the importance of inner strength, persevering under impossible conditions, overcoming doubts, and recovering from mistakes. The same logic applies to stories of empowerment, identity, development, imagination, and healing. Selecting the right story and offering it to another may serve as medicine to a patient in need of treatment:

> [I]n traditional Hindu medicine a fairy tale giving form to his particular problem was offered to a psychically disoriented person, for his meditation. It was expected that through contemplating the story the disturbed

person would be led to visualize both the nature of the impasse in living from which he suffered, and the possibility of its resolution. From what a particular tale implied about man's despair, hopes, and methods of overcoming tribulations, the patient could discover not only a way out of his distress but also a way to find himself, as the hero of the story did. (Bettelheim, 1989, p. 25)

Employing "grammatical resources" to persuade, inspire, or heal, leaders emphasize one or more narrative themes in their stories to influence people, promote change, and take action. While religious leaders offer parables drawn from sacred texts and oral traditions, secular leaders use the narrative resources available in their individual, organizational, or cultural traditions (including spiritual stories) to help interpret experiences and work with others engaged in leadership through the exchange of stories. Stories lay down a path to follow and invite us to take the journey.

The persuasive story answers five questions: "What was done (act), when or where it was done (scene), who did it (agent), how he [or she] does it (agency), and why (purpose)" (Riessman, 1993, p. 19). Each question contributes to the central message and purpose.

For example, the qualities, experience, expertise, and accomplishments of the main character influence the value and interpretation of the story. If you heard a story about a young girl who knew at age twelve what her life's work would be, would you take it seriously? What if her name was Mother Theresa? The story gains power from the teller and main character.

The scene and actions flesh out the context or situation, providing useful background information for understanding, locating an appropriate comparison, and later applying the lessons learned from the story to other circumstances. Because the 9/11 attack could be compared to similar circumstances experienced by Londoners during the nightly air raids in World War II, the stories about their experiences were invaluable to New Yorkers. During World War II, Londoners refused to abandon their city to the enemy. Carrying out as much of their daily business as possible, they remained resolute in their efforts to hold out against the nightly attacks and rebuild their city. Drawing us into the moral of the story, the action taken by Londoners and the reasons behind it offered a way to make sense of the crisis and provided a path for New Yorkers to follow.

Rudy Giuliani, mayor of New York during the World Trade Center attack, returned home during the first night of the crisis and read a biography of Winston Churchill. In a CNN interview, he shared how he used the story and Churchill's experience to figure out what to do:

> "Winston Churchill was a great source of strength and influence for me going through September 11," he recalls. "That night I got out his biography and I read it to try to see how he gets through the Battle of Britain. Maybe there were some lessons that I could apply to how New York was going to get through this terrible battle that was thrust on us." (Lessons in crisis management, 2004, pp. 10–11)

The "shelf life" of stories goes beyond the immediate recall of an event due to its usefulness and application to present-day experience. Stories propel people to action and shed light on ways to adapt to changing circumstances.

Baldwin (2005) describes four gifts of story: (1) story creates context, (2) context highlights relationship, (3) context and relationship change behavior and lead to holistic and concerted action, and (4) connected action becomes a force for restoring/restorying the world (pp. 64–67). "Context is the *lived* experience of understanding that resides underneath the *spoken* experience. Context sets events in time and place" (p. 64). Once the listener understands the setting, the storyteller introduces people and their relationships to each other, then what happens to them—"a real scene with real people involved" (p. 66)—causing listeners to identify with the person(s) who appear to be more like them:

> When these elements combine into real scenes, real persons, real inspiration, the personal becomes universal—the characters lose their specificity and become everyman/everywoman . . . . Like the story of the Good Samaritan, it is an archetypal story that reminds us that the choice to be our best self is always with us, waiting for that skid in the road. (p. 67)

THE INTERACTIVE AND TRANSFORMATIONAL NATURE OF STORY

The content of our stories tells us how to accomplish leadership. Sharing stories about how leadership might be made more authentic, ethical, and transparent, leaders use story to support their development and also as a process for preparing and including others in leadership. Stories move us from the factual and literal to the symbolic form in which the metaphor organizes the storyline, opening up the meaning-making process through imagery and analogous stories. The "metaphors in use" create an expectation of the narrative possibilities and structure.

The storyteller creates and frames a story with the intent of communicating meaning, and the listener in "narrative mode" interacts with the story, simultaneously assigning multiple layers of meaning to it based on his or her experience (Bruner, 1990). Story listeners anticipate how the story unfolds by calling forth their knowledge and experience of the situation described, using the words and images apparent to them from even the barest introduction of the storyline. *Story, whether a true or fictional narrative, describes an event and offers an account of an experience with the intent of communicating meaning.*

In addition to layers of meaning implicit in each story created and told, multiple possibilities exist for interpretation and response based on the story elements and the narrative themes contained within the storyline (Riessman, 1993). When someone tells a story, the "listener" vicariously participates in the story along with the "teller" and (along with the teller) creates his or her own meaning of it almost in the moment. The teller constructs and shares the story, creating meaning for himself or herself in the "storying" process, while the listener simultaneously reacts and responds (sometimes in a different way than intended), understanding the story from his or her perspective and applying multiple meanings to it.

The "sense or significance of a narrative stems from the *intersection of the world of the text* [story] *and the world of the reader*. The act of reading thus becomes the critical moment of the entire analysis" (Ricoeur, 1991, p. 26). Stories offer a new "world horizon . . . which includes the actions, the characters and the events of the story" (p. 26). We imagine this new world through creative interpretations of the story and later combine it with the realities of our lives, interpreting and integrating the story with our life experience. These elements make the story "exchange" transformational in nature.

The listener holds the story *under review*, revising or expanding it based on his or her response. If the listener doesn't believe the story and asks questions, that may cause the teller to do some "narrative repair" (Robinson & Hawpe, 1986). The process of constructing the story proceeds with multiple "tellings" until a well-honed, plausible, and convincing story has been created. After meeting the story "standards," the listener may show his or her connection to the story by describing an insight gained or sharing a new and related story based on his or her experience. The listener now becomes the teller, offering his or her own perspective, causing the teller (now the listener) to change, and an entirely new process occurs.

Familiar with "narrative structures" as a result of cultural tradition and experience, story listeners expect the story to include important ingredients or elements to be complete and credible:

> A "fully-formed" narrative includes six common elements: an abstract (summary of the substance of the narrative), orientation (time, place, situation, participants), complicating action (sequence of events), evaluation (significance and meaning of the action, attitude of the narrator), resolution (what finally happened), and coda (return the perspective to the present). (Riessman, 1993, p. 18)

When these elements appear, a satisfying story is told. The following story about Lance Armstrong's professional and personal victories illustrates all the narrative elements described above.

LANCE ARMSTRONG'S VICTORIES

The story of Lance Armstrong's struggle with cancer and his ability to win the Tour de France (1999–2005) even after undergoing chemotherapy contains all the elements of a "fully formed" narrative structure. In "abstract" we hear the story about Armstrong, a spectacular competitor who not only wins the Tour de France but also defeats cancer. In "story sequence" we hear about his record, struggle, and victories. The "orientation" provides details of the race and his battle with cancer. His dual victories, winning the race and defeating cancer, serve as the "resolution" of the story.

The storyteller encourages us to imagine ourselves in the race along with Armstrong, achieving what he accomplishes ("evaluation"). Armstrong races against time for a stunning and unprecedented seventh win after having already conquered the fight against death. His faith helps him overcome the limitations of his age and illness. Returning to the present, appearing healthy and whole on the final day of the race, Armstrong stands at the podium and claims his victory with his children at his side. With an enviable lead, he wins the race for victory and his life ("coda," the dramatic ending).

Crowds show their support and cheer him on, wearing the symbolic yellow wristband originally sold to support Armstrong's racing and now serving as a universal symbol of hope and faith in the struggle for survival. As a leadership story, the themes of empowerment and accomplishment (the "story within a story") inspire people to adopt the qualities of those in the winner's circle in pursuit of excellence.

Storytellers compose stories with an awareness of story elements, selecting characters and storyline to speak for them. The familiar story elements of setting, characters, conflict, plot, and theme resemble a small play:

> One method of constructing [a story] is to develop a story line. During the *opening scene* the main character is introduced as well as the setting for the story action. Next is the *challenge scene* where something causes tension (a conflict, struggle, etc.). After the conflict is introduced, the *turning point scene* shows what happens in response to the conflict. Something must happen to make a difference (an obstacle is removed or there is a change in the course of action, etc.). Finally, the *closing scene* reveals the resolution and meaning of the story. (Allan, Fairtlough, & Heinzen, 2001, p. 244)

The setting grounds us with the questions: Where are we, and what is the context for this story? A human, animal, or supernatural being may serve as the main character or protagonist. Acting as a story organizer, the plot contains a description of the sequence of events from beginning to end and introduces the choices available to the main character during a dilemma or conflict. Conflict represents another feature of story. Conflict, the struggle in the story, peaks during the "rising action" of the story and gets resolved during the "falling action" and ending. Characters experience conflict as either an internal struggle (within one's self) or an external struggle (a force outside one's self). We experience a predictable sequencing of the plot and finally see resolution to the "trouble" (Frank, 1995).

People tell stories from a particular viewpoint and relate to the main point or "moral" of the story, usually disclosed at the end of the story (Armstrong, 1992). Storylines incorporate one or more "narrative themes" (for example, empowerment, change, or healing). The "restitution theme" progresses in the following form: "Yesterday I was healthy, today I'm sick, but tomorrow I'll be healthy again" (Frank, 1995, p. 77). The restitution theme contrasts with chaos or quest themes in "illness stories":

> Restitution stories attempt to outdistance mortality by rendering illness transitory. Chaos stories are sucked into the undertow of illness and the disasters that attend to it. Quest stories meet suffering head on; they accept illness and seek to *use* it. (p. 115)

Several narrative themes emerge in the Lance Armstrong story. The Armstrong story calls us to face adversity in the same way a world champion faced his struggle with cancer, accepting the illness and "defeating" it through strength of will and personal belief. Many narrative themes and lessons found in Armstrong's story relate to leadership. His story offers wisdom about how to overcome "illness," experience healing, become empowered, achieve goals, and embrace core values. These "mini-stories" within the larger story create the soul of the story, giving us important knowledge about his experience in the world and advice about how to live.

In a deliberative and creative process, storytellers compose stories by choosing a narrative form, theme, and style:

> Genres of narratives, with their distinctive styles and structures, are modes of representation that tellers choose (in concert with listener's expectations, of course) just as filmmakers decide, based on their intentions and the market, what form the script will take, and what conventions will be used to represent character and action. . . . They make us care about a situation to varying degrees as they pull us into the teller's point of view. (Riessman, 1993, p. 18)

A close examination and analysis of the following story, recorded as part of a national project aimed at recording stories of American people (see StoryCorps at www.storycorps.net), provides another example of story elements. The themes of "identity" and "wounding" found in the story show how critical and wounding incidents shape and define our identity.

DRINKING IN ALL THIS DEMOCRACY

Erza Awumey asked his grandfather, Mike Harmon, "What was the saddest day of your life?" (Awumey & Harmon, 2004). Harmon described one of the most painful moments of his life to his grandson in the following story. The story takes place in the 1950s, when Harmon and several shipmates toured Washington, D.C., while on leave. Harmon, a person of color and a sailor in the U.S. Navy, drove a group of fellow shipmates to the capital and served as the designated driver.

After spending most of the day touring the nation's capital, he had the painful experience of being denied entrance into a movie theater:

> I went up to buy a ticket, there's a glass there, a ticket seller behind it and off of the glass reflected the capitol dome. And I just thought to myself, "What a great way to end the day, drinking in all this democracy." I called for the ticket, she was reading, she punched the machine. I reached [with] my hand to get the ticket, and lay down the money and she pulled it back. She said, "You can't come in here." She saw my black hand and refused to sell me the ticket. The capitol dome was superimposed on her angry face, angered that I would have the temerity to ask to buy a ticket. And I just walked the streets crying all night. That's the saddest, without any exception, it's the most painful recollection of anything that's ever happened to me that I have. (Awumey & Harmon, 2004)

Harmon's story contains the narrative themes of identity, survival, change, and learning. Focusing in on the identity theme, the listener learns about Mr. Harmon—who he is and the impact of a critical life experience. The leadership narrative theme of identity progresses in the following form: "This is who I am (as an individual and as a member of many social groups). This is [or was] my life experience and the current [past] situation. These are the challenges I face [or faced]. This is how it is changing [has changed] me. This is who I am now [or becoming]."

After establishing the situation, Mr. Harmon describes the "trouble" (being denied entrance to the theater because he was black) and its effects (he recounts it as the saddest day of his life). You can hear the cadence of Harmon's story told to his grandson as the narrative progresses. First a calm voice sets the stage, and then the rising action of the "trouble" warns of its effects on the storyteller, who now speaks in a hushed tone.

As bystanders are drawn into the scene, we enter the story and experience the storyteller's pain. The teller slows down the storyline (much like a train passing through a sleepy town at night) and draws us into the story to experience it before moving on. The teller and listener, silent for a moment as the train slows and then passes, momentarily unite in mutual protest against what occurred.

The long, low whistle of the train picks up speed as it exits the town, disappearing from our view. During these few moments, the identity of the storyteller and the meaning of his experience reveal how that moment changed his life. After the train disappears, listeners reflect on the story, understand his experience, and learn *who he is now*. Listeners also experience racism in a personal and collective sense through Harmon's story.

Harmon's story illustrates how the power of story changes us. The authors have played a recording of this brief story to their students several times. It takes just under two minutes to play it after the website is located. It is an emotionally charged story, and many who hear it shed a tear. Harmon's voice, tone, and moral authority silence listeners. Sharing his pain despite the elapsed time and distance of the story from his present-day experience, we understand what caused Harmon to feel this way, becoming more sensitive to his position and recognizing that some wounds never heal. Because of its life-changing effect on Harmon, the story serves as both a wounding and an identity story.

Learning about ourselves through the self-story (Frank, 1995), we also acquire knowledge of others through shared stories:

> The self-story is not told for the sake of description, though description may be its ostensible content. The self is being *formed* in what is told. . . . The self-story is told both to others and one's self; each telling is enfolded within the other. The act of telling is a dual reaffirmation. Relationships with others are reaffirmed, and the self is affirmed. (pp. 55–56)

Harmon tells the story to his grandson, forming himself and building his relationship with his grandson Awumey. Awumey learns about his grandfather's identity and also participates in the legacy of his story. Because the story defines his grandfather, it also defines him, establishing a cultural and generational bond.

We can learn quite a bit about people from the stories they tell. Whose voice do we hear? Not hear? What "power relations" are maintained or exposed when we deconstruct the story? How might the story be interpreted by various others?

Inclusive leaders might use Harmon's story to explore the importance of being fully included in democratic communities—challenging us to see how a single rejection can bring a lifetime of pain to someone. Identities, developed from the way we see ourselves and the way others see us, become known through visibility and authentic expression. Ellison, author of *Invisible Man*, describes the source of the narrator's pain, his invisibility: "I am invisible, understand, simply because people refuse to see me" (1995, p. 3). Story allows us to be seen and known by others.

Armstrong's and Harmon's stories illustrate how a personal story engages us in experiencing and reflecting about leadership. We don't have to be in the race for our lives or experience the assault of racism in the 1950s to appreciate the meaning of their stories and learn something. Listening to their stories causes change within us.

Personal stories reveal character and intentions, causing people to realize their capacity and motivation to engage in leadership with others. The narrative process of creating, telling, listening, reacting, interpreting, responding, and sharing stories moves us to self-discovery and the realization of individual and collective potential.

Carr (1985) explains how stories can help us realize our potential:

> In planning our days and lives we are composing the stories or the dramas we will act out and which will determine the focus of our attention and our endeavors, which will provide the principles for distinguishing foreground from background. . . . We are constantly explaining ourselves to others. And finally each of us must count himself [or herself] among his [or her] own audience since in explaining ourselves to others we are often trying to convince ourselves as well. (p. 117)

Riessman (1993) describes the *self as narrative:* "Individuals *become* [emphasis added] the autobiographical narratives by which they tell about their lives. These private constructions typically mesh with a community of life stories, 'deep structures' about the nature of life itself" (p. 2). We accomplish more through the exchange of stories beyond the construction of identity: We impart cultural knowledge, tell moral tales, solve problems and accomplish healing. Stories of identity allow us to move across the borders (Greene, 1988) that divide us.

Personal and cultural stories reveal personal and social identities, giving a personal account of our life experience, its meaning and value. Stories tell listeners what changed us and why. Beginning with relationships, we learn about each other through story, establishing trust by listening to stories and responding emphatically. The disclosure of personal stories facilitates mutual understanding and support for common goals because people now see themselves as group members, replacing personal distance with engagement in the lives of others. We tell stories individually as autobiography or collectively as history, storing them in memory for future use. Fundamental to most human activity, story expresses engagement with others and actions in the world, including the individual and co-meaning we make of it.

Cultural tales, legends, myths, and historical accounts help explain our origins and establish identity, offering guidance on how to live and find meaning in our experience. They also explain and reconcile the disparate and confusing events in our lives. Traditional stories provide introduction to our family and social group(s). Such stories often describe the movement of people to a particular place, family members struggling against the elements and surviving, preserving culture, and providing stability to the community. Becoming visible and revealing more of our authentic selves to others, storytelling provides a way to express our motivations and actions as well as to understand the experience and values of others.

Personal family stories and fairy tales introduce developmental challenges and offer children a way to understand them:

> Fairy tales, unlike any other form of literature, direct the child to discover his [or her] identity and calling, and they also suggest what experiences are needed to develop his [or her] character. Fairy tales intimate that a rewarding, good life is within one's reach despite adversity—but only if one does not shy away from the hazardous struggles without which one can never achieve true identity. (Bettelheim, 1976, p. 24)

"In a fairy tale, internal processes are externalized and become comprehensible as represented by the figures in the story and its events" (Bettelheim, 1976, p. 25). Fantasy tales evoke imaginary worlds, describing the actions of spiritual beings, even explaining natural and supernatural events, tribal origin, and cultural traditions. Tales help children to "bridge the gap between their inner experience and the real world" (p. 66), serving as a means to negotiate gaps in knowledge and uncertainty.

Personal stories about family and cultural history offer additional layers of understanding beyond the obvious assumptions people may make based on appearance, titles or positions, and public accomplishments. Beginning with our personal or "origin" story (who we are and where we came from) told to us by family members and culminating with the eulogy or closing story told about us by our descendants (who we were and how we lived), stories help us and others make sense of our experience. Between beginning and ending stories lie the stories we tell others, revealing experiences and the meaning made of them. "These encounters with life cause us to create new stories and change existing ones" (Angus & McLeod, 2004, p. 195).

Constructed from the interpretation and integration of life experience, personal stories leave an imprint on individual and collective consciousness. Submerged just below the surface of personal and cultural memory, stories explain our actions and experience to others, sometimes merging our individual story with the collective, cultural stories of communities. Individuals accomplish developmental life tasks such as forming identity or becoming a family member through story.

We become our self-story; composing and sharing our personal story with others helps form an identity in motion. The stories we tell others influence their development as well as their decision to participate in our leadership. Writing about narrative inquiry in qualitative research, Candinin and Connelly (2000) suggest that a good narrative has an *explanatory, invitational quality, authenticity, adequacy,* and *plausibility* (p. 185). The same criteria may apply to the mutual exchange of stories in leadership.

Stories should explain what happened, invite others to experience and make sense of them, reveal an element of truth or honesty, provide enough well-organized information to create a coherent and understandable storyline, and offer a reasonable interpretation of events. When some or all of these elements are present, the story released by the teller and interpreted by listeners may transform us all—setting free its power to the universe as interpretations of life, sometimes as wisdom, or perhaps as a prayer for the next generation.

4

PERSONAL AND CULTURAL STORIES: SOURCES OF AUTHENTICITY IN LEADERSHIP

The world is filled with stories impressed on people's hearts. We have only to speak out to set the stories free. Like smoke from burning candles stories rise up. In the base collective unconscious, stories amass; they bump into each other calling out to us.

—Benitez (2006, p. 67)

We visit our stories like old friends, drawing comfort, meaning, and understanding from them. Reflecting on our life experiences through story allows us to understand not only who we are, but also where we are now and how we got here. In a sense, our lives are constantly being staged in front of us (and others) as a developing story, a life epic with occasional dramatic episodes.

Much like playwrights, we script our story in one-act plays, cast ourselves in the starring role, and then stage them in our virtual memory. Intimately aware of the main character's history and motivations (the play is about us after all), we watch vicariously as our life "dramas" unfold, drawn viscerally into the action and emotion of each scene as a participant-observer.

As directors, we wait nervously in the wings, hoping the audience identifies the central themes and resonates with our life experience.

Fearing the drama critic who appraises our performance with detachment and a critical eye, often questioning our authenticity and actions, we anxiously wait for feedback about our performance. A critical "friend" tests our version of the truth, perhaps insisting on a more honest account of the story.

The inner critic helps us discover "narrative truth" by engaging us in reflection about our choices. Serving as both a mentor and conscience, the inner critic closely inspects our choices and their effects and confronts us with a new reality. These ruminations and reflections may ultimately move us to change the course of our lives. "Stories are the single best way humans have for accounting for our experience. They help us see how choices and events are tied together, why things are and how they could be" (Taylor, 1996, p. 2).

Our lives would drift from one circumstance and event to another, seemingly without meaning or control, without the element of choice and its antecedent effects. "If we see ourselves as active characters in our own stories, we can exercise our human freedom to choose a present and future for ourselves and for those we love that gives life meaning" (Taylor, 1996, p. 2).

Leaders use story to (1) make sense of their experience and developing adult personality and character, (2) provide an honest accounting of themselves to others, (3) progress in learning and wisdom, and (4) avoid distorted (and untrue) views of self due to unmanaged ego demands and acts of self-deception. Searching for the authentic and meaningful moments in our lives leads to the discovery and realization of our identity and core values. It also provides an opportunity to reflect on experience and learn.

Operating from a theory of "inside out," personal and cultural identity stories reveal the authentic self, drawing us into the world to take authentic action as an expression of our "true and real" self (Terry, 2001, p. 5). The authentic self emerges through self-discovery and the mutual exchange of story, allowing us to be fully seen and included in leadership. Failure to authentically engage with others may create "a misfit between the leadership role and one's identity, or between the role and reality of work life, [can] diminish[ing] a leader's chance of being genuine" (Ackerman & Maslin-Ostrowski, 2002, p. 9).

Staged like a small play with several acts, stories of personal transformation explain our development to date, establishing our adult character and capacity to serve as leaders and participants in leadership. Elizabeth's personal story of her progression to adulthood reveals her character and passion for leadership. She presents episodes of her life experience, tracing the emergence of her adult identity and core values. The opening scene begins with her last three years of high school.

ELIZABETH'S STORY OF PERSONAL TRANSFORMATION

In the following series of mini-stories, a twenty-six-year-old woman, Elizabeth, tells about how her last years in high school and a critical life incident influenced her occupational choice. Moving three times in high school because of her mother's career (her parents were divorced), Elizabeth describes the moves as "defining moments" even though they took place over a period of several years:

> I recall having a difficult adolescence, full of emotional turmoil and distress. My mother and I moved several times. I went to three high schools in three years. I had difficulty forming new friendships. Eventually, I learned how to make new friendships despite the fact that we moved to a small town and most of the other students had friendships that went back to grade school.
>
> The most difficult times were during lunch when I would have to sit alone. Fortunately I attended my last few years in a rural high school where students were allowed to leave school during lunch. During the first few days of my third move in three years, I often left school to have lunch with my mother, who had an office nearby. She understood how I would feel and encouraged me to leave until I wanted to stay at school during lunch. Eventually I managed to make a couple friends and overcome my shyness, abandoning the practice of eating with my mom.
>
> Although I still feel awkward in some social situations and find it difficult to make friends sometimes, I survived high school, earned a diploma, and went away to college. The frequent moves during high school gave me courage to go away to college despite the fact that I would be on my own again and no one from my senior class would be going with me. In the fall

I packed my car and left for college, more confident about moving and making it on my own. (Elizabeth Smith, personal communication, December 21, 2006)

Coming-of-age stories trace our life stages, depicting us as "works in progress." Elizabeth tells a story about living with her boyfriend several years later, breaking up, and adjusting to living alone again, showing how she conquered a different kind of fear:

At first I found not having a boyfriend to be debilitating. I was afraid to be alone at night in my new apartment. Upset about the big change in my life and feeling scared in a ground floor apartment, I spent many sleepless nights trying to conquer my fears. I learned to overcome my fear of living alone by putting in safety locks, listening to ocean sounds playing in the background to drown out the night noises, talking myself out of being scared, and getting a dog. I also learned how to do things that I would normally have a boyfriend complete.

Simple tasks such as finding the right screws to fasten license plates seemed complex because of my depression and the overwhelming financial and emotional burden of living alone. After about six months, I learned to do things for myself, reclaiming the independence I gave up when I entered into the relationship. Having this time to develop my identity and focus on my career path without focusing on a relationship caused me to become a more confident and assertive young woman. This time has allowed me to reassess what criteria I would seek in a man and gave me confidence to be more selective when choosing romantic partners. (Elizabeth Smith, personal communication, December 21, 2006)

These two stories show how Elizabeth accomplishes the tasks of achieving adulthood. Although the events are common enough (family moves, a parent's divorce, and a romantic breakup), her experience is unique to her, revealing something about how she developed into the person she is today. The next story introduces a critical life event that changes the direction of her life and explains her passion for her current profession:

When I was eleven years old, my sister was critically ill and lost her sight due to a medical injury at age thirteen. Our family lives were turned upside down, first by my sister's loss of sight and our adjustment to it, and

later by my parents' divorce. My sister also developed emotional disabilities, suffering from depression, anxiety, and stress. This unfortunate and
traumatic event dominated most of the remaining years of my adolescence and guided me into a human service career. Being raised with a sibling with a disability taught me many lessons. I had to learn to accept
someone whose behavior was not always normal, often becoming more of
a caretaker than a sibling because my sister always needed additional help.
Learning how to accept her disability and adjust to changes in our family
lifestyle, I became more of a compassionate person who is most at ease
around people with disabilities. (Elizabeth Smith, personal communication, December 21, 2006)

The story reveals another dimension about Elizabeth's life and her
development, causing us to wonder about its effects. Although we listen
with curiosity to the tumultuous experience of surviving adolescence,
her story takes on more interest with a painful life event. We know this
story is more likely to change her than a breakup or family move. The
effects of her sister's injury influence Elizabeth's search for a part-time
job in college and eventually her choice of occupation. In the following
story, Elizabeth tells us about the nature of her work and, indirectly, her
character:

I worked in a group home for adults with significant disabilities during
college and delivered direct care to clients living in a group home. The
work was challenging. I once rescued a client who experienced a seizure
while taking a bath. I held her head firmly above the water despite her violent and uncontrolled responses, keeping her from hurting herself. I felt
proud of myself for rescuing her. I also reported a situation in a group
home where I worked when a client did not receive a daily bath and was
often ignored by a staff member in charge of the client. I didn't care about
the consequences; it was wrong. (Elizabeth Smith, personal communication, December 21, 2006)

After graduation, Elizabeth took a position in a local hospital, this time
working as a psychiatric aide with patients with emotional disabilities:

While working at a hospital in a psychiatric unit, I once interrupted a patient attempting to take his life using a bedsheet. He was trying to figure out
how to do it. I don't know if he could have actually figured it out. I ignored

what he was doing, quickly distracted him, and called for help. I later left
the hospital when a client attacked a co-worker and I realized the working
conditions were unsafe. I contacted hospital administrators and told them
that they needed to put better systems in place to protect the clients and the
employees. I left the hospital and moved from direct care to case management. Now I write plans for clients and ensure they receive good care. I try
to use the same standards of care for my clients as I would for my sister.
(Elizabeth Smith, personal communication, December 21, 2006)

The human side emerges as layers of stories are piled one on top of
another. Elizabeth unveils her life, tells us what happened, how she
changed, and why. Explaining changes in life circumstances, the resulting fears, and the actions taken to overcome adversity, Elizabeth
emerges as a more confident and mature person; however, not without
a paying a price for each life lesson. Her stories serve as defining moments because she recalls them as significant events and tells us what
they mean as she integrates her "ethic of care" into her adult personality and life work (Gilligan, 1993). We know who she is now.

Even if Elizabeth had neglected to explicitly share the meaning of her
stories (not the case here), we would know something about her circumstances, including the underlying theme of fear, after the first few
sentences. Sentences such as "I went to three high schools in three
years" or "I was afraid to be alone at night in my new apartment" set the
stage for a story about overcoming fears. These "life stage" stories,
drawn from accomplishing developmental milestones, serve as a rich
source of material for constructing a leadership story.

Elizabeth's story covers several aspects of her "family and relationship
history" from her high school years to her emerging adulthood. Introducing a milestone (graduation, leaving home) and several critical life
events, the themes in her story unfold. In hearing her life story, listeners see her authentic self and also find ways to relate to her story. Her
experience with cultural difference, as a sister of an adult with significant disabilities, affects her. Describing her sister's pain and disabilities
as well as the loss she experienced as a family member, Elizabeth traces
the effects of these events on her identity and character. The added burdens of responsibility and sometimes embarrassment associated with
her sister's disability defined her adolescence. Her statement, "I'm now
most at ease around people with disabilities," shows the hard-won ma-

turity extracted from the circumstances and the motivation for her current work.

Elizabeth's story shows how thinking about the important events in her life helped her discover her authentic self, including her capacity and motivation for leadership in her chosen field. "By changing the lens of developmental observation from individual achievements to relationships of care, women [like Elizabeth] depict [her] ongoing attachment as the path to maturity" (Gilligan, 1993, p. 170). Elizabeth makes these connections between her work and relationships with others. Her leadership serves as an outward expression of her authentic self. "Authentic leaders look inward to assess their motivations, potential, and experience, and they look outward for opportunities to lead in ways that are consistent with their internal world" (Noonan, 2003, p. 100).

IDENTITY AND AUTHENTICITY

acting and behaving on core values

Stories come back to us like old friends, familiar, yet somehow changed because we change and see them differently. Traveling back home to our memories, we visit our stories often to reflect on their meaning and grow in wisdom and leadership. Sharing our stories with others helps us to enter the arena of leadership, engaging others in understanding their life callings and locating the future direction of the community.

Much like plays, our life stories, scripted in one-act plays, cast us in the starring role, allowing us to stage them in virtual memory. Sitting in the audience, we vicariously watch our life "dramas" unfold, drawn viscerally into the action and emotion of each scene. Waiting nervously in the wings, we secretly hope the audience will really see and understand us. Sometimes an internal drama critic appears, reviewing the play with detachment and a critical eye. Challenging the way the play is staged or how the plot unfolds, the critic may question the actor's authenticity and actions. The internal critic serves as a critical friend, scrutinizing our actions and often insisting on a more honest account of the story.

Taking us beyond the direct experience of one person and involving more than the mere recall of events or experiences, real stories help us accomplish the work of leadership because of the lessons contained in the story. "It is the way wisdom gets passed along" (Remen, 1996, p. xxv).

Leaders in diverse communities possess an intimate knowledge of story and facilitate exchanges of cultural stories to reduce barriers and locate common purposes and direction.

Affirming the importance of individual and cultural (social) identities, leaders expand the collective capacity of people to successfully collaborate through the exchange of story. Stories convey the purposes and desired outcomes of leadership and, when shared in communities, help to establish a bond between and among people, encouraging their participation in the process.

Becoming more authentic prepares us for leadership and helps us continue our life search for meaning and its expression. Often submerged below conscious awareness, core values become part of authentic identity and influence the way individuals react to issues and events. Common descriptions of authenticity include being genuine, living truthfully, possessing self-awareness, and knowing and being oneself. These facets of authenticity reflect the concept of "the inner core" or the central aspect of our being.

Fakery causes a loss of support for our leadership. Inauthentic (and unethical) storytellers, trying to paint a favorable impression of themselves to others or perhaps win support for self-serving goals, immediately lose their moral authority when their dishonesty is exposed. It's not only what kind of stories we tell, but also what we ask others to do after hearing the story that matters. Arrien (as cited in Moxley, 2000) describes the many ways we conspire to present a false self and lose the trust of others:

> We feed the false self by editing our thoughts, rehearsing our emotions, performing what we think other people want to see or hiding our true selves. We feed the false-self system whenever we are unwilling to tell the truth, say what is so, or give voice to what we see. (p. 127)

Stories push the boundaries of our everyday thought worlds and constructions, causing us to see the future possibilities while simultaneously making sense of our past and present circumstances through the close inspection of our personal transformation. Future stories, like interrupted dreams in the night, startle us to wakefulness, warn of fears, and hint of desires, yet swiftly retreat from our immediate inspection. Setting our imaginations to work, our visions in the making, when shared, can help us know the unknowable and detect new possibilities.

The exchange of stories helps leaders and members locate their identity and purpose within the scope of personal, family, and community lives. Engaging people in the mutual and shared exercise of meaning-making, storytelling aids the development of our individual potential, membership in communities, and participation in leadership.

Leaders examine important life events, featuring them in the form of a "quest narrative" to account for and explain changes in their identity and life purpose. While personal and cultural identity stories explain the course of our development (perhaps including a few defining moments), quest narratives emphasize the time when we took risks, learned new skills, and acted with courage, leaving a "stable" state and rising to the occasion. These life-changing events, described in the next chapter, serve as significant episodes of deep learning.

5

THE QUEST NARRATIVE AND THE CALL TO ADVENTURE: DEFINING MOMENTS, REFLECTIONS, AND EPIPHANIES

The shape of my life is, of course, determined by many other things; my background and childhood, my mind and its education, my conscience and its pressures, my heart and its desires.

—Lindberg (1955, p. 23)

Defining story as "the significant actions of characters over time," Taylor (1996, p. 15) gets at the heart of a life narrative. Rather than disconnected bits of experience, we thread our life experiences into an evolving story, assigning meaning to the shape and pattern of our lives through interpretation and producing a meaningful self-portrait. Stories facilitate the ongoing dialogue with others and self, helping us negotiate our subjective reality with objective experience.

Stories help us to know and explain the developmental progression of our lives (and our current state of being), enabling us to make decisions and take action based on life purposes. These actions and their effects change us and in a circular fashion reshape our individual and cultural identity. The progression proceeds in this manner: Knowing who we are (identity) causes us to establish core values (purpose) and pursue them (goals), choosing among alternative approaches (choices), taking action (action), and experiencing their effects (effects). The experience of living changes us, creating an expanded and altered identity. In this way a life or social history emerges from experience and constantly changes. Stories help us keep track of what happened, its meaning to our development as leaders, and its effects.

The quest narrative organizes the circumstances of our personal transformation into story form. Campbell (1949) offers a three-stage description of the hero's journey: (1) departure and the call to adventure; (2) initiation, including the challenges and trials associated with the journey; and (3) the return home, including the meaning of the journey and the personal changes that have occurred. The quest narrative emphasizes the need for people to take risks by moving out into the world to experience growth. The decision to heed the call to adventure and act ensures that the story becomes about personal transformation rather than a tale of lost opportunity.

Told in story form, the quest narrative also appears as "stage theory" in scholarly literature related to adult learning and change. Again, the story proceeds like the quest narrative in linear fashion. Prior to change, the adult experiences (1) "relative stability" in his or her life and environment (Knox, 1977, p. 536). Changes within themselves or the environment come to consciousness, causing adults to (2) "anticipate change" (and often fear it). The (3) " actual change" occurs, serving as a departure point. Leaving the old routines and comforts, adults experience (4) "disorganization," when accomplishing change. Moving through the change and reflecting on is effects, adults (5) "return to [a state of] relative stability" (p. 537). In cyclical fashion, the return to stability prepares us for the next adventure.

Turning to research on human development, a developmental perspective offers yet another way that the quest narrative can be organized—as stages in ego development (forming a personality) or as a life stage (for example, moving from childhood to adolescence) (Knox, 1977). Each adult stage presents a developmental challenge that must be mastered to evolve, otherwise development becomes arrested and growth ends. The quest narrative serves as a progress report on our life experience and its effects. We become the story of our lives.

Whether the story describes the hero's or heroine's journey or a significant episode of learning in the development of an adult personality, or gets told as a life stage or passage story, the pattern remains the same.

A "stable identity" experiences change, encounters chaos, learns, becomes someone new, and returns home. Pearson describes the goals and
purpose of this journey:

> to find the treasure of your true self and then home to give your gift to help
> transform the kingdom—and in the process your own life. The quest itself
> is replete with dangers and pitfalls, but it offers great rewards: the capac-
> ity to be successful in the world, knowledge of the mysteries of the human
> soul, the opportunity to find your unique gifts in the world, and to live in
> loving community with other people. (in Bolman & Deal, 2001, p. 106)

Leaders know their story, so they can be honest with themselves and
others regarding their identity and character. Sharing stories to explain
their life purpose and motivation as well as illustrate their capacity to
lead others, leaders tell others how they "rose to the occasion" and met
challenges facing them:

> The genesis of the quest is some occasion requiring the person to be more
> than she has been, and the purpose is becoming one who has risen to that
> occasion. This occasion at first appears as an interruption but later comes
> to be understood as an opening. (Frank, 1995, p. 128)

The "opening" refers to the learning made possible because leaders
answered the call and met the challenge. The quest story, as an identity
story, tells people about origins, capacity, and motivation for leadership.
Members or followers demand to know not only *what* they are asked to
do but also *who* is asking. Story serves as a vehicle to influence others
and engender their trust.

Life experience, framed as the call to adventure, draws us away from
our current existence to experience change. Rising to the occasion and
overcoming life's challenges prepares us to participate in leadership.
When experiencing trials and tribulations, the quest seems like a threat
to identity and existence. When presented with the call and the challenge, a choice must be made: to retreat and lose the opportunity to
progress, or to face and meet the challenge. Changed as a result of
meeting the challenge, the hero or heroine returns home with new insight and goals. All stories contain the basic components of a quest narrative: the call, the challenge, the choice, the resolution, and the return

home. We must experience change *in the world* with others to progress, mature, and acquire wisdom. Our life story as a "quest narrative" explains in chronological order the significant events or defining moments in our lives and their meaning. Locating these events in autobiographical form and analyzing their impact helps leaders to identify the source of their values and life purpose. The quest narrative essentially serves as a life story organizer, marked by defining moments and our interpretation of their meaning.

The search for defining moments takes us on a reflective journey to locate core values and the sources of authenticity. Self-aware leaders identify the way core values exert a powerful influence on their perspectives. Naming and claiming important values helps form a moral identity and serves as a springboard for action.

Awareness of core values puts leaders on alert. Core values serve as "triggers," often determining our response to dilemmas as well as serving as an undetected explanation for leadership decisions. Core values may also serve as traps, blocking other viewpoints and taking leaders down a path of self-proclaimed righteousness without engaging others in a meaningful dialogue regarding their values.

Guarding against the dangers associated with an automatic response or an excessive emotional reaction, wise leaders recognize when deeply held values are challenged by others and monitor their responses to conflict. Knowledge of core values helps leaders guard against an automatic versus well-considered response to difficult situations. Core values emerge from our life story and come to our dramatic attention in defining moments, tracing the source of our core values and the journey of our personal transformation.

"Defining moment" stories succinctly and sometimes poignantly explain our adult development and identity, often told as a mini-series of life stories. Delving into our family and relationship history, critical life events, accomplishments or milestones, and experience related to cultural difference (Noonan, 2003), we quickly locate episodes of deep learning and pivotal turning points in our lives.

An ordinary story takes on meaning when the subject reveals what happened and what it meant to him or her. As authors of our stories, we "read" them for meaning, interpreting them as a part of our inner work to become more self-aware by reflecting on the meaning of our experience.

After locating significant experiences and discerning their meaning, we may later share them with others as a way of introducing ourselves to them. Our life stories, when composed by us and told to others, reveal our inner character and life purpose to people who matter to us. Because we progress through life stages in predictable ways, our individual experiences often carry universal themes such as struggle, fear, achievement, and growth.

The following story of "Big Grace" illustrates how a defining moment and reflection helped Dawn, the narrator, become a more ethical leader.

BIG GRACE

Considering my early school years, I remember otherness more in those who came to us from "outside" the community. I remember a new, large girl who was quite a bit older than us, who didn't speak English well and was placed in our grade level as a result. She was one of several children from a migrant family who seemed to overflow a tiny, dirty, and broken down two- or three-room house at the end of our row of houses. Their toilet was a ramshackle outhouse sitting next to the cattle yard.

She was dubbed "Big Grace," since when she came into our school we already had another Grace as a schoolmate. Big Grace wasn't there long, but I remember a particularly heated game of tetherball. I was the reigning champ and our newcomer had a powerful arm; it was inevitable that we should square off at some point. She was gargantuan next to me; it was a David and Goliath battle. I found myself the favored one of my schoolmates and it was my place to defend the turf against her as she defeated my peers one by one. My goal was set. There was something in her eyes that told me this win was important to her.

Though not highly competitive, I sensed it was up to me to defend our community standing from any intruder. I needed to outplay her skill and wit. Back and forth the game went for a while until I finally gained ultimate control. As I slammed the rope-tethered ball round and round the pole and out of her reach, I glanced at her face to strategically size up my opponent. She knew it was over. I felt a pit in my stomach because somehow I realized winning was really going to be losing this time.

I didn't need the win as much as she did. It was probably her only hope to measure up to something that seemed to matter since academic and social skills were not going to. She walked away from her loss, head down, amidst the cheers for me, and mostly unnoticed by the rest of the children. That scenario has never left me because in my heart I came to realize she was no different from me as far as needing a feeling of belonging and people who supported her. It was a defining moment for me in leadership, too. I will err on the side of deep human need before I will win at all costs for the organization and the crowd. (Olson, 2006, pp. 8–9)

Like Dawn, we seek to become someone else when, upon reflection, the person we see is not to our liking. To "become" we venture from home into the world. Later, returning with new stories, we see ourselves differently. Like time travelers, we may journey back further to examine our formative experiences with a new and more critical lens. Most things look different after leaving and later returning home.

But the "walk about" doesn't end when we return home. On a kind of forward and backward journey, we frequently reflect to peel back the protective layers of memory and inspect the past with a more discerning eye, allowing a new self to emerge. Sometimes a valuable lesson is not learned while wrestling with the present, but only later, looking back on the events and our previous interpretations of them. Some stories leave an indelible mark on the way we treat others as leaders or, as is the case in the next story, may cause us to temporarily disengage from others as a result of the treatment we receive.

THE LEADER OF THE BAND

Paul shares a story about his first experience as a band director in a Midwestern community, illustrating the importance of distance and time in reflection. A young, outstanding percussionist, Paul's musical talents provided him with an entrée into several careers related to music. A successful college band student and classroom teacher, Paul pursued the next logical step in his career path, seeking a position as a band director. Striving in his new role, Paul advanced in his field and later moved to a different school district to develop a new band program and serve as its first director.

After accepting the position, Paul eagerly established a new band program from the ground up. He hired two colleagues, formed a team, and worked diligently with them to increase student participation in the band program. Remarkable program growth and student success paved the way for even more impressive accomplishments. Dramatic increases in band membership and staff positions led to the first state championship, earned at the close of the third year. Over the next few years, Paul continued to build the program, seeing yet another state championship added to the program's accomplishments.

Despite this dramatic success, Paul became increasingly troubled about several staff members who challenged his leadership, the program, and its future direction. Even more disturbing, the original "team" excluded him from some of their plans and meetings and finally challenged his leadership by staging a coup in the principal's office. Although they were unsuccessful in their attempt to take control of the program, relationships shattered and the team never functioned as well as in the early years. Paul continued to lead the program for the next several years and later accepted a position to serve in a larger leadership role.

Looking back on the years spent with the program, Paul saw the cause of some of the team's problem staring back at him in the mirror. His colleagues had challenged his leadership in the principal's office, disappointed with his actions as program director. Paul reflected on his leadership and his hard-won wisdom in the following account:

I did not want to be the type of director that took credit for all of the program's accomplishments. I gave all team members an equal vote when it came to creating vision for the program, and while I attempted to share my personal vision for next steps, it became apparent that we did not always agree. It is interesting to look back on that time, because in my interest to be different from what I clearly saw as [a] dysfunctional . . . [situation in my previous position] . . . I can see now that I created some [of the] dysfunction. . . . I was the most experienced and most educated member of the [location deleted] band staff. I was hired for my leadership, yet in some ways I chose not to lead.

The program grew quickly and experienced a great deal of band competition success. I did try to honor any requests that would come from any of the team members, and at times that created inconsistent instruction, and did not always allow for full-group goal setting and completion. We tended to bounce around from one relatively good idea to another, not seeing that without a common vision for the staff, the long-term success of the program would be jeopardized because the team did not always agree on the next steps. I, as the leader, needed to lead. The staff grew to become a group that spent more time questioning each other's thinking than sharing a common vision for success. . . .

[They] . . . seemed to be in constant disagreement with my thinking, but I now see that it would not have happened if I had been a stronger leader. Collaborative teamwork and shared decision making does not always mean that equal votes must be cast by all members. My lack of true team leadership created a situation where student achievement could have been damaged because of the lack of communicated direction for the program. I expected them to fall in line with the direction I supported, but I needed to communicate that direction well. (Gausman, 2006, pp. 5–7)

Both Paul's and Dawn's stories illustrate how wisdom emerged from reflection on the defining moments in their lives. Paul learned how to collaborate with others while maintaining his leadership only after he learned the effects of his actions on team members. Dawn learned the importance of justice and caring the moment she watched "Big Grace" walk dejectedly from the playground. Their stories show us how an episode in their lives caused an "epiphany," or turning point. Their experiences changed them.

In the language of theater, the defining moment serves as the dramatic scene in the play. Exposing the actor's character, the audience challenges the actor's version of the truth, balancing his or her story with other perspectives. As the curtain falls, the main character contemplates what has changed and its meaning. Despite an immediate awareness of the potential impact of a critical life event, it may take years to fully understand its full effects. Defining moments and reflection on their meaning may change core values and life purpose.

Critical incidents, "particular, concrete, and contextually specific aspects" of our life experience (Mezirow, 1990, p. 180), cause deep personal change. The epiphany happens during reflection when we experience an "aha!" moment; suddenly perspective, direction, and values change. Later we explain this change by sharing the story of the defining moment with others, helping them see how we changed and why. The events and epiphanies leave indelible marks on our identity.

Unforgettable and often relived incidents substantially transform us (Denzin, 2001). Even a series of minor events can result in a major epiphany. For example, listening to racist or sexist jokes can have a cumulative effect. The "last straw" event causes an eruption due to brutal effects of small, repeated incidents on our well-being. The product of reflective labor, insights gained from either major or cumulative epiphanies reveal the powerful impact of critical incidents in shaping our internal and world views (p. 37).

From critical incident to reflection and the experience of epiphany, we reconstruct our internal worlds from the raw data of our experience. Changing internal assumptions about ourselves and the world, epiphanies move us to tell a new story and lead in a different way. Mezirow (1990) describes the importance of this reflection in learning: "Critical incident responses stand alone as primary data sources, giving insights into learners' assumption worlds in expressions that are indisputably the learners' own" (p. 180).

As authors of our stories, we rummage through the attics of our memory to locate those defining moments, which serve as the raw material for our transformation. The "relived" story and subsequent reflection may result in a reinterpretation of the story. Because we change, the meaning of these defining moments may also change. Remen (1996) notes the importance of the reflective process and the potential to see new insights when we revisit our stories for a second reading: "Revisiting such stories over the years, one wonders how one could not have seen their present meaning all along, all the time unaware of what meaning a future reading may hold" (p. xxx).

Honest reflection resides at the center of our experience, asking us to struggle against the natural inclination to see ourselves in a more favorable way or continue to hold a distorted internal view of ourselves despite evidence to the contrary. Lopate (1995) describes the "difficult climb into honesty" in the personal essay. The same criteria apply to composing and sharing personal stories of transformation:

> So often the "plot" of a personal essay, its drama, its suspense, consists in watching how far the essayist can drop past his or her psychic defense toward deeper levels of honesty. One may speak of a vertical dimension in the form: if the essayist can delve further underneath, until we feel the topic has been handled as honestly, as *fairly* as possible, then at least one essential condition of a successful personal essay has been met. . . . If, however, the essayist stays at the same flat level of self-disclosure and understanding throughout, the piece may be pleasantly smooth, but it will

not awaken the shiver of self-recognition—equivalent to the frisson in horror films when the monster looks at himself in the mirror—which all lovers of the personal essay await as a reward. (pp. xxv–xxvi)

Transformational stories do not require us to expose all of our darkest secrets; however, our stories must offer an honest account of our lives, revealing our "habits of thought" in the way they are selected and told (Lopate, 1995, p. xxvii). The material for stories comes from life experience and includes "how the world comes at another person, the irritations, jubilations, aches and pains, humorous flashes" (p. xxvii). Processing its content, we also "learn the rhythm by which the essayist [storyteller] receives, digests, and spits out the world" (p. xxvii). The teller becomes the story.

Hagberg (2003) offers a leadership development model with the following stages: (1) "start" (static stage), (2) move out (take a risk), (3) move up (acquire skills and experience), (4) move in (live your life courageously), and (5) move beyond (achieve a state of grace) (p. 276). The quest narrative appears again in yet another form. The ultimate goal of the quest narrative involves acquiring wisdom and living in grace (a form of spirituality, authenticity, self-discovery, and the pursuit of moral goodness). Acquiring wisdom moves us to abandon self-interest and serve a higher purpose or calling. Self-awareness leads to greater goodness and a higher calling.

Calling up the defining moments in our lives and sharing these stories with others is central to becoming and serving as a leader. Defining moments, composed in story, show how the choices made, actions taken, and meaning assigned to them mark out our life history and its meaning. Our self-story "requires editing. Editing is the constant process of updating who we think we are and how we speak about our histories and ourselves" (Baldwin, 2005, p. 128). The "edited" self emerges in leadership with a purpose and goals. Gornick's (2001) definition of memoir and advice about how to write one offers valuable guidance regarding how a personal story becomes meaningful to the writer and reader:

A memoir is a work of sustained narrative prose controlled by an idea of the self under obligation to lift from the raw material of life a tale that will shape experience, transform events, deliver wisdom. Truth in a memoir is achieved not through a recital of actual events; it is achieved when the reader comes to believe that the writer is working hard to engage with the experience at hand. What happened to the writer is not what matters; what matters is the large sense that the writer is able to *make* of what happened. (Gornick, 2001, p. 91)

Identifying the pivotal moments in our life through story allows us to compose an intimate portrait, a memoir of experience, revealing our inner self as well as the outer persona.

Providing a useful tool for analysis, Baldwin (2005) depicts the experience of change and its meaning in a graphic model called the "spiral of experience" (p. 100). Illustrating how individuals experience change, Baldwin describes three stages: (1) something happens, leading to (2) questioning, and moving the storyteller to (3) resolution with his or her experience. The "something that happens" might be a chaotic or shocking experience or a moment of surprise or delight.

During the questioning phase, individuals explore the effects and meaning of their experiences that ultimately cause changes in identity and purpose. When the experience and reflection become integrated, a new self emerges and the spiral continues (see http://storycatcher.net/storycatcher_spiral.html for an illustration of the spiral). Individuals achieve a state of grace when a peaceful resolution of changes within and outside of us occurs:

> The self-story must go beyond simply claiming changes in character and demonstrate these changes. Much of the success of the story—its impact both on others and on the self—depends on how convincing this display of changed character is. Readers pick up published illness stories for all sorts of reasons, but the moral purpose of reading is *to witness a change of character through suffering.* In this witness the reader both affirms that change, which is one sort of moral duty, and gains a model for his own change, another moral duty. (Frank, 1995, p. 128)

According to Frank, the "new self" "is not so [much] newly discovered as newly *connected* to its own memory. The past is reinterpreted in terms of the present and takes on an enhanced meaning" (1995, p. 128). Rooting through experience and memory, stories serve as a significant source of wisdom.

Because we rarely control the context or circumstances requiring leadership, or even the people we work with to accomplish it, "leadership as a way of being" refers to the only thing we can control: our identity and the nature of the gifts and service we bring to leadership. Much like conducting an archaeological dig, the search for clues about our past requires us to carefully remove layers of material to locate artifacts that tell a story of how we lived in another time. We do this to say who we are today—as a way of being.

The steps in composing your life story require you to locate defining moments, recall the experience and its effects, assess its meaning, and describe the values incorporated into your identity. One quick method involves imagining your life in book form and dividing the events into chapters. Begin each chapter with a story about a significant episode or experience that explains your current success. Reflect on the following questions: "What did you do to earn your success, and what important values did you discover? How do these events define you?" Think about the importance of this experience in forming your core values and identity. Several methods may help you locate important events in your life story. Another strategy, the life walk, uses the metaphor of a journey to locate these important events.

THE LIFE WALK

Setting out on a personal journey of discovery, imagine that you are taking an extended walk along the path of your life with a close friend. Visiting and reflecting on the important moments of your life, tell your friend about the important moments of your life and what they mean. Imagine that you are holding a deck of cards in your hands and each card represents one episode or event in your life that was meaningful (Noonan, 2003). Different cards draw your attention to the possibilities for locating your leadership story. The first card, "family and relationship history," causes you to think about childhood memories, school years, first loves, and friendships. Influential people and events flood your thoughts.

A second card, labeled "milestones and achievements," reminds you to consider how the accomplishment of significant goals or failure to achieve has changed you. Whether winning an award or always running last in long distance running, experiences in achieving goals shape your work habits and aspirations.

The next card, "critical life event," floods you with memories of seminal events in which you likely experienced intense emotions as well as deep learning.

Wondering what else might stir your memory, you select the last card, "cultural difference." You immediately recall moments in your life when experiences related to diversity changed you. Memories of inclusion and exclusion surface along with moments of joy and pain.

Once the cards are drawn, the second aspect of the walk occurs. A reflective companion pauses with you at each stop on your life map, helping you interpret on the meaning of the event.

Experiences relating to and interacting with others during our formative and adult years concern aspects of family and relationship history (Noonan, 2003). Look for stories about family members, friendships, dating, and major transitions (for example, from daughter to wife). The following questions help make the connection between this history and its impact on our development:

> What did your experience as a family member teach you about relationships? What stories illustrate this lesson? How did your childhood relationships with people outside of your family influence you? What positive and negative experiences shaped your learning? How do your adult relationships shape the way you interact and relate to others? How does this history relate to the leadership your offer others? (Noonan, 2003, p. xx)

Life stories, drawn primarily from family and relationship history, relate our formative experience to the development of important aspects of personality and core values. The following story describes a moment in grade school when a young girl learned an important lesson about justice and fair treatment.

> Every day during Lent we left my Catholic grade school an hour before lunch to walk swiftly to the parish church. Sister set a brisk pace and we half-walked, half-ran the eight blocks to church. As soon as we settled in the pews, my second grade classmates and I watched Father emerge from the sanctuary, advance to the altar and say his third Latin mass of the day.

Nearing the end of the mass, Father moved to the railing and offered Communion. We received the body of Christ in the form of a Communion wafer, a 25-cent sized circle of unleavened bread, bowed our heads, reverently returned to our seats, knelt down and prayed.

As the Communion line was ending, a sudden movement caught my eye—Gregory spat out the Communion wafer on the church floor. Like a stealth bald eagle plucking fish out of a deathly still nature lake, Sister flew toward the offending student, nabbed him, drew him into the folds of her habit and swiftly exited out the side door. It was over before we knew what happened. Well, it wasn't really over. The next morning we witnessed Gregory's trial and punishment.

Walking into the classroom with Gregory in tow, Sister ordered us to kneel next to our desks and pray for him. Gregory knelt beside Sister while she grimly outlined the nature of his offense and sin against God. Next, Sister told us to stand and raise our arms away from our sides just like Jesus did when he was nailed to the crucifix. Interminable minutes went by and our arms grew sore as we complied. Somehow Gregory's punishment became ours. Finally Sister ended the exercise, banished Gregory to the cloakroom open to the hallway and ordered him to stand in the crucifix-like position for various intervals throughout the day.

After Gregory exited the room, we went on to reading, mathematics, religion, and lunch. Never far from our minds, we caught glimpses of Gregory standing in the cloakroom throughout the day as we entered and exited the classroom. I can still see the forlorn figure of Gregory in the cloakroom, standing idle and looking terribly alone. I wondered then and now at the cruelty I witnessed when I was seven years old. Despite my young age, I knew it was wrong. Gregory's shame had become my shame.

This was the first time I learned that religious people—people with God's authority, could be wrong—even abusive. Like fine gossamer cloth, my delicate faith in people and the Church began to tear at the seams. We never learned why Gregory spat out the Communion that day, but years later I wonder how it affected him. As I matured, I learned that many of us (myself included) who sometimes wear the cloth of authority, may abuse our power. When we drop a hammer too hard and severely punish the offender, justice, dignity, and moral authority are lost. (Confidential submission, personal communication [SN], 2006)

Claiming the sources of our core values through story allows us to see their meaning and explain why they are important to us. The actions

taken to accomplish milestones or significant accomplishments reveal
the process and the price of success, whether achieved individually or
collectively.

Developmental milestones and notable achievements, marked by significant effort and struggle, tell a story of achievement accomplished
through diligent effort. A business owner features the importance of individual effort and teamwork as primary themes in his and his company's
success story:

> Standing in front of employees at an annual holiday party held at a ski
> lodge, the company owner choked up as he related the company's history,
> pointing with pride to 30 years of hard work in providing service to their
> customers. Looking out at the adjacent ski slope, he noted that the place
> of the company party was the site of their first major job. Company elec-
> tricians first wired the ski lifts and later installed night lighting using an
> old line truck. The owner said, "The brakes didn't work on the truck so we
> just got it to the top and slowly worked our way zigzagging down the hill."
> Emphasizing hard work, the owner said, "The brakes didn't work, but we
> made it work."
>
> Carrying the company spirit to recent history, a second story affirmed
> the value of hard work. A foreman in charge of a large job received a call
> from a supplier at 5:00 A.M. about a delivery of supplies. The supplier said
> he was on-site and asked where the foreman wanted the supplies
> dropped, assuming he was en route for the normal 7:00 A.M. starting time.
> The foreman replied, "Why don't you just drive around back, I'm already
> here." The foreman lives an hour and a half away and was already on the
> job. When the foreman stood up to receive a small holiday gift, the em-
> ployees cheered. (personal communication, January 19, 2007)

Whether working alone or with others, stories of hard work and accomplishment reveal a lot about someone's character. Serving as a developmental landmark on one's life map, achievement stories show how personal qualities and hard work contribute to the achievement of
significant goals. The following questions help to compose achievement
stories: "What was the goal, and why was it important to you? What sacrifices did you make and obstacles did you overcome to achieve this goal?
What did you learn from the pursuit and accomplishment of these goals?
How did your accomplishment add to your personal and professional

confidence and competence as leader?" The questions apply to individuals as well as organizations. Significant accomplishments tell us what we are capable of doing as a result of substantial effort. But achievements often come at a price, as evident in the next story about a critical life event.

A critical life event shakes us to the very core, often resulting in a dramatic change in perspective or goals. The story should answer at least some of the following questions: "What event in your life had a significant impact on you? What happened, and why do you consider it a life-changing event? What choices or decisions can you trace back to this event? How did this experience influence you as a leader or participant in leadership?" Columnist Nick Coleman recently shared a story about his youthful experience as a school bus driver, illustrating how one incident casts a shadow over a lifetime:

> I was 19 or 20 when I got the keys to a big orange machine and maps to schools in Maplewood and Roseville that I had never of. At that age, I could hardly drive my 1961 Corvair around town without crashing into mailboxes, so I would never have thought it wise to put 60 children in seats behind me. (Coleman, 2007, p. B7)

During a frightening episode in which he thought he might have run over a young girl, he drove for two miles before he finally had the courage to stop, utterly terrified about what he might find. Coleman said, "I thought about it for two horrible miles before I stopped the bus on the highway shoulder and crawled underneath to look for any shred of her that might stuck under the bus" (2007, p. B7). Coleman shares what the experience meant to him:

> She was on her corner the next morning, as usual. But I never forgot the total fear of believing you may have killed a little kid who just wanted to bring a water-color rainbow home to her mommy. . . . So whenever I hear of a school bus accident, I try not to blame the driver before we find out what happened. (p. B7)

The horror of this event still appears in his dreams. The experience changed him, causing him to resist judging someone too harshly. He's been there, too. Years later, Coleman used this event to caution others about judging a bus driver too swiftly, evidence that he recognizes the benefits of inspecting his actions first. Crucial life events help us grow in wisdom, forever changing perspective and future actions.

Membership in social groups, much like our family and relationship history, affects our self-esteem, security, and sense of belonging. Continuing with the life walk, the last "life card" relates to cultural differences, helping you recall how your experience with cultural difference changed you.

Cultural identity stories and experiences related to cultural difference further define adult development. Individuals possess a personal culture composed of their membership and experience in social or cultural groups. Cultural factors of difference include race, ethnicity, religion, place and country of origin, age, occupation, education, mobility, gender, and sexual orientation. Our stories might describe how power, privilege, and position advantaged or excluded us. The following story illustrates how cruelty leaves lasting effects, particularly when inflicted on vulnerable children by adults who are supposed to know better.

One day, I got stuck on a problem of how to get a golf ball out of a narrow, deep hole. For days I would come up with what I thought were fairly creative ideas, but the teacher and my classmates kept telling me I was wrong, and should be able to figure it out. My mom was a cocktail waitress at the local golf course, but I had never stepped outside of the kitchen. I'd never played golf or even held a golf ball in my hand. I didn't know that they were light and could float, and the correct answer was to fill the hole with water.

Well, in this small town of fewer than 1,000 people, my family was known to be the "poor white trash." My parents were frequently kicked out of establishments for being drunk, my siblings and I were the worst dressed kids in school, and it generally wasn't a pleasant place to be. And, after this week of torture for not knowing about golf balls, one of the local mothers approached the school and asked that I be removed from the class. Clearly, she said, I wasn't smart enough to make it, and she didn't want her daughter to be exposed to a lower class of people like myself. Yuck! Talk about people trying to put you in your place for purely class reasons.

But this incident and all of the times I mispronounced something had a significant impact on my communication style. I became careful not to expose my true self, lest I be found out for the imposter I am, and I hold a bitterness towards people who treated my family poorly simply because of our class. (Confidential submission, personal communication [SN], January 1, 2007)

Unfortunately, stories of exclusion, frequently experienced by some individuals or marginalized members of culturally different groups, seem to be ever present in the human condition. It seems unnecessarily cruel when the exclusion is based on cultural differences such as race, class, or gender, the result of birth origin or differences in opportunities completely out of the control of individuals. These stories help us understand people's reluctance to trust others or make themselves vulnerable in relationships and groups. Some need to wear protective armor to defend against cruel assaults on their dignity.

Cultural identity stories allow us to explain the painful and joyous moments in our lives, through tales of family and community life, celebrations, and ritual, as well as distancing events, cruel acts, and experiences in living at the margins. These stories expose others to differences in life experience and values. The following questions help us locate and extract meaning from our experiences related to cultural difference: "How does your cultural identity and experience influence your beliefs, values, and ways of interacting with others? How have your experiences with cultural difference affected the way you seek or retreat from opportunities or challenges? How does your cultural upbringing and experience influence your motivation and capacity to serve as a leader or participant in leadership?"

Asking and answering reflective questions about our lives calls upon leaders to lead a serious life. "A serious life, by definition, is a life one reflects on, a life one tries to make sense of and bear witness to" (Gornick, 2001, p. 91). By organizing and then reflecting on personal transformation stories, leaders and members return to a state of stability wiser because they have recalled their journey, identified what happened and its effects, and claimed the changes in identity and life purpose. Leaders account for the past, live in the present, and imagine the future, using story as a personal and organizational tool for self-discovery and purposeful action.

Members expect leaders to describe some of their defining moments to learn who they are and whether they are worthy of their trust. Judging their capacity to lead based on their life experience and ability to reflect and learn from it, leaders gain or lose credibility based on the stories they tell. People avoid extending too much trust until they've learned something about others and checked out the facts. We also want to learn from their wisdom—do they have something to teach and inspire us?

Anne Morrison Lindberg, international aviator and pioneer, wrote *Gift from the Sea* (1955) to clarify her life purpose. An international bestseller, she introduced her book with the following words. "I began these pages for myself, in order to think out my own particular pattern of living, my own individual balance of life, work and human relationships" (1955, p. 9). She describes the shape of her life and her goal to find inner peace after reflecting on her life experience and locating her authentic self:

> The shape of my life is, of course, determined by many other things; my background and childhood, my mind and its education, my conscience and its pressures, my heart and its desires. I want to give and take from my children and husband, to share with friends and community, to carry out my obligations to man and to the world, as a woman, as an artist, as a citizen. But I want first of all—in fact, as an end to these other choices—to be at peace with myself. I want a singleness of eye, a purity of intention, a central core to my life that will enable me to carry out these obligations and activities as well as I can. I want in fact—to borrow from the language of the saints—to live "in grace" as much of the time as possible. I am not using this term in a strictly theological sense. By grace I mean an inner harmony, essentially spiritual, which can be translated into outward harmony. (Lindberg, 1955, p. 23)

Leaders and members discover their authentic selves through the exchange of personal transformation stories, expressing their authenticity in the ethical acts of leadership carried out with others. Our innate goodness and ability to collaborate with others to promote the common good and expand the "moral core" emerge from our collective authenticity and determination to live in grace. "The ultimate aim of the quest must be neither release nor ecstasy for oneself, but the wisdom and the power to serve others" (Campbell, 1988, p. xv).

As a "story ethic," the stories we tell must serve others rather than ourselves. The following story, told by former President Bill Clinton, shows how his story, honestly told, can serve as a catalyst to change not only an individual life but also symbolically representing change atti-tudes on a global scale. President Clinton tells how the gift of a shirt be-came his symbol for the importance of helping others.

THE GIFT FROM A STRANGER

Invited to speak at the University of Minnesota before a crowd of 5,000, former President Clinton focused on the importance of global humani-tarian work and the need for interdependence between the United States and other countries (McCallum, 2005). Because world economies are closely tied together, Clinton argued that our future economic suc-cess may depend on our ability to establish favorable relationships and improve the declining image of the United States in the world:

> Clinton said the U.S. can't kill or jail all of its enemies, and should work to create more partners and fewer foes. "We should be trying to build a world, at this unique moment in history, that we would like to live in when we're not the only big dog on the block," Clinton said. (McCallum, 2005, pp. 6–7)

Clinton's gift for storytelling became evident when he shared a defin-ing moment when leaving Ghana after working on an economic project with the president of Ghana. Walking toward his plane and preparing to board, he heard someone calling him. "President Clinton, don't go, don't go!" (From Ghana, with gratitude, 2005, p. A4). Clinton stopped and walked toward the woman, then shook her hand. The woman expressed her gratitude for his support of the Africa Trade Bill, telling him that she was one of 400 women who now made shirts and supported their fami-lies from the revenue.

She offered him a shirt to express her appreciation and Clinton, now free to accept it as private citizen, decided to take it home. The shirt now hangs in his closet, serving as a daily reminder of the importance of en-suring that the well-being of others is an integral part of a shared future.

> And I took that shirt home and . . . put it in my closet in a place where I literally have to look at that shirt every single day. You know why? Because every time I see that shirt I remember: That woman's not mad at me. Or you. She doesn't resent America or the West period. She knows she'll

never be as rich as you are, but she thinks we're on her side and pulling
for her and we want her to be part of a shared future. So she doesn't want
her kid to fight in a tribal war. She wants her child to stay in school, get a
college degree and do better. She is living her version of what we used to
call in this country the American Dream. And it didn't cost very much
money. It's a lot cheaper than fighting a war. (From Ghana, with gratitude,
2005, p. A4)

Reflecting on the gift and its meaning, Clinton shared a defining moment as a public story, revealing how his moment can be become our
moment when a nation lends a helping hand to those less fortunate. Beginning with the foundational core of leadership, *leadership as a moral
endeavor*, the importance of moral goodness and loving action toward
others and ourselves serves not only as a strategy for our continued survival but also as a life-giving force for the future.

6

"I AM ANOTHER YOU": LEADERSHIP AS A MORAL ENDEAVOR

The Mayan greeting, "In La'kech," means, "I am you and you are me. I am another you."

—*In La'kech* (2005)

In what was more like an episode from *Superman* than a real-life tale of heroism that occurred inside the New York City 137th Street/City College Station on January 2, 2007, Wesley Autrey rescued twenty-year-old Cameron Hollopeter from certain death. After watching Hollopeter fall off the platform between the subway rails, Autrey leapt off the subway platform to rescue Hollopeter.

As he tried to pull the man to safety at the Harlem stop, Autrey looked up:

I saw the two white lights, and said, "Whoa, you ain't got no time," Autrey said. Autrey, 50, grabbed Cameron Hollopeter, 20, in a bear hug and the pair landed in a shallow trough in the track bed, with Autrey on top. (Strickler, 2007, pp. 3–4)

Autrey protected and saved Hollopeter from being crushed by the train. As the screeching wheels of the subway train ground to a halt, Autrey used his weight and position to hold Hollopeter down in the two-foot-deep trough located between the rails. "In my mind, I believed, I hoped, the train had enough clearance," Autrey said. "It didn't hit my head; it just nicked my cap" (p. 6). The train rolled over the top of them, missing Autrey by inches and entrapping them for twenty minutes before they were rescued from their nightmarish captivity.

Shouting out to shocked bystanders, Autrey thought of his two little girls and asked people to tell them he was okay. Autrey, an "ordinary" construction worker on his way to meet his wife with his four- and six-year-old daughters in tow, performed an extraordinary act of courage.

Just moments before the fall, Autrey and two women had observed Hollopeter convulsing on the platform, causing Autrey to run for help. Returning to Hollopeter's side, Autrey borrowed a pen to pry open the man's mouth because he was having difficulty breathing. Autrey thought his rescue for the day was over, when Hollopeter, disoriented, unexpectedly lost his balance and fell from the platform, causing Autrey to once again get involved. However, this time Autrey placed his life in peril, making a split-second decision to rescue a stranger.

Autrey, an ordinary construction worker, performed an extraordinary act of courage. When asked about his heroism, Autrey said, "I'm just saying, I saw someone in distress and went to his aid" (p. 19). Although spectators expressed their approval with cheers and congratulations, Autrey's response showed his humility:

> While spectators cheered Autrey, hugged him and hailed him as a hero, he didn't see it that way. "I don't feel like I did something spectacular; I just saw someone who needed help," he told the *Times*. "I did what I felt was right." (Associated Press, 2007, pp. 14–15)

Because Autrey saw the stranger as his neighbor and acted quickly to save him, he serves as an example of a leader with "moral insight" (Royce, 1865 in Goodpaster, 2007). Defined as the foundation of the golden rule, moral insight means recognizing that there are other people in the world and "treating one's neighbor unselfishly" (Goodpaster, 2007, p. 52). Autrey's amazing rescue of Hollopeter at the 137th Street Subway Station illustrates moral leadership because he demonstrated all the qualities of a moral leader, defined in the next section.

THE PURSUIT OF GOODNESS AND LOVING ACTIONS

Leadership as a *moral endeavor engages us in the pursuit of goodness realized through loving action toward others and ourselves.* The following questions help us examine the degree to which our actions are both moral (based on ethical principles) and loving (largely aimed toward the well-being of others).

1. Who do we define and include as members of our moral community? How do they benefit from membership in the community?
2. What moral purposes and goals are established and achieved? What loving actions are required?
3. What are the immediate by-products and long-term effects of our moral endeavors?

The Mayan greeting, "In La'kech," translated as "I am you and you are me. I am another you" (*In La'kech*, 2005), reinforces the bond among community members. If I am you and you are me, then we are both the same and equally worthy of membership in the tribe. Moral leaders use the widest possible definition of membership in their "scope of justice" (Clayton & Opotow, 2003, p. 301), sometimes extending membership to those they will never meet or know. Autrey's actions at the 137th Street Station in New York City serve as an example of someone who saw the stranger as a member of his community and risked his life to save him. Members within our moral community receive "considerations of fairness," a "share of community resources," and benefit from willingness on the part of the members "to incur sacrifices to help them" (p. 301).

When we identify others as members, we treat them in loving ways because of their membership. The first condition of moral leadership involves seeing distant others as potential members of our community, which is more easily accomplished when the stranger is similar to us than when the stranger is someone who challenges us and our way of life due to cultural differences:

> [Identifying] others is much easier when we can assume a degree of common cultural ground with them. Family members, members of the same community, religious tradition, ethnic group or nation—these are "neighbors"

with whom identification poses the least severe challenges. (Goodpaster, 2007, p. 58)

The famous parable of the Good Samaritan (Luke 10:25–37, King James Version) provides an answer to the question, "But who is my neighbor?" While others passed by an injured and suffering man, the good man from Samaria stopped to aid him. Nursing his wound, providing housing and food, and offering further assistance, the Good Samaritan provides an example of accepting the stranger as a member of our moral community. Acting from such virtues as compassion, kindness, and goodwill, leadership as a moral endeavor requires treating others as neighbors, family members, and friends.

Moral leaders examine issues of fairness and justice, asking: "Who is likely to benefit or be harmed by my actions? Do cultural differences such as race, ethnicity, sexual orientation, religion, or gender negatively affect my decisions about who becomes a member of my moral community? Do I include some and exclude others based on cultural differences?" In Autrey's case, he saw beyond a "color" or "stranger" divide and rescued another person, recognizing their shared humanity.

Those who fail to help others experiencing peril do so because they do not see them as members of their moral community or choose not to put themselves at risk for another's safety or happiness. When individuals risk themselves seemingly without thought, we detect the capacity for moral leadership. Moral leadership "is more than an intellectual insight, it is profoundly practical. In order for it to guide our choices and our behavior, it must be anchored in our will . . . as it is in our belief system[s]" (Goodpaster, 2007, p. 62). Autrey's instantaneous inclusion of Hollopeter as a member of his moral community led him to take action, going from belief to practical action.

In the pursuit of goodness, the purpose and strategies employed must pass both a moral "means" and an "ends" test to qualify leadership as a moral endeavor. "Focusing on the development of moral intelligence, imagination and character, leaders frame issues, examine alternative ethical perspectives among competing choices and take action out of *goodness* toward others" (Noonan & Anderson-Sathe, 2006 p. 9). Evaluations regarding their leadership should be based on whether leadership "elevates" through purposeful moral action.

Burns (1978) describes leadership as "moral but not moralistic. Leaders engage with followers, but from higher levels of morality: in the enmeshing of goals and values both leaders and followers are raised to more principled levels of judgment" (p. 455). The capacity to provide moral leadership depends on the development of moral character.

Rest (1986) describes four psychological processes necessary for moral behavior: (1) moral sensitivity, (2) moral judgment, (3) moral intention, and (4) moral action (pp. 3–18). Evaluating Autrey's leadership using Rest's criteria shows all of the psychological processes outlined by Rest. Autrey sees Hollopeter in trouble (sensitivity), quickly determines it is his duty to do something (judgment), decides to help by rescuing him to fulfill his duty (intention), and jumps in front of a subway train and saves Hollopeter (action). Autrey's loving action, based on his capacity to move from his beliefs to action, serves as an exemplar of moral goodness.

Moral leaders apply their knowledge of ethical philosophy, values, and beliefs to real-world dilemmas, determining morally justifiable actions. After taking action, the short- and long-term effects of leadership shape the third condition of moral leadership: whether what is accomplished is both morally good and worthy of us in the long run.

Moral leaders ask whether they have accomplished worthy goals and affirmed their core values. They ask the following questions: "Did the benefits outweigh the costs? Were the human and capital resources expended wisely and the fruits of the labor fairly distributed? Were opportunities to achieve our potential distributed fairly among us?"

Although leadership often involves taking action to accomplish goals, its short- and long-term effects go beyond reaching a target or finishing an activity. Moral leaders ask: "Did the activity create more or less trust, more or less commitment, and more or less engagement in future work?" The answers to these questions, vital to the "ends" test of moral leadership, help evaluate the immediate short-term effects of leadership as well as its contribution to the moral culture present in the environment. Members often choose goodness over self-interest when fully included and engaged in work carried out in an ethical manner. The long-term survival and the expansion of moral capacity within people, organizations, and communities serve as the basis for evaluating leaders: "Were the goals, actions and resulting effects worthy of our efforts? Did

our actions help us survive and expand our capacity for loving actions toward others? Did leadership elevate the human condition and serve us
both in the short and long term?"

Moral leaders recognize the necessity of an equally valuable "new
bottom line" of moral action in leadership—moving us beyond the mere
pursuit of money and power to such outcomes as "love and caring, ethical and ecological sensitivity, kindness and generosity, non-violence and
peace" (Network of Spiritual Progressives, 2006, p. 2). The pursuit of
goodness requires seeing a situation as moral, identifying a course of action that passes moral scrutiny, and accomplishing worthy goals that
serve us now and later. Autrey's actions also meet the third test of moral
goodness related to effects of leadership on others.

Stunned by the level of Autrey's risk and sacrifice, many examined
what they might do under similar circumstances. Autrey's actions move
us to higher levels of moral sensitivity and engagement. His story, as a
universal story of sacrifice and selflessness, inspires and elevates others.

Although we can't measure the exact effects of the change based on a
"Good Samaritan Index" or the golden rule, we know Autrey's actions
made a difference—certainly to Hollopeter's family and his heirs. Consider also the positive effects on Autrey's children and others. His behavior serves as a moral guide to his family and community. His leadership expands the moral core, serving us all because of its inspiring and
rippling effects on others.

FORMING A MORAL CHARACTER

Moral identity, defined as the character and capacity of people to lead
morally good lives, forms as individuals and social groups progress and
mature. The moral core, defined as the capacity to exercise moral judgment as well as the motivation to take action based on moral impera-
tives, serves as a collective resource for moral agency and action. Shaped
by individual, family, and social values, formed by developmental experiences and their effects, and combined with aspects of our personality,
character is an integral component of identity. Character reflects an innate goodness based on past actions and revealed when individuals exhibit qualities of "ego strength, perseverance, backbone, toughness,
strength of conviction and courage" (Rest & Narváez, 1994, p. 24).

Individuals as well as communities have a moral core of goodness and capacity for ethical action. Experiences and past actions shape the size of the moral core and affect the future capacity of people to live morally defensible lives. When individuals or communities participate in leadership, their actions either expand or contract the moral core. A community or nation increases or decreases its moral core based on its character, capacity, and collective actions. The capacity to expand the moral core rests with individual and collective leadership. In this view, leadership serves as a life-giving force for an ever-shrinking, morally bankrupt activity. The possibilities depend on what we do together.

For example, when strangers offer help, their agency increases the capacity for moral action due to their efforts. Hurricane Katrina, 9/11, and tsunami stories come to mind immediately. Empathy allows us to see the plight of another while compassion causes us to act on it. Sacrifices generally produce exponential effects when they become visible and their effects on others are known or imagined. The moral core expands when we see others as members of the human family and extend them loving care. The same logic applies to all aspects of leadership as a moral endeavor. The more we pursue goodness, the greater the effect will be. When we move away from goodness and our innate moral core, we lose the capacity for moral action in our own eyes and the eyes of the world.

History provides us with many examples of how the move from innate goodness eventually causes the demise of individuals and entire civilizations. On the world stage, people both individually and collectively have committed atrocities against others. Stories of murderous acts, squandering resources, hate crimes, incidences of abuse, and dishonest and self-serving conduct daily march across the front page of the newspaper. These examples of large and small reductions of the moral core abound in our daily life. Individuals and groups bear responsibility for these acts due to the rule of law and human decency. Although examples of evil abounded in the twentieth century, the most evil and violent in human existence, we find the moral agency the only plausible response to these atrocities.

For example, the recent death of a beloved journalist, Hrant Dick, who fought for the rights of the Armenian minority in Turkey and paid with his life, caused an entire community to do some soul searching. Dick refused to follow "Article 31" in Turkish law, which bans "insulting Turkishness" (Borg & King, 2007, p. A4). Jailed for speaking out about the killing of 1.5 million Armenians (the first genocide of the twentieth century), Dick lost his life because he spoke about the Armenian deaths. Ogun Samast, who may have been influenced by "nationalist militants," allegedly murdered Dick (p. A4).

Dick's widow, Rakel Dick, appealed to mourners to find a moral response to his death:

> Her husband's death, she said, must not become a catalyst for more hatred. "The murderer was once a baby," she said. "Unless we can question the darkness that turned this baby into a murderer, we cannot achieve anything." (Borg & King, 2007, p. A4)

His death and his wife's response expand the moral core, calling on us to examine our actions and do something to reduce the evil in our lives.

Whether famous or largely unknown, the courageous actions of some expand the moral core. Transformational leaders like Nelson Mandela, Martin Luther King Jr., and Mother Theresa call us to action, showing by their example and sacrifice the path to a moral life. They challenged members of the world community to fight oppression and care for others. The everyday actions of good people, who are neither famous nor powerful, also inspire members to action. Autrey's actions in a New York subway, which took place in the short span of a few minutes, inspired a nation and earned him an invitation to the Hall of Congress alongside national leaders to serve as an example of courage. Recognized by President George W. Bush during the 2007 State of the Union address, Autrey contributed in some immeasurable way to the moral core. Connecting the moral core to leadership, activities such as seeking justice, achieving goals, listening, learning, reflecting, healing, and understanding either expand the moral core or reduce the capacity to live moral lives.

Sometimes moral opportunities present themselves clearly, like Autrey's moment in the New York subway. At other times, it might take several years to recognize an opportunity for moral leadership and respond to its call. Another subway rider, Jody Williams, found inspiration as she left a New York subway. After reading a leaflet on global activism handed to her as she exited the station, Williams recalls being inspired by its message. It wasn't until a few years later that her desire to work toward humanitarian goals coincided with an opportunity. Heeding the message and call to leadership, Williams embarked on a life-alerting journey to save the lives of others through her humanitarian efforts.

JODY WILLIAMS, NOBEL PRIZE WINNER

The founding coordinator of the International Campaign to Ban Landmines (ICBL), Jody Williams helped to organize an international campaign beginning in 1992 to ban the use of antipersonnel landmines and eliminate them in all conflict areas. Landmines, first used during World War II to maim soldiers, reduced enemy resources by causing troops to care "for an injured soldier on the battlefield [rather] than deal[ing] with a dead soldier" (*History of Landmines*, n.d., p. 4). Landmines, dangerous to soldiers and civilians alike, maim people and threaten lives during and long after a conflict:

> After a while, antipersonnel landmines began to be deployed on a wider scale, often in internal conflicts and started being **aimed at civilians** [bold in original]. They were used to terrorise [sic] communities, deny access to farming land and restrict population movement. The practice of marking and mapping minefields was no longer followed strictly. As a result, civilians, peacekeepers, aid workers and soldiers alike had no way of knowing if they entered a minefield. Rain and other weather often shifted minefields. So without clear records, and with the impacts of weather and time, clearing up the mess after a conflict became even harder. (*History of Landmines*, n.d., pp. 5–7)

Later dropped from planes, landmines fell indiscriminately in unmapped territories (p. 8). Today, more than a hundred million landmines (*Nobel Peace Prize*, 1997, n.d., p. 2) still threaten the safety and peace of people worldwide despite the accomplishments of an international campaign to eliminate them. Ultimately the efforts of Jody Williams and the ICBL led to an international treaty banning the use of antipersonnel landmines. Sharing the Nobel Peace Prize in 1997 with the organization she coordinated, Williams described her motivation to serve based on altruistic purposes awakened when she read a leaflet on global activism and also her early years defending her brother, who is deaf (*This I Believe—Jody Williams*, 2006).

Giving credit to the efforts of others and the importance of action in leadership, Williams tells a story of faith, collaboration, and change:

> If I have any power as an individual, it's because I work with other individuals in countries all over the world. We are ordinary people: My friend Jemma from Armenia; Paul from Canada; Kosal, a landmine survivor from Cambodia; Haboubba from Lebanon; Christian from Norway; Diana from Colombia; Margaret, another landmine survivor from Uganda; and thousands more. We've all worked together to bring about extraordinary change. . . . For me, it's about trying to do the right thing even when nobody else is looking. . . . I believe that worrying about the problems plaguing our planet without taking steps to confront them is absolutely irrelevant. The only thing that changes this world is taking action. I believe that words are easy. I believe the truth is told in the actions we take. And I believe that if enough ordinary people back up our desire for a better world with action, I believe we can, in fact, accomplish absolutely extraordinary things. (*This I Believe—Jody Williams*, 2006, pp. 6–10)

Williams' story illustrates the power of moral action and its effects on others. Seeking justice expands the moral core. When Williams saw those threatened by landmines as part of her moral community, she embodied the spirit of the Mayan greeting, "In La'kech," translated as, "I am you and you are me. I am another you" (*In La'kech* 2005).

Williams serves as "a morally exemplary individual, one who substantially integrated over the long term, moral understanding into [his or] her sense of personal identity" (Bergman, 2002, p. 123). Her individual legacy, along with those of many others who engage in humanitarian work, expands the moral core. Jody Williams and the members of the International Campaign to Ban Landmines (ICBL) tackled one of the world's most invisible and deadly enemies, antipersonnel landmines, effectively reducing the threat of violence to thousands of people worldwide. Acts of personal commitment expand the moral core.

We next compare the lives of two men who served as cabinet members in the Johnson administration during a time of great social change and war. Both led during dangerous times and affected the moral core. Acts of leadership must be considered and measured in light of their influence on the moral core. Fundamentally, when actions fall short of the moral standard, the people who engage in leadership also fail, largely due to the way they conduct themselves and their lasting effects.

A MOMENT OF MADNESS: LEADING IN
DANGEROUS TIMES

On September 29, 1972, Robert McNamara, Secretary of Defense during the Vietnam War and then president of the World Bank, boarded the *M.V. Islander* ferry docked at Woods Hole, Massachusetts, for the forty-five-minute trip to Martha's Vineyard (Hendrickson, 1996). Making his way to a small dining counter, McNamara ordered a drink and chatted with a companion. A short while later a young bearded man, unknown to McNamara, approached him and said, "Mr. McNamara, there's a phone call for you. Please follow me" (p. 5). McNamara followed the stranger along a narrow walkway, ostensibly heading for the pilothouse to take the call, when the stranger turned on him.

Grabbing McNamara by his belt and collar, the stranger attempted to throw him overboard. Caught by surprise, McNamara held on for dear life and started screaming, "Oh, my God, no" (Hendrickson, 1996, p. 8). McNamara struggled to stay on board, locking his hands firmly onto the railing with a vise-like grip, barely thwarting the stranger's attack.

Although the motivation for the stranger's assault was unclear, McNamara was saved when help arrived and pulled the violent stranger off him. After escorting McNamara back to the dining hall, the crew notified the police, who ordered them to detain the assailant. But the assailant, helped by someone sympathetic to his cause, jumped off the back deck and disappeared as the ferry docked. Although the police searched for the assailant, they never found him, and the incident received little public notice as a result of McNamara's desire to put the episode behind him, refusing to press charges.

Years later, biographer Paul Hendrickson, aware of the "legend" regarding this assault, tracked down the story and located the unknown assailant by ferreting out potential candidates. Showing up at his door, Hendrickson convinced the reluctant assailant to talk about the incident, securing his cooperation with a promise of anonymity. In a moment of madness, the attacker had nearly changed the course of his life and the life of his intended victim because of his belief that McNamara's actions regarding the Vietnam War unnecessarily caused countless deaths. His desire for retribution overtook him when the opportunity

presented itself on that fateful night. He wanted McNamara to acknowledge his culpability:

> You see what got to me in the first place is here's this guy crossing Vine-
> yard Sound on a ferry one Friday night whose very posture is telling you,
> "My history is fine, and I can be slumped over a bar like this with my good
> friend . . . and you'll just have to lump it." Well, I got him outside, just the
> two of us, and suddenly his history wasn't so fine, was it? (Hendrickson,
> 1996, p. 356)

The struggle between the two men symbolizes the conflict over Vietnam, including the debate about moral accountability for the decisions
and results of McNamara's leadership. The accusations leveled at Mc-
Namara's leadership include excessive loyalty to Lyndon Johnson resulting in deceptive policies; denying that there was troop escalation in Vietnam and the escalation of the war effort as a result of extensive bombing
in North Vietnam; ignoring the advice of military experts, resulting in a
failing strategy in Vietnam (and knowingly continuing the effort); manipulation of the Joint Chiefs into endorsing policy they did not, in fact,
support; and lack of a human response to the tragedies and loss of
American lives in Vietnam (Herring, 1995).

In *In Retrospect: The Tragedy and Lessons in Vietnam* (1995), Mc-
Namara attempts to "put before the American people why their government and its leaders behaved as they did and what we [the reader]
may learn from that experience (p. xviv). In the prologue to his book,
McNamara asks a central question, hinting at his failure to offer capable
leadership:

> My associates in the Kennedy and Johnson administrations were an excep-
> tional group: young, vigorous, intelligent, well meaning, patriotic servants
> of the United States. How did this group—"the best and the brightest"—
> as we eventually came to be known in an ironically pejorative phrase—get
> it wrong on Vietnam? (p. xviv)

Although this passage serves as a good beginning, many felt the book
fell short of an authentic and credible apology to the American people,
as evidenced by the controversy that accompanied McNamara's book
tours, editorials in leading newspapers, and critical reviews. McNa-

mara's book tours opened wounds, as revealed in a dramatic episode at Harvard on April 25, 1995. John Hurley, a combat veteran who came to hear McNamara, rose from the audience and, losing control of his emotions, called the book an "obscenity":

> My friend, my commander, Bert Bunting, died in Vietnam. McNally never saw Wyoming. Alan Perrault never saw Needham, Massachusetts, again. Sonny Davis didn't come home. They were torn to shreds, they were ripped apart. You ripped the soul out of the family of 58,191 families in this country, sir. And you remained silent. You said nothing. You let thirty years pass. (Hendrickson, 1996, p. 380)

On the third day after McNamara's book's release, the lead editorial in the *New York Times* called McNamara "morally dead and spiritually bankrupt" (Hendrickson, 1996, p. 379), holding McNamara accountable for his actions:

> Mr. McNamara must not escape the lasting moral condemnation of his countrymen. . . . His regret cannot be huge enough to balance the books for our dead soldiers. . . . What he took from them cannot be repaid by prime-time apology and stale tears, three decades late. (p. 379)

Kneeling in the confessional of history and asking for forgiveness, McNamara's attempt to apologize and "set the record straight" fell on deaf ears; he simply took too little responsibility far too late. The "moment of madness" that took place on the *M.V. Islander* ferry was a moment of reckoning for McNamara and only the beginning of a lifetime overshadowed by his failure in Vietnam. McNamara left his position as Secretary of Defense on February 29, 1968. Although he subsequently served as president of the World Bank, he rarely escaped questions about his role in Vietnam.

Appearing as a guest on *Larry King* in 1986, McNamara was asked to discuss his public service. They discussed generally the conduct of public servants. The following dialogue ended with a damaging admission by McNamara:

> King said, "Always be honest."
> McNamara replied, "Always be honest."

King added, "And not always say everything."

McNamara said, "Well, no. I think at times it's perfectly permissible to withhold information, so long as one doesn't lie, but one should never mislead." (Hendrickson, 1996, p. 377)

In the interview, King asked McNamara why he never quit his position as Secretary of Defense when it was evident that he did not fully support the war effort. McNamara replied:

> Well, I had questions, but when one is asked by a president to serve and when one can continue to voice his concern privately, and when the president wishes to consider that, and weighed in a balance with other things, I think one has an obligation to continue, and I did. (p. 377)

McNamara's decision to support the president despite his concerns substantially diminished his reputation and legacy as a leader. The painful effects of this decision followed him through the remaining years of his life.

In contrast, John Gardner, Secretary of Health, Education and Welfare (HEW) during the Johnson administration, reached the opposite conclusion. While serving as HEW secretary during the escalation of the war in Vietnam, Gardner told the president that it was not right to serve a president he could no longer support and offered his resignation. Gardner did not believe Johnson should run for reelection, and told him so.

JOHN GARDNER'S RESIGNATION

In November 1967, President Lyndon Johnson planned to run for a second term as president. After contemplating his position, John Gardner concluded that he did not support Johnson and that he would need to resign because he thought the president deserved loyal people serving in his cabinet:

> Then, in early January, I wrote a very brief letter of resignation and delivered it by hand to the president. He read it and asked me why. I said that in my judgment the course of events had so damaged his capacity to lead that he could not unite the country in the struggles that lay ahead. . . . I

explained this to the president as best I could. It wasn't easy. I gave him great credit for what he had achieved in my Department, but I kept returning to my point. I said that in an election year, a president contemplating re-election deserved the wholehearted backing of his entire team, and that I could not give it. (Gardner, 2003, p. 26)

Remarking years later on the impact of his decision and resignation on his relationship with President Johnson, Gardner thought it strengthened it. "Having told him forthrightly just about the hardest thing one could say to a president, I think he trusted me more. We remained on terms of friendship and mutual respect to the end of his life" (2003, p. 27). The reputations of Gardner and McNamara differ dramatically. Although both McNamara and Gardner initially supported increasing troop strength in Vietnam, Gardner alone recommended full public disclosure of this decision. He also favored a plan to educate the public about the need for increased financial support of the War (McNamara, 1996, p. 206), something Johnson loathed doing. The escalation of the Vietnam War remained temporarily concealed from public knowledge. McNamara participated in the subterfuge.

McNamara's choice to publicly support Johnson despite his increasing despair about the war caused a breakdown in public trust. McNamara's silence and Johnson's deception "embarked [the country] on a course carrying it into a major war [that] was hidden" (McNamara, 1996, p. 206). The legacy of this deception, along with others in both the public and private sectors, has expanded cynicism about leadership and the breakdown in public trust. McNamara also endured a lifetime of accusations of wrongdoing regarding his actions, in contrast to Gardner's legacy of ethical leadership and concern for the common good. Although both men engaged in leadership during the same difficult historical period and worked for the same president, their choices placed them on dramatically different courses.

McNamara's unwillingness to stand for what he believed because of his loyalty to Johnson cost him the respect of the American people and jeopardized his life. Facts about the escalation of the war in Vietnam, hidden from the public, damaged trust. To carry out the deception, he silenced those who objected and refused to hear alternative views (McNamara, 1996). In contrast, Gardner's style, participatory and inclusive, diminished barriers and welcomed alternative views.

Gardner expanded the involvement of agency personnel during his years at HEW to search for solutions for poverty, health, and educational issues. He later established Common Cause to provide a way for common people to have a voice in influencing policy (Gardner, 2003). In contrast, McNamara disliked the media, participated in keeping information secret, and refused to meet with those holding opposing viewpoints (McNamara, 1996).

Their stories illustrate important aspects of moral leadership, contrasting different values and approaches to leadership during tough times. While Gardner serves as an exemplar of moral and collaborative leadership, McNamara serves as a reminder of the many ways misguided loyalty and an unwillingness to engage with others to find alternative solutions can be dangerous to the leader and those who must live with his or her decisions. Beyond loyalty to the president, there is a higher loyalty to the American people.

Frankel (1995) summarizes the ethical challenges in McNamara's leadership, pointing out his responsibility to the soldiers as well as to the president of the United States:

> McNamara blames Johnson for going to war furtively, with no regard for the rights of Congress and the public, but he rejects any obligation to resign in protest or, once out of office, to share his policy disagreements with the country. Cabinet officers, he contends, should have a constituency of one: the president—from whom they derive all authority and through whom alone they can be held accountable. That is surely the right ethic for normal times. Unelected officials should not steal their president's mandate to pursue an independent course. But a thousand dead Americans a month create their own constituency. Even military discipline admits a higher duty than hierarchical loyalty when power is badly used and puts lives at risk. (pp. 17–18)

The contrast between the ethical decisions and actions of Gardner and McNamara stands out as a useful comparison in thinking about leadership as a moral endeavor. McNamara's and Gardner's stories raise several important issues about moral leadership: (1) the role and importance of moral authority, action, and accountability in leadership; (2) the importance of moral intelligence and action and its effects on others; (3) the potentially disastrous and often dangerous effects of misguided leadership on self and others when "morally bankrupt" decisions are made; (4) the enduring nature of suffering; and (5) the timelessness of public memory in recalling some of the most devastating episodes in human history.

Ciulla (1995) defines "good leadership," addressing both moral actions as well as effective performance in achieving goals:

> [T]he ultimate question in leadership studies is not "What is the definition of leadership?" The ultimate point of studying leadership is, "What is good leadership?" The use of the word *good* here has two senses, morally good or technically good or effective. These two senses form a logical conjunction. In other words, in order for the statement "She is a good leader" to be true, it must be true that she is effective and she is ethical. (p. 13)

We assume moral leadership precedes "effective" leadership, while also recognizing that moral leaders must also be "technically" good to achieve the goals of ethical leadership. Leaders and members accomplish the goals of leadership through collaborative, relational, inclusive, sense-making, and futuristic actions. Leadership, an outward expression of an inner moral core of our individual and collective authenticity, addresses universal challenges ever present in the human condition.

Although many proposed definitions and conceptions of leadership exist, dating from the earliest times in human history to the present, Bass's suggestion that leadership should be based on "the purposes to be served by the definition" allows for many interpretations of leadership (1990, p. 20). We can't imagine a more important purpose of leadership than the pursuit of goodness through loving actions toward others and ourselves. Leaders and members engage in such activities as telling the truth, acting with integrity, listening to each other and learning, seeking social justice, and dealing with change, expanding the moral core through ethical actions.

Colby and Damon (1992) describe the interpersonal styles of moral leaders, including:

> (1) a manner that encourages collaborative activities with others, (2) a determination to find colleagues that share one's most fundamental moral goals (3) a toleration of, and interest in, the alternative perspectives of colleagues who share one's fundamental goals, (4) an eagerness to communicate with

colleagues and others about values, (5) an active seeking of new knowledge and strategic skill from others, [and] (6) an ability to take on aspects of the other while not losing the integrity of one's own long-standing commitments. (pp. 198–199)

These styles emphasize the integration of "reflection and action to live out [their] moral commitments" (p. 310). Moral commitments go beyond self-interest and instead emphasize the greater good, achieving a state of grace and authenticity. Moral leaders seek to expand the moral capacity of entire communities by "hand[ing] one another along through the moral leadership we show or through how we support it in others" (Coles, 2000, p. xii).

SEEDS OF MORAL COURAGE AND CULTURAL CHANGE

The hardy sunflower grows on the borders of country roads, in fields, and next to front entrances of homes, welcoming visitors. North American Indians cultivated the sunflower and later shared it with Spanish explorers. Europeans used it for oil production, Russians bred it to reach a "mammoth" size, and then North Americans later reintroduced it as a crop again (*All about sunflower,* n.d.). Planted in shallow soil, it takes just a few inches of moist dirt to support a sunflower. Quickly growing wide and deep roots, the sunflower reaches a fantastic twelve feet in height during a single season. Each sunflower holds densely packed, colorful seeds:

Each sunflower head, or inflorescence, is actually composed of two types of flowers. What appears to be yellow petals around the edge of the head are actually individual ray flowers. The face of the head is comprised of hundreds of disk flowers, which each form into a seed (achene). . . . Sunflower heads turn with, or track, the sun early in their development, but later stay east-facing before facing downwards. (*Sunflower: A Native Oilseed With Growing Markets,* n.d., p. 7)

At night, the sunflower closes up, protecting itself from cooling temperatures. Forming an equiangular spiral, the seed core expands from the center outward in equal increments in an almost perfect, symmetrical pattern. It widens from the base, expanding outward, adding increasingly more seeds to its core.

Just before harvest, the sunflower faces downward, protecting itself from predator birds. Sunflower plants yield high-energy food for living things, serve as a source of oil, and provide a decorative element in dress and design. Arguably one of nature's perfect foods, the sunflower continually serves as a source of new uses ready for human invention.

The sunflower can represent an image of leadership as a moral endeavor because of its adaptability to different environments, shape and growth pattern, hardiness, and "seed core." Beginning with the idea of where sunflowers are planted, whether on the borders, in the fields, or next to our homes, leadership grows around us and serves many purposes.

The sunflower, a product of cultural collaboration, grows large through adaptation in and innovation to changing environments. Methods and people, transplanted into new environments, thrive due to their exchange of learning and technologies. Spreading itself rapidly after being planted in shallow soil, the sunflower grows deep roots and anchors itself in the soil. While the growing season remains relatively constant, the yields and quality increase through collaboration and invention, resulting in an improved hybrid.

The seeds of our collective endeavor must be firmly rooted in nutrient-rich soil and allowed time to reach full maturity. We, like sunflowers, follow the light, pursuing moral goodness and strategically retreating from the darkness and the detrimental effects of misguided actions. Colorful seeds located in the center of sunflowers are actually individual flowers contributing to the "moral core," the individual actions hidden in the flower petals. The size of the seed core determines the quantity of the harvest.

Drawing nutrients from the mix of rain, soil, and light to dramatically increase size in a single summer, the sunflower and our moral lives expand when we experience life-giving forces. As we seek justice, the moral core expands. As we innovate, our capacity to develop and share resources expands, allowing us to care for others. Understanding causes us to see ourselves in another (I am you) and treat others respectfully, expanding their capacity to contribute. And so on. The harvest extracted from the sunflower is life giving and healthy, producing many benefits.

The soul of leadership, captured in the moral core, is expressed in authentic action in the world, producing moral by-products such as justice, love, and caring.

Moving outward from our moral core, we express our capacity and authenticity in our collective endeavors. Story serves as a nutrient for the moral core. Different types of stories expand the core by drawing our attention to the various purposes of leadership described above, affecting the quality of the moral endeavor. Some stories have enduring value as a source of inspiration or a painful reminder of what happens when we lose "due north" on our moral compass. Forming an equi-angular spiral, the seed core, like our moral core, expands from the center outward, increasing its size based on our moral actions, demonstrating how collaboration and moral action expand the moral core.

Bergman (2002) describes the motivation to act in moral ways by connecting moral action to identity: "I can do no other and remain (or become) the person I am committed to being" (p. 123). Outward actions reflect inner character.

A SPECIAL BOND BETWEEN DOCTOR AND PATIENT

On a mission of mercy in El Salvador, Dr. Samuel Weinstein, a New York heart surgeon, made a special donation to Francisco Calderon Anthony Fernandez, an eight-year-old boy who not only needed heart surgery to save his life but also blood of a rare type, B-negative, to survive. After eleven hours of surgery, Fernandez had lost too much blood. His surgeon, Dr. Weinstein, who had B-negative blood (only 2 percent of the population have this blood type), stopped operating, left the room, donated his blood, and returned to finish the operation.

> "We realized he might bleed to death, so I asked what blood type he was and they said he was B-negative and I said, 'You know, I'm B-negative.' Dr. Robert Michler, founder of the group, was standing next to him and said, 'I support you'." "Weinstein, who said he was an occasional blood donor—'but never like this'—said the interruption lasted about 20 minutes. 'It's not like I was going to lie down and have cookies,' he said."
>
> But after he gave his pint, "They gave me a couple of bottles of water and a cardiologist who has more important things to do came out to check

on me and gave me a Pop-Tart. Yeah, I think surreal is the right word."
(Associated Press, 2006a, ¶ 6–10)

Making worldwide headlines, Weinstein's story of personal sacrifice inspires others. His actions embody the qualities of a moral leader.

Silverman (2006) divided story actions into a five-sided star to help leaders locate and use story to inspire others, using the following categories: (1) find stories, (2) dig into stories, (3) select stories, (4) craft stories, and (5) embody stories (p. 215). The final point of the star refers to the way moral leaders must live the promise of leadership as they portray it, establishing their credibility and gaining support of others. Weinstein's personal donation of time and blood sets an example for future doctors and others who decide to follow his example of moral leadership.

Ethical leaders secure the commitment of followers by acting in ways that are consistent with moral values. In contrast to Weinstein's actions, some leaders fail a moral test due to self-serving motives and actions. As a result, the willingness of members to participate in leadership wanes. In the next chapter stories about the difference between telling the truth and telling lies (even small ones) may help leaders distinguish the sometimes thin and confusing line between honesty and deception, an important aspect of moral character.

7

OFFICIAL STORIES, COVER STORIES, AND DECEPTIONS: TRUTH, LIES, AND EVERYTHING IN BETWEEN

A lie gets halfway around the world before the truth has a chance to get its pants on.

—Winston Churchill (Quote DB, n.d., c)

Leaders often use story to explain their roles, decisions, and actions while serving in an official capacity as well as to describe and explain the meaning of important events, directions, and activities of the organization. Serving as the public face of the organization, leaders communicate about the history, performance, and vision of their organizations through story. The stories they tell must be worthy of themselves, the organization, and its private and public members. Because stories must pass the scrutiny of various audiences, leaders must be able to distinguish between telling the truth and lying and then, to the degree possible, tell the truth. This is no simple matter.

Bok (1979) describes a "clear-cut lie" as a lie "where the intention to mislead is obvious, where the liar knows that what he [or she] is communicating is not what he [or she] believes, and where he [or she] has not deluded himself [or herself] into believing his [or her] own deceits" (p. 17). The distinctions between telling the truth and telling lies contains two dimensions: the general truth or falsity of the speaker's statements and whether or not the speaker's intent is to mislead others.

Distinguishing between Plato's "noble" lie (for example, a morally justifiable action told to save a life or a country) with the outright fabrication of a self-serving story to limit damage to oneself or an organization, leaders must be aware of the range of "truthful" responses and stick as closely as possible to a truthful recounting of facts, recalled without an intent to mislead (Bok, 1979, p. 176). Imagine a continuum of truthfulness, on one end of which would be a close and honest account of the story with no intent to deceive, while at the other end would be located those stories that are loosely and carefully crafted to mislead and deceive others. Official stories are authorized accounts released, explained, and defended by legitimate representatives of the organization. Prepared for internal and external consumption, official stories serve as descriptive statements of the central events and actions of the organization.

More than mere statements of fact, official stories reflect the values of leaders and the organization. They must bear the burden of Bok's truth-telling standard: The "official" story must contain reasonable and accurate statements of fact and be honestly told. An official story becomes a "cover story" when one or both conditions change: Someone does not fairly represent the facts or he or she intends to mislead others. Rarely used unless trouble looms, the cover story exists as a type of crisis story. The cover story seeks to minimize the anticipated or actual consequences of a tragic event or disappointing performance, offering a different version of the "truth" for public consumption.

For example, when leaders emphasize certain "facts" and leave others out, the story becomes factually suspect. When the order of how things actually occurred changes (revising history to suit the deception), the story becomes factually suspect. A story can be factually "correct" but untrue. In situations like this, the deceiver arranges facts to promote the deception, disguises the real events, shields culpable parties from scrutiny, and prevents damage to individuals or the organization. Deception lurks somewhere in the background, causing us to question all the facts presented and what might be missing from the story.

In the following "fictional" story, locate what aspects of the story might cause us to question its placement on the "truth-deception continuum" described previously.

While attending a hastily called staff meeting, the superintendent waited uncomfortably with his colleagues to hear the administration's "official" story regarding a recent crisis. Just weeks after the school district had received a national award, news of the district's dismal financial performance leaked out. Deeply disturbed and embarrassed, the chief executive officer prepared a press release to explain why the organization was in "statutory operating debt."

Taking responsibility for the problem and offering a public apology, the superintendent offered the following reasons for the failure:

1. School funding has reached crisis levels.
2. There was a change of personnel in the business office.
3. Financial documents submitted to the board and administration were estimates of the operating budget and proved to be incorrect; the problem wasn't noted until after the next fiscal year was already in motion, making it far too late in the fiscal year to make budget reductions.
4. A higher than anticipated fuel bill increased district expenses by $1 million.
5. The fund balance steadily declined over the last few years to maintain a high-quality educational program.
6. There was no misuse of funds; the district merely spent more revenue than it collected from the taxpayers.
7. Choosing not to release the preliminary and disappointing findings until after a referendum (a request put before the voters to support an increase in taxes) was held, a district official stated that the timing of the report's release was unrelated to the referendum.

Imagine opening up the morning newspaper and reading this account. Although some might accept the story without questioning its veracity, others might question the truthfulness of the preceding statements. All too familiar with public officials who obscure the truth by arranging facts to mitigate poor financial performance, the reader might reject the "official story" and ask more questions about what really happened.

Unfortunately, the "real story" happened to Dr. Michael Kremer, Superintendent of Schools and the Hopkins School District in Minnesota (Kremer, 2005). The preceding statements were drawn from Kremer's press statement issued to the public. Kremer found himself swimming against a sea of disbelief. Releasing information about poor financial performance after a referendum received approval raised doubts among the voters about Kremer's honesty, causing them to challenge the official version of events.

Perhaps the most damaging aspect of this story was the belief of some that district officials withheld information to influence the outcome of the vote. Immediate disclosure about the financial performance before the referendum might have removed all doubt about the motivations of those involved. (Who could doubt their honesty if it was most likely to be damaging to themselves or the district?) Unfortunately, it might have caused the sound defeat of the referendum at the polls, a double penalty. Even appreciating the difficult position of the district and superintendent doesn't change the "truth-telling" standard: Be particularly forthcoming with crucial information that will be likely to influence choices.

Cover stories attempt to minimize the potential damage of a failure that carries a high penalty by trying to avoid the costs of mistakes. "These avoidance tactics may stall the damage in the short term, but can cause greater damage for the executive or organization in the long run when the public learns of the deception" (Noonan, 2003, p. 148). Right or wrong, the failure to fully disclose will be viewed by some as a deliberate deception. Once people challenge the story, things fall apart and may never be the same again. The incident damages the teller, the members of the organization, and the larger community. In this case, the superintendent resigned and the board established "their new plan to implement the 'Three Rs' for the School District: Restore financial stability, Renew trust and Refocus the District" (*Hopkins School Board Accepts Superintendent Kremer's Resignation*, 2006, p. 6).

Widely acknowledged as a very dedicated and capable superintendent with an excellent track record, Superintendent Kremer likely lost his job because the official story fell on deaf ears. His story serves as a lesson on the full and early disclosure of bad news to the public. In the next story, a "cover story" lands the superintendent in trouble with the public and city government.

THE CASE OF THE BROKEN WATER MAIN

Worried about a rumor related to school violence and collaborating with board Chair Bruce Richardson and high school Principal Robert Laney, Superintendent Debra Bowers of St. Louis Park, Minnesota, decided to close school for a day due to the potential for school violence rumored among students. Creating a "cover story" about the real reason for the closure to avoid compromising the investigation, they told the press and public that a broken water main necessitated the school closure. The next day, school reopened and Superintendent Bowers and Principal Laney posted the following press release on the school district website:

October 2, 2006

Late Sunday night, we announced that all classes were canceled at our senior high school on Monday, Oct. 2, reportedly due to a broken water main. We were dealing with a different situation and we decided to cancel school for the safety of our students. Student safety is our top priority and last night's measures were taken, in part, due to recent national events. We apologize for any concern or confusion this may have caused.

A student notified high school administrators at 8 P.M. Sunday of a rumor that a student or group of students intended violence in the school on Monday, and that a weapon or weapons could be involved. Between 8 and 10:30 P.M. St. Louis Park police and high school administrators interviewed seven students and determined there was no substance to the allegations.

At 11:30 P.M., St. Louis Park police informed high school principal Bob Laney of a call from dispatch from a different student making similar allegations. With the new situation occurring at 11:30 P.M., we announced classes were canceled to allow police to complete their investigation. Monday morning, police verified that there was no substance to the second allegation and that it was related to the scenario they investigated earlier Sunday evening.

Measures we are implementing to ensure student safety upon their return on Tuesday include restricting student movement around the building and having additional safety monitors at the senior high. We thank the students who came forward with their concerns and we'd like to remind you that you can help by talking to your students about the importance of sharing information if they believe a potentially dangerous situation exists.

There is no evidence of a threat at the high school, or any other district building at this time. Today's afterschool [sic] and evening district and Community Education activities, including childcare, will be held as scheduled. Again, we apologize for any inconvenience this may have caused, however, student safety is a top priority for our schools. (St. Louis Park Schools, 2006)

Once the deception and the real reason for the school closure became public, a debate ensued about the decision to deceive the press and public. Initially, Superintendent Bowers rigorously defended her decision, claiming the higher interest of student safety. She soon learned that people had serious concerns about the public deception. Some argued that the safety of the students justified the lie, even though such a ruse would be unlikely to work again. Others argued that the public deserved to know the truth, describing the greater harm in lost trust due to deception.

The Institute for Global Ethics (Kidder, 2006a; Kidder 2006b) published an online newsletter and issued two weekly columns about the deception written by well-known ethicist Kidder. Kidder invited online readers to submit their views in the October 23 column and then summarized the arguments in his October 30 column:

> The power of the arguments on both sides reminds us why this is a tough right-versus-right dilemma. To one group, the notion of the "well-placed lie . . . for the public good" raises troubling ghosts of Watergate and Clinton–Lewinsky—not to mention current stories of riots in Hungary and political entanglements in Poland, both springing from deception by government officials. To the other group, the assertion that it "seems so simple" appears dangerously close to risking children's lives for the sake of an abstract principle. (2006b, p. 6)

The obvious problem, lying to the public even in the interest of public safety, was only the beginning of what developed into the nightmarish aftereffects of a poor decision. The school officials had failed to notify city officials about what they were doing, and the government center was inundated with requests for information from the general public. Some residents called to ask, "Should residents stay home to guard against the potential for their water lines being damaged during the repair of the water main? How long did the public works employees think the repair would take? Did they anticipate a total shut down of water during the immediate and near future? Is the water likely to become contaminated?" Because of various considerations, the decision failed to meet the test of wisdom and instead appeared more like a "rookie" mistake.

Public pressure mounted and eventually the following Associated Press (AP) story appeared on October 2, 2006:

> A school superintendent who lied to students, parents and the media about why St. Louis Park High School was closed on Monday, apologized today.
>
> Superintendent Debra Bowers said, "I want to apologize," after spending 24 hours thinking about her decision to put out the story that the school was closed due to a water main break, when actually there were rumors that someone wanted to commit violence.
>
> School administrators said last week's school killings in Colorado and Wisconsin played a part in their decision to put out a cover story. (Lonetree, 2006, pp. 1–3)

"Good lies" must be examined within the context of other competing values. Kidder frames the debate on the importance of weighing honesty with other values, offering wisdom on how to measure decisions in the future, beginning with a question:

> Can the "well-placed lie" ever be the basis of sound policy? Even the intelligence services, which work hard to deceive the enemy, draw a sharp line at deceiving their own citizens. While the line unfortunately may be breached now and again, the policy is clear: Don't lie to Congress and the public.
>
> Were I on that school board, I'd engage the discussion about policy with the following question. "We're willing to do *whatever it takes* for the sake of school safety and security, but not at the expense of *X*. In St. Louis Park, what is *X*?"
>
> One such *X* might be shutting down all schools for the rest of the year—the safest option of all, but not one any board could contemplate. What else wouldn't we shut down? Our academic class work? Our sports program? Our commitment to freedom of movement? Our respect for one another? Our candor in communications? Classes and sports could be shut down temporarily during a threat. But respect and candor, once closed, aren't easily reopened.
>
> The soundest policy is one that gets stronger with every use. It makes each application easier, not harder, than the last. It sets an example you'd like others to follow. It provides clear guidelines. It speaks with one voice, striving to say the same thing to everyone. And it helps you leave the ethi-

cal woodpile higher than you found it—a metaphor that the good people of Minnesota, with winter approaching, already understand. (2006b, pp. 8–11)

Correcting the public deception early reduced the damaging potential of this episode not only for Bowers, but also for the school district and board of education. Public lies are rarely acceptable.

The effects of a perceived or actual "public lie" on the teller are considerable, including the loss of personal integrity (individuals live with the knowledge of the lie) and the confidence of one's peers (Bok, 1979). Adding to the teller's burden is the fact that more lies may be needed to keep the story going. "The first lie 'must be thatched with another or it will rain through'" (p. 26). Ultimately the teller who seeks to maintain power by minimizing the negative effects with some kind of deception often loses power when the deceived learn of the deception and demand a more honest account—this includes internal and external audiences. The first audience for the official story includes internal members, who have the most at stake in preserving the organization's reputation with the public.

COVER STORIES

Leaders might attempt to co-opt members in the deception by sharing the official story with them, using it as a kind of dress rehearsal for the public release of the story. If the members question the story, it might be revised in its first reading. We've all witnessed leaders trying to maintain a story no one believes. After several objections, the leader might even ask us to help him or her edit the story, indirectly asking us the question: "What might be said that would be closer to the truth but still be not as damaging as the truth?" Using the rationale that the "official story" is in the best interest of the organization, compliance is sought from the members. At the very least the leader assumed we would agree with the story by not contradicting it.

Asking the members to swallow a fundamentally untrue story, the teller moves the deception to them. When the story is released to the public and isn't denied by the members, it gains weight and credibility. When the deception is revealed, the members also share culpability in the deception and the lie grows, lending credence to Churchill's famous quote: "A lie gets half way around the world before the truth has a chance to get its pants on."

When individuals lose their opportunity for freedom and choice because of unknown alternatives and consequences, they also lose faith in public institutions and leadership. When deceived, the community loses the precious commodity of social trust: "a social good to be protected just as much as the air we breathe or the water we drink. When it is damaged, the community as a whole suffers; and when it is destroyed, societies falter and collapse" (Bok, 1979, p. 28).

When a new, official version of the events contains excuses, rationalizations, distortions, and omissions, members suffer from living the lie. Leaders offer an official version of the story and, like runway models, test the response to the new design with internal audiences. Leaders sometimes use the authority of their positions to craft a deceptive story, selling their version of the truth as a way to "protect" the organization (and apparently all of us). In this process the truth isn't told, and the responsible parties are not held accountable. These acts produce declining morale and a culture lacking accountability for actions. The cover-up extracts a heavy price when the causes of failure are buried before a forensic doctor performs an autopsy. Causes of poor performance must be catalogued before grieving can commence, a funeral takes place, and the body receives a proper burial.

While official stories spin the events into the most favorable light, cover stories often misrepresent elements or omit facts, with the intent to mislead others by altering perceptions of an event. An outright lie is a complete fabrication: The statements made are not true and the teller intends to deceive; the teller's motivation is to survive.

One of the more famous "lies" in recent public memory is President's Clinton's assertion that he "did not have sexual relations with that woman"—a public lie that nearly cost him the presidency. In his now famous, "I have sinned" speech, Clinton attended a breakfast for religious leaders held in the East Room of the White House on September 11, 1998, and addressed his falsehood:

> First, I want to say to all of you that, as you might imagine, I have been on
> quite a journey these last few weeks to get to the end of this, to the rock

bottom truth of where I am and where we all are. I agree with those who have said that in my first statement after I testified I was not contrite enough. I don't think there is a fancy way to say that I have sinned. (Bennett, 1998, pp. 3–5)

In a fascinating study of presidential lying, author Eric Alterman (2004) offers the following advice to future U.S. presidents (and anyone who serves in a public role):

Protect genuine secrets by refusing to answer certain questions, certainly. Put the best face on your own actions and those of the politicians you support, of course. Create a zone of privacy for yourself and your family that is declared off-limits to all public inquiry. But do not, under any circumstances, lie. (2004, p. 314)

Even a close reading of this now-famous speech reveals that Clinton's apology fell short of an actual admission of his deception. His private failing became even more public with the repeated lies told about his personal choices, which compromised his ability to lead.

Although the truth is hard to hear, perhaps the opposite is also true: The lie may also be hard to hear in the long term because of its damaging effects, causing us to lose trust in people and institutions. "[T]rust in some degree of veracity functions as a foundation of relations among human beings; when this trust shatters or wears away, institutions collapse" (Bok, 1978, p. 33). Bok offers the "principle of veracity" to guide us in our truth-telling decisions: "[I]n any situation where a lie is a possible choice, one must seek truthful alternatives" (p. 32).

In the following two stories, reporters Jayson Blair and Jack Kelley violated the public trust in the media by plagiarizing and fictionalizing their work. Their stories reveal how a pattern of misconduct gets started and who contributes to it by failing to hold people accountable for their actions. When a big lie gets told over and over again, others often indirectly participate in it.

The Blair story illustrates how an excessive desire for success, when combined with mental illness, a powerful addiction to drugs, and poor judgment, led to the early demise of a young reporter at reputedly the world's "best" newspaper, *The New York Times*.

JAYSON BLAIR AT *THE NEW YORK TIMES*

Jayson Blair started his career at *The New York Times* as a summer intern in 1998, returning to college in the fall. Because of dropped classes, Blair actually had more than a year of coursework to finish and struggled when invited by the *Times* to return for a second, six-month internship. He never finished his degree and later avoided telling Rule, director of reporter recruiting, that he never graduated (Blair, 2004). He received an appointment as an "intermediate reporter" in 1999. Despite concerns over the quality of his work, the *Times* promoted Blair to the position of full-time reporter in 2000.

Just three years later Blair resigned in disgrace due to a "blatantly plagiarized" story he submitted that was largely lifted from the work of Macarena Hernandez, a reporter for the *San Antonio Express-News*. Hernandez wrote a story about the family of a young marine who was missing in action. Listing details from Hernandez's story, Blair left an impression that he had actually been to Texas and interviewed the family. It turned out he never went to Texas or to half the places he wrote about in his fabricated and plagiarized stories submitted during his tenure at the *Times*.

In *Burning Down My Masters' House: My Life at The New York Times,* Blair describes the extent of his plagiarism, fabrication, and deception in the opening lines:

> I lied and I lied—and then I lied some more. I lied about where I had been, I lied about where I had found information, I lied about how I wrote the story. And these were no every day little white lies—they were complete fantasies, embellished down to the tiniest detail. I lied about a plane flight I never took, about sleeping in a car I never rented, about a landmark on a highway I had never been on. I lied about a guy who helped me at a gas station that I found on the Internet and about crossing railroad tracks I only knew existed because of aerial photographs in my private collection. I lied about a house I had never been to, about decorations and furniture in a living room I had only seen in photographs in an electronic archive maintained by *Times* photo editors. In the end—justifies—means environment I worked in, I had grown accustomed to lying. I told more than my share of lies and became as adept as anyone at getting away with it unquestioned and unscathed. I suspected that the truth would either set me free or kill me. (Blair, 2004, p. 1)

When initially questioned on April 28, 2003, about a story he had submitted about the family of a young marine, Blair substantially denied any wrongdoing to *Times* officials, promising to bring in his notes and expense records to prove his innocence. Blair carried out his charade for several days, trying to lie his way out of it while painting himself solidly into a corner, until he finally resigned on May 2, 2003. Following his resignation, the *Times* created an investigative committee to look into the deceptions. Combining the facts assembled by the *Times* committee and Blair's admission in his memoir, the depth of his deceptive acts mystifies even his most sympathetic supporters.

Blair lied about the plagiarism, going to great lengths to cover up his deception with even more lies. He "reconstructed" reporter's notes to convince others that he actually wrote the story, claiming that he merely confused his notes with research acquired from other news sources. He also said his brother had the receipts for his expenses incurred while traveling to Los Fresnos (Blair, 2004). The lying continued despite pleas from others for the truth. Because Blair wrote the story about a missing marine and his family in response to a request made by Jim Roberts, the national editor at the *Times*, Roberts felt somewhat responsible for finding out the truth and correcting errors made under his supervision. In a meeting with Blair, Roberts demanded to know the full story:

> "Jason, I'm tired of this bullshit!" "What do you mean, Jim? I am not bullshitting you. The Associated Press story is in the computer files I gave you, and I think that and other stuff has been mixed up. Listen, do you not believe me?" "I am not saying that. I want you to answer me honestly—were you in Los Fresnos?" "Listen, Jim, I was there. I remember the beads that hang in the archway between the kitchen and the room where a shrine is. I remember the pictures in one of the daughter's rooms. I remember the back door of the kitchen leading to the patio. I remember the furniture. . . . I remember a ton of details." (Blair, 2004, p. 17)

Roberts also recalls the meeting. Documented in the *Times* report about Blair's deception, Roberts said, "Look me in the eye and tell me you did what you say you did" (Times Reporter Who Resigned Leaves Long Trail of Deception, 2003, p. 138). Blair blames himself and quite a few others for his downfall. In *Burning Down My Masters' House: My*

Life at The New York Times, Blair recounts his story and admits his lies, but then proceeds to explain his deceptions based on his drug use, bipolar depression, pressure to produce stories along with unreasonable work hours, a culture of deception at the *Times* (more about this later), and discriminatory practices against African Americans. The title of Blair's book implies that his "masters" at the *Times* controlled his life, enslaving him as a lowly and struggling reporter.

A close reading of the memoir offers another picture—the "masters" of Blair's life might also include alcohol, cocaine, and the pursuit of personal pleasures over his duties at the *Times*. The combination of Blair's early rise to stardom at the *Times*, powerful drugs, and mental illness explains quite a bit. However, his need to feed his personal "hungers" (Heifetz & Linsky, 2002), traced to an abusive childhood by Blair's own account, offers further insight into the root causes of his deception and his willingness to risk all (reputation, career, friends, colleagues, and integrity) to succeed.

Although Blair received treatment for his drug addiction and was clean when he wrote the story about the lost marine, his pattern of deception, undetected for so long, was firmly engrained in his work habits. This, combined with his lack of ability to see beyond his own self-interests (perhaps caused by addictions and mental illness), put him on a collision course. Rational persons, assessing the risk and consequences of his conduct, might easily predict the likely result of Blair's choices as self-destruction. Tragically, because of his addictive and self-destructive habits, Blair could not imagine a future beyond the next day, and that never changed.

While Blair claims racial discrimination and intense pressure to produce at the *Times* as reasons for his demise, his colleagues and reviewers of his memoir often blame him for his pathological deceptions and subsequent denials. As a young, rising African American writer, undoubtedly Blair experienced racism. How does Blair, an African American, survive in a climate in which his capabilities are likely to be questioned daily? He also bears the unfair burden of symbolically representing his colleagues of color. Many among the first to rise to the top from the marginalized justifiably complain of the intense scrutiny and additional burden of being the designated representative of a cultural group.

Blair's lack of experience and desire to succeed certainly influenced his decision to deceive others. In his defense, Blair claims that a culture of "half-truths" prevailed at the *Times*. According to Blair, famous reporters failed to credit stringers who substantially contributed to their stories. Often reporters briefly crossed a state line (a "toe touch") to give the impression that they were reporting from a location instead of actually writing the story from a laptop computer somewhere in New York or elsewhere in the world (Blair, 2004, p. 254). Blair viewed his transgressions as an extension of an already unethical environment:

> The cognitive logic of my belief that I could get away with not visiting a city I was supposed to be writing from can easily be understood, though not excused, by the thing I had done and witnessed so far during the sniper shootings. I had seen correspondents perform toe-touch and no-touch datelines, and watched some write stories from hundreds of miles away from where they were supposed to have been. (p. 254)

Blair's conduct must be considered in the context of the newsroom practices that allowed his deceptions to go unchecked for so long. The *Times* report described other factors that contributed to Blair's deception:

> [These factors included] a failure of communication among senior editors; few complaints from the subjects of his articles; his savviness and his ingenious ways of covering his tracks. Most of all, no one saw his carelessness as a sign that he was capable of systematic fraud. (Times reporter who resigned leaves long trail of deception, 2003, p. 13)

Instead of trying to reconcile these positions, most likely the truth lies somewhere between the two views. Although some seek to pillory him, Blair and others mitigate his conduct due to his self-destructive abuse of drugs, the presence of a mental illness, and the after-effects of an unfortunate, abusive childhood. Clearly talented, Blair's problem was not an inability to write; it was that he wrote fiction in lieu of fact and lifted the work of his colleagues, using it as his own, breaking a sacred trust placed in him by his profession and the public.

A less notorious but equally damaging story about another journalist, Jack Kelley, provides more insight about lying and the importance of integrity in leadership. A pattern of reckless conduct occurs when certain propensities within the individual combine with less-than-accountable environments.

JACK KELLEY: A STAR REPORTER RESIGNS

Quickly following on the heels of Blair's misconduct, the exposé of Jack Kelley's comparable transgressions at *USA Today* appeared in the headlines of the *Baltimore Sun* (Banville, 2004). Brian Gallagher, the executive editor of *USA Today*, received an anonymous complaint against Kelley in May 2003. The caller complained about Kelley's flagrant violations of ethics, citing his excessive use of "unnamed sources" (helping him fabricate his stories) and plagiarism of story details from other news sources (p. 2). Kelley denied the accusations, defended his record, claimed a hostile work environment, and finally resigned from his position. He initially issued the following statement:

> "I walk away from *USA Today* knowing that in 21 years I have never had a correction or retraction printed," Kelley said in the January statement run by the paper. "Every story published under my byline was accurate based on what I saw, the interviews conducted and the details available at that time." (p. 27)

On the heels of the Blair story and under pressure from the *Baltimore Sun*, the *USA Today* management launched an investigation, which later revealed the extent of Kelley's violation of journalistic standards:

> As part of the internal review, *USA Today* reporters closely scrutinized more than 100 of Kelley's articles, narrowing their investigation from the 720 articles that the review board first checked for plagiarism and fabrications. Seven weeks into their investigation, *USA Today* issued a series of scathing articles that eviscerated several of Kelley's most notable stories, including an Aug. 10, 2001 story about a suicide bombing in Jerusalem that Kelley falsely claimed to witness and a Nov. 26, 2001 story on terrorist training camps run by Osama bin Laden that Kelley had actually plagiarized from several news sources. (Banville, 2004, pp. 29–30)

Later, Kelley retracted his story and apologized to the public, taking responsibility for his mistakes and recognizing that the public assessment of his journalistic contributions would suffer because of his deceptions.

The extent and nature of Kelley's and Blair's misconduct serve as examples of how individual deceptive acts breach the trust extended by professional colleagues and the public. This misconduct can significantly compromise and damage the integrity of an organization. *The New York Times* and *USA Today* unwittingly cooperated with this reckless conduct by turning a blind eye to complaints and failing to uphold the journalistic standards described in newsroom policy and commonly upheld in professional practice.

The *Times* investigation showed Blair's work riddled with errors, causing some to doubt his suitability for promotion to full-time reporter in 2000. Compounding this situation, there was a clear lack of communication between departments and editors about these errors (Times reporter who resigned leaves long trail of deception, 2003, p. 145). The inquiry into Kelley's work "criticized a culture of fear that made reporters loath to question the paper's star reporter and a lax editing structure that allowed Kelley to use unnamed sources in violation of the paper's own rules" (Banville, 2004, p. 41). When organizations lack sufficient oversight of the conduct of individuals and the quality of their work and fail to respond to the signals of an impending crisis clearly evident in poor practices or uninvestigated complaints, they participate in their own demise.

Having learned how systems contribute to deception by failing to uphold standards, both *The New York Times* and *USA Today* implemented better systems to address these gaps in developing and implementing ethical standards. The aftermath of these stories—editors fired, credibility lost, and public trust damaged—illustrates the impact of lying on others. The damaging effects may extend to professional journalists and erode the public trust in the media.

Describing the impact of the Kelley scandal, Ken Paulson, editor of *USA Today,* cautioned, "When a newspaper's credibility is damaged, it's never quite over. We have to be vigilant and protect the integrity of *USA Today* on a daily basis" (Banville, 2004, p. 49). Fueled by fear and the pressure to succeed in a difficult profession, Blair and Kelley's circumstances partially explain their motivation to deceive others:

> Anyone who has spent five minutes in a modern-day newsroom knows fear
> is part of the fuel that powers our daily work: fear of getting "scooped" by

a competitor; fear of becoming irrelevant to the community; fear of losing profits; fear of losing our credibility. (Deggans, 2004, p. 23)

Fiercely competitive and less-than-accountable cultures create reasons and opportunities for deception. The pressure to succeed and achieve more than what may seem reasonable under difficult circumstances contributes to the downfall of many good people. Failing to promote and inspect professional standards also contributes to the problem. An honest culture upholds a high truth-telling standard through its policy development and actions. While the actions of Kelley and Blair fail to meet the test of journalistic ethics, the harm caused by their individual actions resulted in damaged trust, not lost lives. When matters of life and death are at stake, individuals and leaders of organizations must make a concerted effort to reduce the potentially adverse effects of foolish mistakes, poor choices, and instances of reckless conduct that have the potential to harm or even take a life away.

The decision to deceive and ignore the truth-telling standard can sometimes have disastrous consequences for individuals and organizations. What makes some seemingly intelligent people make jaw-dropping mistakes despite their cognitive capacity to do otherwise? How do they get away with it? The psychological and cognitive traps associated with foolish mistakes, poor decisions, and acts of reckless conduct described in the next chapter offer some explanation. Many poor decisions, based on egocentric or ethnocentric views, result from seeing only ourselves in the story.

8

FOOLISH MISTAKES, POOR DECISIONS, AND RECKLESS CONDUCT: AVOIDING TRAPS AND ACTS OF SELF-BETRAYAL

Nothing in all the world is more dangerous than sincere ignorance and conscientious stupidity.

—Martin Luther King (Quote DB, n.d., a)

Broadcast as a "World" story on National Public Radio (NPR) using the tagline, "Ambulance Crew Entranced by CPS Navigation Machine," the following story describes an ambulance crew who lost their way when they foolishly placed all of their faith in technology and ignored their common sense.

> A British ambulance crew had a simple job. They were supposed to ferry a mental patient between two hospitals in London. The hospitals were only 10 miles apart. The ambulance crew relied on a GPS [Global Positioning System] navigation system to lead the way. And they kept trusting the computer as it took the ambulance the wrong way. By the time the ambulance reached Manchester, England, about 200 miles away, the crew finally realized something wasn't right. (*Ambulance Crew Entranced by GPS Navigation Machine,* 2006, p. 1)

This embarrassing episode illustrates many aspects of Langer's (1997) description of mindlessness "characterized by an entrapment in old categories, by automatic behavior that precludes attending to new signals; and by action that operates from a single perspective. Being mindless, colloquially speaking, is like being on automatic pilot" (p. 4). Surely the crew must have observed the city in its rearview mirror as it traveled a substantial distance into the countryside (not to mention the time elapsed for an ostensibly ten-mile trip), yet they ignored the warning signs in the environment, placing their faith in a fascinating technology. Reminding us of our fallibility and humanness, mistakes come from our experience of living and often help us grow in humility and understanding. The following "foolishly lucky" story took place in Oak Park, Michigan.

> A man who awoke inside a garbage truck that was about to compact its load was rescued after making a frantic cell phone call to police, authorities say. The man, who is unemployed, was scavenging for bottles Thursday when he fell asleep in a dumpster. (Associated Press, 2007a, p. 2)

Unable to identify the exact truck, the man described the location of the dumpster where he failed to get the attention of anyone outside of the truck. Unbelievably, the cell phone battery dislodged and the trapped scrounger lost his only means of communication. Here's the rest of the story:

> "An officer went and pounded on the side of the truck and somebody pounded back," Pousak [one of officers looking for the trapped man] said. The man appeared to be unhurt except for a scratch, Pousak said. "If I was him I would go to church and play the lottery because today was his lucky day," the police officer said. (p. 2)

Exchanging stories about foolish mistakes and poor decisions promotes learning by causing us to examine how individually and systemically we sometimes contribute to our own demise, taking on a humorous quality only when no one is harmed, but we gain wisdom because of the experience. Most foolish mistakes that have some element of mindlessness to them often result in an embarrassing moment with less-than-tragic effects on others. More like missteps, mistakes temporarily distract us from a goal but don't permanently damage individuals and organizations. In fact, some mistakes lead to growing wisdom and innovation, helping us learn from them or leading to an insight that may have been unrealized if not for the mistake. Like parents of teenage drivers, we hope that our mistakes and those made by our colleagues or family members replicate a minor accident rather than a fatal crash causing a loss of life or limb.

Foolish mistakes, made when we are caught "off guard," leave a faint impression but rarely an indelible mark. We swap our foolish tales with others to create an environment in which making mistakes, considered a "low-risk" activity, serves as an opportunity for reflection and learning. In contrast with foolish mistakes, poor decisions may have longer-lasting and sometimes disastrous effects.

Made as a result of poor information, limited perspective or experience, or faulty thinking and judgment, poor decisions may derail a career or threaten the stability of an organization if we do not take corrective action early in the process. If the poor decision causes significant harm, the action may also be designated as an act of reckless conduct. However, no matter what the causes or the consequences of poor judgment, leaders should at least tell the truth and accept responsibility for their actions.

Eight minutes changed the life of Commander Scott Waddle, the lives of nine people who died in a tragic and wholly preventable accident, and the lives all those directly and indirectly affected by this event and its consequences. It's the kind of story we all fear we might have to tell one day: the story of how the unimaginable happened to us. In a split-second moment of poor decision making, Commander Scott Waddle (Retired) of the U.S. Navy caused irrevocable harm to others in a tragic accident at Pearl Harbor. Waddle's mettle was tested when he had to face the consequences of his grievous actions. From his experience we learn about the importance of telling the truth when it counts.

COMMANDER SCOTT WADDLE

Born into a military family, Scott Waddle wanted to attend the Air Force Academy to become a pilot (Waddle, 2002). Because of a medical condition, he was not accepted for pilot training but later tried to become a pilot in the Naval Academy after being admitted as a candidate. Disappointed twice in his first career choice, Waddle finally decided to pursue a career as a submarine commander. Working diligently, Waddle earned recognition for his academic and professional success. Graduating at the

top of his class at Annapolis, Waddle spent twenty years in the construction, maintenance, and operation of nuclear-powered submarines before
being selected from a competitive field to command the USS *Greeneville*
and manage a 140-man crew.

Under Waddle's capable command, the USS *Greeneville* became one
of the most successful submarine units in the Navy. They often assigned
poorly performing sailors to serve on the *Greeneville* as a way to salvage
their careers. Successful in turning around poor performance and gaining commitment from his crew based on his model of ethical leadership,
Waddle's success and reputation grew.

Recognized as a capable and impressive commander, Waddle often
took distinguished visitors on a submarine tour and ride to impress them
with the submarine's capabilities. Public relations work was an important part of Waddle's service because the Navy was constantly in conflict
with other agencies in seeking congressional support (Waddle, 2002). As
part of a public relations event and lobbying effort, dignitaries boarded
the *Greeneville* on February 21, 2001, at Pearl Harbor for a special ride
on a premier attack submarine under the command of Commander
Waddle (Kakesako, 2001).

Specially provisioned like a cruise ship rather than a fighting ship, the
Greeneville was stocked with fine food to please the guests. A routine
check of the operating equipment showed everything in good working
with one exception: an improperly working sonar screen, which served
as a backup to using the manual, visual inspection of the surface with a
periscope. After noting the needed repair, Waddle proceeded with the
tour and cruise, not worried about a malfunctioning backup system on
such a short visit.

The *Greeneville* performed flawlessly that day. Excited by the thrill of
riding in a pitching and swerving submarine, the guests expressed their
delight. Wishing to impress the visitors even more, Commander Waddle
decided to do a dive-and-surface maneuver. He raised the periscopes
and did a 360-degree survey of the surface and did not see any other wa-
tercraft. The submarine shot down 400 feet. As a final maneuver, the
submarine resurfaced, blowing out the air from the lungs of the ship and
making a rapid ascent to the surface (Kakesako, 2001). Saving the best
experience for last just before surfacing the submarine, Waddle asked a
guest if he wanted to handle the controls for the procedure to resurface
(Waddle, 2002).

The guest readily agreed. Waddle issued the order to surface, beginning an anticipated dramatic closure to an impressive joy ride. The submarine began its rapid ascent to the surface. Calling out the depths as
they rose faster and faster, Waddle commanded the vessel to the surface. Just as they neared the water's surface, they heard a loud bang.
They immediately raised the periscopes, which to their horror revealed
that the *Greeneville* had hit a 180-foot Japanese trawler loaded with a
precious cargo of adults and high school children (Kakesako, 2001).
Waddle watched through the periscope as the ship sank. The malfunctioning screen and his decision to turn over the controls to a "guest" had
contributed to the accident, along with the risky and unnecessarily rapid
ascent to the surface (Tempesta, 2004).

Claiming the lives of nine people, the horrific accident became an international incident. President Bush apologized on behalf of the American people and formed a court of inquiry to investigate the accident.
While all those serving below the role of commander were granted im-
munity, Commander Waddle was charged with dereliction of duty, haz-
arding of a vessel, and negligent homicide. Choosing to accept responsibility for the accident, Waddle apologized to the parents of the children
who died as well as the Japanese people (Kakesako, 2001). Despite legal
advice to the contrary, Waddle took the stand in his own defense and
claimed responsibility for the accident without offering excuses or blam-
ing anyone else. He told the truth with the certain knowledge that what
he said in the inquiry would be used against him (Tempesta, 2004).

Commander Waddle, later found guilty of all charges except the negligent homicide charge, narrowly avoided a prison sentence (Kakesako,
2001). He retired from the Navy, ending a brilliant and promising career
as a naval officer. Since the incident and his retirement, Waddle has received thousands of sympathetic cards and letters because he willingly
told the truth despite its potential cost to his family, career, and life.
Waddle reports moving through despair (even considering suicide at
one point) and described his decision to tell the truth as the right and
only thing to do under the circumstances.

Because deceptions and often avoidance of blame by elected officials
and members of elite groups occur frequently, when Waddle actually
told the truth and took responsibility for his actions, he made headlines.
Commander Waddle's story shows what can happen when a full admission of the truth occurs after a grievous error. While the effects of a poor

choice may never fade from memory (nine people lost their lives), some respect can be regained, and forgiveness earned, when someone takes responsibility for the circumstances and consequences of a poor choice. Leaders who acknowledge a poor decision early may recover some valuable assets lost as a result of their decision by admitting errors and changing course immediately.

Why did Commander Waddle make a poor decision that day that caused the death of nine people? At least a part of the answer involves the "fallacy factor," ways in which highly successful people think and deceive themselves, sometimes becoming victims of their success.

FALLACIES AND SELF-DECEPTIONS

Smart and often highly successful people may make poor decisions because of fallacies in their thinking and an exaggerated belief in their knowledge and superiority over others. The following fallacies help to explain the range of poor decision making, whether a foolish mistake, a poor choice, or reckless conduct: (1) fallacy of egocentrism, (2) fallacy of omniscience, (3) fallacy of omnipotence, and (3) fallacy of invulnerability (Sternberg, 2003, p. 160). Lured by the fallacy of egocentrism, some believe the world centers around them and use their power to satisfy their every want (omnipotence), believing in their own invulnerability. Clearly some or all of these elements were present in Waddle's story.

Accustomed to being highly rewarded for their intelligence or talents, those falling victim to omniscience often "lose sight of their own limitations" (Sternberg, 2003, p. 160). Because leaders often have expert knowledge or plentiful resources at their disposal, they may ignore gaps in their knowledge or place too much confidence in the knowledge they hold (omniscience). The following quotes from famous "experts" illustrate this problem:

Man will never reach the moon, regardless of all scientific advance.—Dr. Lee Forest, inventor of the vacuum tube, 1957

I think there is a world market for maybe five computers.—Thomas Watson, chairman of IBM, 1943

There is no reason for any individual to have a computer in their [sic] *home.*—Kenneth Olsen, president and founder of Digital Equipment Corporation, 1977

Airplanes are interesting toys, but of no military value.—Marshal Ferdinand Foch, French military strategist and future WWI commander, 1911

Television won't be able to hold on to any market it captures after the first six months. People will soon get tired of staring at a plywood box every night.—Darryl F. Zanuck, head of 20th Century-Fox, 1946 (Langer, 2005, p. 92)

While these examples show limitations in thinking resulting from a lack of openness to alternative viewpoints, the shortsightedness of their proclamations may only prove that none of us has a crystal ball. Wise leaders know that they can avoid being trapped by their own thinking by staying open to learning and listening to others with counterviews. The fallacy of omniscience demonstrates the potential limitations in our thinking, while the fallacies of egocentrism, omnipotence, and invulnerability relate to failures in self-perception and character.

Lacking the practical knowledge or experience to read some situations intelligently, people often make poor choices when their inability to make good choices combines with the naked pursuit of their needs. They lack the desire to judiciously balance the interests of self with the legitimate interests of others, creating opportunities for foolishness. "Foolishness is an extreme failure of wisdom" (Sternberg, 2003, p. 236), arising from "the faulty acquisition of or application of tacit knowledge [as] guided by values away from the achievement of the common good" (p. 236).

The culprit or co-conspirator may be egocentrism, omnipotence, or belief in our invulnerability. Egocentrism develops from a narcissist and unrealistic appraisal of our worth and place in the world. Lacking an ability to see others as contributors to our success may cause us to steal recognition or reward from others. Omnipotence accompanies egocentrism, fueling egos with false pride, earned in the dubious belief that we hold the power and our colleagues and adversaries lack the ability to successfully compete with our knowledge, position, or prior success. The two may contribute to a feeling of invulnerability; both great and strong, that nothing bad can come from our ill-advised decisions. We want what comes from meteoric and unattributed success: money, fame, power, and the pursuit of pleasure.

Often the social power and recognition that accompany positional leadership contribute to this distorted view. Many famous people describe difficulties in adjusting to sudden fame or power. Ill equipped to handle the shift from being "ordinary" to having access to resources and becoming famous, people often change almost overnight. These factors contribute to instances of reckless conduct, which stands in a category by itself.

To qualify for nomination in the "reckless conduct" category, those who exhibit reckless conduct must deliberatively choose a course of action with the knowledge that their actions fail to meet the standards of professional and personal ethical codes of conduct. Violating widely accepted social norms and values, those exhibiting reckless conduct do so for self-serving motives, despite the costs and negative effects of these indulgences on others. Fueled by a powerful drive for personal gain, recognition, or advancement, or perhaps carried out to feed an addiction to drugs, alcohol, or sexual desires, episodes of reckless conduct occur when these desires or ambitions are combined with poor judgment.

Unfortunately, the reckless conduct category needs no stories; the discouraging conduct of many people in public and corporate life offers plenty of examples. The prevention of misconduct merits discussion. Leaders understand how acts of misconduct occur, gaining insight into and warning about how to avoid cognitive and psychological traps that lead to acts of self-betrayal. Guarding against individual acts of reckless conduct, leaders establish more accountable systems to prevent such acts.

TRAPS AND SELF-BETRAYAL

Many egocentric people, seduced by a need for recognition in their profession, "need affirmation, but accepting accolades in an undisciplined way can lead to grandiosity, an inflated view of yourself and your cause" (Heifetz & Linsky, 2002, p. 169). The pressure to succeed may be one probable cause for people to engage in risky behavior. However, this doesn't explain why some violate ethical standards and moral codes, while others maintain standards despite these pressures. Stories about people who follow a self-destructive path fascinate and warn us about the consequences of valuing our needs above others in extreme cases. These stories attract our attention, pointing out our potential vulnerabilities and root causes. We use the "I can't believe they did this . . ." type story to guard against errors in judgment and see the traps inherent in satisfying our needs in dangerous ways.

Once misbehavior is identified, the way individuals conduct themselves during the inquiry and resulting crisis also matters. Executives, athletes, and public figures in a variety of fields experience a crisis of reputation due to errors in judgment. Wishing to avoid the consequences of their mistakes, leaders are often overconfident in their assessment of their ability to "see" what's going on and to survive the crisis. Unaware of others' perceptions, leaders may misjudge the seriousness of their failure and declining support for their leadership. Wise leaders listen to others and recognize their vulnerabilities during a crisis.

Kusy and Essex (2005) studied the failures of prominent leaders and their efforts to recover from their mistakes, similar to the fallacies described above. Two fatal errors that derail leaders, thwarting their efforts to recover from the consequences of human mistakes, are (1) "aberrations of trust that compromise leader integrity" and (2) "a pattern of foolish mistakes that indicates gross incompetence" (p. 127). Fatal errors involving these conditions meet our previously described criteria for reckless conduct. These include deliberatively choosing a course of action with the knowledge that their actions fail to meet the standards of professional and personal ethical codes of conduct and violating widely accepted social norms and values for self-serving reasons, despite the costs and negative effects of these self-indulgences on others.

Whether a foolish mistake, a poor decision, or an instance of reckless conduct has occurred, leaders and organizations must guard against a climate that allows disappointing and often damaging choices to happen or continue. Heifetz reminds us of the dangers inherent in success and a false belief in our invincibility:

> We get caught up in the cause and forget that exercising leadership is, at heart, a personal activity. It challenges us intellectually, emotionally, spiritually, and physically. But with the adrenaline pumping, we can work ourselves into believing we are somehow different, and therefore not subject to normal human frailties that can defeat more ordinary mortals on ordinary missions. We begin to act as if we were physically and emotionally indestructible. (Heifetz & Linsky, 2002, p. 613)

When hearing a story about reckless conduct, some may blame and shame. Wise leaders ask instead: "What causes people to engage in reckless conduct, and what can be learned from its tragic effects? What conditions might cause people to act in a similar vein, going against their core values and professional ethics? How can lax standards and a climate of fear create opportunities for misconduct?" These questions, when asked by ethical leaders, promote professional standards and ensure accountability for choices and actions.

Leaders share stories to reveal the dangers of the ego-driven fallacies, using them to reflect on their actions as well as warn us about cultures that fail to provide healthy expectations and appropriate mentoring to their members. Not only are individuals accountable for poor behaviors and choices but also organizations, for tolerating them. Changing a lax and poorly performing organization into a more accountable one requires capable and systemic leadership.

Professional standards, when adopted and incorporated into policy, ensure higher standards of accountability and reduce the opportunity for human error or ego. The cognitive and psychological aspects of human error and poor decision making must be identified and guarded against through professional knowledge and accountability systems. Examples of diligent efforts in medicine and aviation to reduce human errors and increase accountability appear next. These stories illustrate how the efforts of leaders can save lives.

EXERCISE CAUTION: HOSPITAL ZONE

Dr. Semmelweis, head of Vienna General Hospital's First Obstetrical Clinic, tried to solve a puzzling and highly disturbing mystery (*Ignaz Phillip Semmelweis*, n.d.). After entering the hospital to deliver their babies, some healthy women gave birth and then unfortunately died within a few days after the birth from a mysterious illness called puerperal fever or childbed fever (*Ignaz Phillip Semmelweis*, n.d.). Comparing mortality statistics between two clinics in the same hospital, Semmelweis found that the mothers' survival rate was nearly three times higher in an obstetrical clinic staffed by midwifery students than in the clinic staffed by medical doctors and students.

Even though their caretakers had higher levels of education and experience, patients were dying at an alarming rate under the care of medical doctors. Pregnant women knew about the differences in mortality rates, and some gave birth before entering the hospital, while others begged to be admitted to the midwifery clinic (*Ignaz Semmelweis*, n.d.).

Semmelweis tried to discover the reason for the differences in performance between the two clinics. Although hospital supervisors opposed his investigation because they didn't believe the fever was preventable, Semmelweis persisted in his study. Semmelweis tried to eliminate every conceivable variable and isolate the cause, but to no avail. The answer evaded him for some time. After taking a leave from the hospital for about a month, Semmelweis returned to find that, much to his surprise, the mortality rate had actually declined during his absence. Semmelweis finally figured out the answer to his puzzle after losing a close friend, Jakob Kolletschka, who died "from an infection contracted after his finger was accidentally punctured with a knife while performing a postmortem examination" (*Ignaz Semmelweis*, n.d., p. 7).

An autopsy revealed that Kolletschka had died from puerperal fever, like the mothers in the clinic staffed by medical doctors. Seeing the connection between the death of mothers and his friend, Semmelweis hypothesized that some kind of material in cadavers was passed on to patients from cadavers, causing the fever. Semmelweis's discovery occurred before the official discovery of germs in 1847.

Semmelweis ordered medical doctors and students to thoroughly wash their hands "with a chlorine solution before making an examination and the death rate plummeted" (*Ignaz Phillip Semmelweis*, n.d., p. 5). For the first time in the history of the Vienna Hospital, the mortality rate at the medical clinic fell below that of the school of midwives (*Ignaz Phillip Semmelweis*, n.d.).

Semmelweis might be surprised and certainly upset to learn that 160 years later more than two million people become infected after being admitted to the hospital, largely due to the problem of "nosocomial" [hospital acquired] bloodstream infections, resulting in approximately 100,000 deaths per year (McGaughey, 2004, p. 22). "The death toll is higher than from AIDS, breast cancer, and auto accidents combined" (p. 23). Lack of hygiene still causes patient deaths today, despite extensive knowledge about infection, including how to prevent its spread.

Doctors and medical personnel still pass bacteria from one patient to another because they fail to wash their hands between patient examinations:

> Bradley Moore of Washingtonville, New York was taken to the hospital with a head injury. He managed to survive swelling and damage to his brain, but while he was in the hospital he contracted an infection. "It was the infection that killed him," Patricia Moore explained, after burying her son. "I am only one voice, one mother, but I know that hospitals can lower their infection rates by implementing simple practices such as handwashing. This problem has been ignored too long." (McGaughey, 2004, p. 22)

Like Moore's death, a disturbing number of "never events" (preventable deaths) (Lerner, 2007, p. 8) occur at least partly as a result of a host environment filled with bacteria as well as the transfer of dangerous bacteria from one patient to another directly through the hands of medical care personnel. Unfortunately, "most hospitals are dirtier places than they used to be" due to the decline in maintaining standards and too much faith placed in antibiotics to take care of the problem (p. 23). Although the remedy for hospital-acquired infections has been known since 1847, the problem is far from eliminated.

The study of never events includes not only the study of human anatomy and biological sciences to understand physical sources of illness but also the behavioral sciences to study the sources of human errors and reckless behavior in health care and management. Tackling the tough issues of accountability in patient care presents some tense moments for Alison Page, chief safety officer for Fairview Health Services.

Working in an environment where errors may cost a life, Page directs systemwide efforts to report errors in the interest of patient safety. A nationwide movement underway to consider the human element in decisions related to patient safety and increase accountability, preventative health care focuses on the actions that lead to negative patient outcomes as well as the effects of medical treatment. According to Page, the Fairview system adopted a program called "Just Culture" (www.justculture.org) to educate medical personnel about the causes and effects of human errors as well as the consequences associated with poor decisions (Alison Page, personal communication, January 15, 2007). Just Culture focuses on creating positive outcomes:

The Just Culture is a way of doing business—a set of standards by which regulators, employers, and employees can work together to create the best possible outcomes. On one side of the coin, the Just Culture is about creating a reporting environment where staff can raise their hand when they have seen a risk, or made a mistake It is a culture that puts a high value on open communication—where risks are openly discussed between manager and staff. It is a culture hungry for knowledge. On the other side of the coin, it is an organization that has a well established system of accountability. (Marx, 2005, p. 1)

According to Page, prior to adopting the Just Cause philosophy, medical personnel were accountable based on the outcomes of treatment rather than the decisions and actions carried out by medical personnel. Explaining the relationship between decisions made by medical personnel and patient safety, Page shared three possible scenarios.

In the first scenario the diagnosis and treatment of a patient follows established practice, and yet the outcome, a patient death, still occurs. An inquiry into the cause of death would reveal that correct decisions were made using all the available information, despite the disappointing outcomes. In this case, supervisors should support and console medical personnel. A disappointing result can occur despite the best efforts of medical personnel because medical knowledge is imperfect and not all negative outcomes can be prevented.

In the next scenario, the diagnosis and treatment provided to the patient by medical personnel fails to follow established practice due to a lack of either knowledge or experience. The patient grows worse, suffers, or dies needlessly. Supervisors respond by admitting error, accepting consequences, and coaching medical personnel to improve their practice and learn from mistakes. While the hospital and its personnel may suffer some negative consequences due to patient suffering and harm, administrators offer leadership during the crisis by investigating the errors, identifying areas of poor performance, learning from mistakes, and putting systems in place to ensure this event never occurs again.

Finally, in the third scenario, patient treatment flagrantly violates established medical practice due to an intentional deviation from established medical procedures, including taking shortcuts, needless risks, and lack of care in performing work. Medical personnel, fully aware of correct procedures, deliberately ignore appropriate practice and threaten or harm patients. In this case supervisors are advised to punish medical personnel, making them accountable for their reckless actions even if no eventual harm occurs. Punishment takes the form of warning, dismissal, or a formal inquiry that may lead to the loss of licenses. (Alison Page, personal communication, January 15, 2007)

Medical personnel have always been accountable for instances of malpractice and gross negligence due to their poor performance through peer review, local or state medical board inquiries, or civil and criminal complaints. However, preventative health care, aimed at improving patient safety, focuses not only on the decisions and actions of medical personnel but also on health outcomes. Outcomes result from either good or bad decisions. If some medical personnel show consistently poor outcomes, their decisions and actions should be inspected to identify causes. If medical personnel do everything right in treating the patient, they are not responsible for poor outcomes. However, even if a reckless act fails to harm a patient, if medical personnel violate established standards, they are disciplined (and sometimes dismissed) to ensure patient safety.

For example, hospital personnel recognize potential for errors in surgery due to stress and fatigue. Safety procedures now require that objects used during surgery be counted and marked on a white board and later recounted at the end of the surgery to ensure that nothing is left inside the patient (Lerner, 2007). The practice is a response to experience with human errors. Another example involves the education of medical personnel. Signs above sinks prominently display procedures to reduce infections and report the negative patient outcomes that result from the failure to comply with hand-washing procedures. Would it make a difference to you if you knew that, unless existing practices are changed, 100,000 people are likely to die every year because of infections acquired in the hospital?

The Minnesota Health Department's website advertises its track record for patient safety (see www.health.state.mn.us/patientsafety/). The website reports the results of state law that requires Minnesota hospitals and clinics to report poor health outcomes. This requirement ensures a higher level of public accountability while also providing patients with valuable information about the safety record and performance of medical personnel. This system works much the same way that the word-of-mouth warnings served mothers when pregnant women avoided giving birth in a Vienna hospital.

How do hospital personnel explain the variance and sometimes deviation of hospital personnel in following established medical procedure? Psychological literature related to human errors contributes to their understanding.

Reason and Mycielska (1982) explore many aspects of human error, describing how common mistakes can have disastrous effects:

> Should we inadvertently switch on the toaster when we meant to turn on the electric coffee pot, the result is mildly inconvenient, but no more than this. Should precisely the same kind of mistake occur on the flight deck of a large passenger aircraft or in the control room of a nuclear power plant, the results can be and sometime are catastrophic. The difference lies not in the nature of the error, but the extent to which its circumstances of occurrence will penalize it. (p. 3)

Errors made in flying aircraft that resemble "absent-minded behavior" include shutting down the correctly performing engine when the other engine malfunctioned, hitting the wrong switch and reducing pressure when more was needed during take-off, and misreading the altimeter (Reason & Mycielska, 1982, p. 4–5). Human errors consist of two types:

> *Errors of judgment and planning.* The actions go as planned, but the plan is inadequate.
> *Actions-not-as-planned.* The plan is satisfactory, but the actions are not those intended. (p. 14).

Actions-not-as-planned explain the disappointing results in medical practice or the airline industry. An airplane pilot does not plan to switch off the engine. "Slips" occur when people who carry out routine activities and perform them automatically become distracted due to competing influences in the environment or show a lack of attention or vigilance in performing the work (Reason & Mycielska, 1982).

Referring to cognitive failures as "demons," Reason and Mycielska describe the factors that "fire up" demons associated with human errors: (1) context (similar environmental cues cause inappropriate automatic responses), (2) the influence of needs or emotions (anxiety or stress accelerates problems), and (3) "neighboring demons" (carrying out identical or similar actions activates automatic and incorrect responses (1982, pp. 58–61). Another factor related to human error is complexity in problem solving.

Reason (1992) describes "the existence of three basic error types: skill-based slips and lapses, rule-based mistakes and knowledge-based mistakes" (p. 95). Skill-based errors result from monitoring failures, while rule and knowledge-based mistakes are associated with problem solving. It turns out that the second type of mistakes related to problem solving occurs because of the misapplication of "good rules" or the application of "bad rules." Review of procedures and their worth (or mischief) reduces humor errors.

Leaders insist on operational debriefing to affirm the value of good rules, developing explicit guidelines for their use as well as to eliminate those rules proven suspect and ineffective (bad rules). Increasing accountability by outlining appropriate procedures to limit human errors, leaders insist on strict adherence to professional standards and guard against human errors caused by "demons" such as errors of logic. Because the behavioral sciences warn about these concerns, leaders who fail to insist on professional practice and collective knowledge and wisdom indirectly participate in failure events. The sources of human errors and reckless conduct, as well as the negative outcomes that result from them, must be investigated and reported.

The aviation industry addresses the concerns described previously in the medical field. A systems approach reduces the risks associated with human error by allowing pilots, crew members, and maintenance personnel to "break the chain" before a mistake happens (Nancy Jacobs, personal communication, February 27, 2007). Redundant systems also reduce the number of errors and tragedies. When personnel notice that something's not right during preflight inspection or flight operation, they can delay or call a halt to the process.

"TIME OUT" AND "KNOCK IT OFF": OVERCOMING HUMAN ELEMENTS

Much like patient safety programs, aviation standards attempt to reduce human errors through established flight procedures and guidelines. Action taken during preflight planning, flight operation, and postflight debriefing reduces errors and expands the opportunities to learn from mistakes. Prior to beginning a mission, Air Force crew members complete a personal risk assessment to determine their fitness to carry out their duties (Chris Hoffman, personal communication, February 22, 2007). Crew members rate their fitness and level of stress from low to high based on whether factors such as family and financial concerns, current level of fitness, and emotional well-being might compromise their ability to think clearly and use sound judgment on the mission.

Once crew members have demonstrated their fitness, they follow guidelines for safe communication during the mission. Recognizing the need for all crew members to participate in maintaining flight safety as well as ensuring that senior officers receive feedback when things go wrong, the Air Force created two ways to communicate about their concerns: "Time Out" and "Knock It Off!" (Chris Hoffman, personal communication, February 22, 2007).

The U.S. Air Force issues instructions to crew members regarding its flying operations, delivered in the form of official instructions issued by order of the Secretary of the Air Force. Instructions outline procedures for flight operations, including communication protocol. The following "Time Out" instruction shows how crew members can reduce errors:

> Instruction 5.12.4.1. "Time Out" is the common assertive statement for use by all crewmembers. The use of "Time Out" will:
>
> 5.12.4.1.1. Provide a clear warning sign of deviation or loss of situational awareness.
>
> 5.12.4.1.2. Provide an opportunity to break the error chain before a mishap occurs.
>
> 5.12.4.1.3. Notify all crew members when someone sees the aircraft or crew departing from established guidelines, the briefed scenario, or that someone is simply uncomfortable with the developing conditions. (Air Force Policy Directive, 2006, p. 56)

"Time Out" establishes the right and obligation of crew members to participate in ensuring safety. When a "Time Out" is called, the pilot in charge (PIC) "stabilize[s] the aircraft and ensure[s] terrain clearance (5.12.4.2.1.)," to allow him or her to listen to the concerns of crewmembers. After discussion of these concerns, the PIC makes the decision to stay the course or change.

A second communication device, "Knock It Off," raises the level of concern one more notch:

> "Knock It Off" serves a similar purpose as "Time Out" but transcends a crew member's voice of concern for safety to an explicit call for immediate corrective action. While it is also designed to break the human chain of error, the "Knock it Off" call is a more imperative form of communication and is generally used after an aircraft has already engaged in a training maneuver. The statement is by definition, "A term any crew member may call to terminate a training maneuver" (Air Force Policy Directive, 2006, p. 273). This lateral control of a situation is of particular importance to aircraft that engage in combat training and tactical formation flying.
>
> Whether it involves two or more fighters simulating air-to-air combat flying or a formation of transport aircraft conducting an actual in-flight airdrop of military personnel and equipment, a loss of situational awareness or an improperly flown procedure can have swift and unforgiving results. The "Knock It Off" call directs all crew members to take corrective action and follow established procedures designed to allow crews return aircraft to safe and level flight where effective problem analysis may take place.
>
> Aviation mishaps, which result in the loss of valuable equipment and irreplaceable human life, have often begun as the result of very insidious failures in the human thought process. On countless occasions, losses in situational awareness and poor human judgment have resulted in catastrophic failure of equipment and loss of human life. The most tragic aspect of all, however, is that many incidents could have been, as demonstrated in numerous accident review boards, easily prevented. The communications procedures outlined in U.S. Air Force flying regulations and instilled in aircrew members through hours of classroom training, simulation, and experience attempt to minimize the occurrences of catastrophic and fatal mishaps by giving crew members of all ranks and experience levels a voice in safe mission accomplishment and aircraft operation. (Chris Hoffman, personal communication, February 28, 2007)

Hoffman personally learned the cost of human errors when a near-fatal crash almost claimed his life and the lives of crew members flying the last flight of the season to McMurdo Station, Antarctica.

THE LAST FLIGHT TO MCMURDO STATION, ANTARCTICA

Early in the bright blue morning of February 22, 2000, the aircraft that I was serving as flight engineer on, call sign Skier 92, departed Christchurch New Zealand for an eight-hour flight south to McMurdo Station, Antarctica. Our assignment along with two other aircraft was to pick up the remaining military support personnel who were scheduled to leave the continent for the close of the 1999–2000 Antarctica season. McMurdo Station has long served as a base of operations for the National Science Foundation's United States Antarctica Program. During peak season the station's population can exceed one thousand people including operational staff, scientists, and aircrew.

The aircraft, manufactured by Lockheed Martin, has honorably served as the South Pole's life link to human civilization and delivery vehicle transporting scientists to research camps scattered throughout the continent. It allows others to thrive in their pursuit of scientific research by delivering fuel, food, and other much needed supplies to international scientists working throughout the summer of the Antarctica season. The LC-130, which is a variant of the U.S. Air Force's C-130 airlift transport, is unique in that this particular model includes large snow skis that allow it to land and take off from ice runways and open fields of snow. To help lift the backbone of the airlift fleet off of ice and snow at heavy gross weights are eight solid-fuel rockets that are attached to the sides of the aircraft's fuselage.

This is the same type of aircraft that in October 1999 our unit, the 139th Airlift Squadron of the New York Air National Guard, used to rescue Dr. Jerri Nielson from the South Pole. Almost overnight the rescue of Dr. Nielson, who at the time had been suffering breast cancer, made international news headlines and the members of the 139th Airlift Squadron national heroes. While my role was quite small in comparison to those that actually flew the Pole mission, I had an opportunity to participate in the rescue by standing alert with another crew and aircraft as a search and rescue asset while the lead aircraft landed at the South Pole and rescued Dr. Nielson.

My own personal adventure began as the aircraft that I was assigned to departed Christchurch on a warm summer morning and headed south for an eight-hour-long flight to McMurdo Station. Antarctica. In front of us were two other aircraft assigned to the same mission. While en route to

McMurdo we would receive weather reports via high frequency radio from forecasters working at the station. The weather forecasts are based on arrival times and not current weather conditions.

The flights generally last between seven and eight hours and involve precise navigational planning that takes into account an aircraft's airspeed, fuel consumption, and wind speed. An imaginary point along the aircraft's flight path is known as PSR or "point of safe return." It allows an aircraft to fly as far south as possible yet enable it to return to Christchurch should weather conditions or maintenance difficulties dictate otherwise. Part of my job during flight was to monitor the aircraft's systems and engines while calculating actual fuel consumption versus predicted. This information, along with that provided by the navigator, was continually assessed to determine our aircraft's range capabilities.

On a number of occasions I had flown on these so-called north-south shuttles that had to return to Christchurch due to bad weather forecasts at McMurdo Station. The letdown could actually be quite intense given the amount of preparation involved in the day's flight and knowing that the process would have to be repeated the next day. Back to back eight-hour flights can be grueling for even the most seasoned aviator.

Our weather forecasts that morning were favorable during the flight. We left New Zealand in trail of two other aircraft and by regulation were supposed to abide by specified takeoff time intervals. Since all of the aircraft departed ahead of schedule, the last two were within approximately half an hour of each other and the lead aircraft. In the flying community, this rule bending is sometimes the result of a phenomenon referred to as "gethomeitis" or "mission hacking." While the intentions of crews leaning forward are good, the results can be hazardous. Landing at closer than specified intervals can potentially make recovery of the aircraft for ground personnel difficult but even more so can create a dangerous situation should weather conditions begin to deteriorate on the continent.

Our first hint of trouble ahead was the level of confusion existing in the weather reports provided to us, as we got closer to our PSR point. While the forecasts were favorable for proceeding past PSR, there was a persistent storm rolling over the continent in the vicinity of McMurdo Station. Our dilemma was that flying past PSR and landing at the station are based on an arrival forecast and not current conditions. While a newly arrived weather forecaster was providing our reports, more experienced non-weather staff members on the continent were expressing grave concerns about the aircraft going beyond PSR. This was based solely on their years of experience while working in Antarctica and weathering the intense blizzards that the climate can create. Speaking for myself, after already experiencing a recent "boomerang" flight, a mission that returns to Christchurch after turning around at PSR because of weather, I wanted to press on and get the job done. In these few sentences lay the first insidious elements in the chain of human error that led to disaster.

The storm grew worse in Antarctica and the aircraft inched closer to the point of safe return without a decision being made. With a good degree of clarity, I can recall how my level of concern slowly increased with every minute traveled closer to our decision point. What's even more remarkable is the silence I remember experiencing between radio transmissions. I honestly feel that everyone knew what needed to be said but no one wanted to say it, "we need to turn back and try it again tomorrow." In repeated tragedies that have been attributed to the human error chain people knew their actions could possibly result in disaster but for many reasons, including pride, intimidation, and inexperience, chose to do otherwise. I was just as guilty as those mentioned above.

After communicating our concerns with each other over an inter-plane radio frequency and with ground staff down at McMurdo via HF radio, further input was sought from the on-scene commander. While this person's intentions were genuinely good and sincere attempts to make a rational analysis of the problem were made, he was still not fully integrated in the situation at hand and in hindsight did not have all of the information necessary to make an effective decision. Nevertheless, structure, roles, responsibility, and chain of command prevailed, and all three aircraft were directed to proceed beyond PSR. Shortly afterward, a more senior weather forecaster arrived on scene and realized the gravity of the situation. The aircraft and crews were flying toward one of the year's worst storms, in close intervals, with no possibility of turning back, and nowhere safe to land.

The lead two aircraft landed in total whiteout conditions near McMurdo Station at an auxiliary ice runway. As a result, they nearly collided with one another. The storm was so bad that after a failed attempt to retrieve the crews from the aircraft, it was decided that they would have to remain in the aircraft until the storm subsided. It would last for many hours beyond that decision.

My aircraft, Skier 92, dangerously low on fuel and out of options, had to work with the radio coordination of personnel at McMurdo to find a suitable place to make a forced landing. The decision was made to land at Wyandot Ridge, which is a research area high on top of a rock-strewn volcanic glacier approximately 150 miles from McMurdo Station. No aircraft had ever attempted a landing in the vicinity. The only aircraft to land near the area in the past were helicopters dropping off research scientists, not 155,000-pound, four-engine aircraft. We prepared the aircraft for the landing by placing all of our cold weather survival gear and clothing near the crew entrance door should the aircraft structure fail during landing. Outside it was well below minus 40 degrees Fahrenheit with unimaginable wind speeds that would send a human body sliding across the ice and rocks.

That day we made two attempted landings at Wyandot Ridge. The first jarring impacts of hitting the undulating rock and ice surface led to the aircraft initiating an aborted landing attempt. The plane literally bounced off the earth's surface. We circled the area several more times looking for a suitable landing site while using the sun and shadows to determine the worst locations of the irregular surface. Eventually it was decided that we were fast running out of options and needed to get the aircraft on the ground.

Each time the aircraft left the surface of the ground and slammed back down, debris flew through the air like small missiles throughout the cockpit and cabin area. On one of the last great impacts, the force pushed me through my shoulder harness and caused me to hit the overhead control panel above head first. Eventually our aircraft, without exploding or breaking apart but sustaining substantial structural damage to the underside of the fuselage and wheel well fairings, came to a stop. To each crew member's credit, not at any time did anyone ever lose composure during our landing or lose faith in the other person's ability to carry out his duties. We were all together and alive.

The twenty-four hours or so that followed our landing were mixed with challenges and emotions. After radioing back to McMurdo Station our disposition, we were told that the storm had completely grounded all operations. The other crews were still stranded in their aircraft and the rescue helicopters that normally work during the season to provide rescue support were already days out at sea shipboard on their way back home. A great deal of invaluable survival training and faith in each other and those needed to help us kept us thinking and moving toward rescue.

We were picked up approximately twenty-four hours later and our aircraft, after being made ready by a specialized maintenance recovery team, was eventually flown back to New York, where it sat in two stages of repair. One stage occurred in Christchurch, New Zealand, and the other Scotia, New York, the home of the 139th Airlift Squadron. The aircraft flew again the following July.

A complete accident investigation took place and reviewed the actions and results of the ground and aircrews that memorable February day in 2000. What was discovered was that a small series of human errors coupled with faulty structural procedures led to an easily preventable mishap. No blame was made or restitutions demanded on the part of command staff, ground personnel, or aircrew members. Instead, a thorough analysis of the incident was taken into account, followed by recommendations for change in command and control and operational procedures that would prevent similar mishaps from occurring in the future.

To this very day, the 109th Airlift Wing and 139th Airlift Squadron of the New York Air National Guard still support the science mission in Antarctica with unparalleled skill and success. (Chris Hoffman, personal communication, February 28, 2007)

Hoffman's harrowing story shows the importance of guarding against mistakes and learning from them. Effective leaders recognize the challenges of psychological and cognitive traps associated with human error and poor decision making. Leaders take responsibility to ensure that, to the degree possible, the circumstance threatening human life, damage to property, or trust in the organization are guarded against. In many cases, their best defense is listening to others who warn of hazards and creating an environment dedicated to learning from errors and improving operations.

The responsibility of members to speak up during hazardous and unwise situations relates to what Chaleff (1998) describes as obligations of "courageous followership." Describing the relationship between leaders, members (followers), and purpose, Chaleff said, "Followers and leaders both orbit around the purpose; followers do not orbit around the leader" (p. 11). Perhaps one of the most difficult roles in followership involves giving negative feedback to leaders. "When giving feedback about behavior, we [followers] must clearly state: what the specific behavior is; what adverse effects it is causing and how serious the potential consequences are should the behavior continue" (p. 86).

The following stages of withdrawing support for leaders due to actions of misconduct or evil behavior provide a decision-making framework:

The first incident or suggestion of violating basic human values must be energetically challenged. If a second incident occurs, it must be responded to with a clear statement of intentions to withdraw support should it reoccur in any form. . . . Repeated incidents should be met by withdrawing support and by public exposure. . . . If followers cannot obtain documentation or corroboration for all their claims, but can for one claim, they should focus public attention on this point; one irrefutable demonstration of a leader's corruption is more powerful than many refutable charges. (Chaleff, 2003, p. 179)

These guidelines provide a method of withdrawing follower support, recognizing that there are times when members must refuse to cooperate with unethical and inhumane directives. The authority for leadership rests with the purpose of leadership, not the person possessing the most power or position. Leaders, accountable to members and constituents, must closely examine their behavior to guard against psychological and cognitive traps.

FAILURE AND ACCOUNTABILITY

Growing in wisdom, leaders "look[ing] out the window and into the mirror" to determine who gets credit when things go well and how to accept responsibility when failure occurs (Collins, 2001a, p. 35). According to Collins, the most successful leaders, "level five leaders," have two important attributes: humility and perseverance in achieving goals when working with others. Persevering leaders, "infected with an incurable need to produce results" (p. 30), accomplish a lot through their tremendous drive to succeed. Leaders with humility credit good fortune to the participation of others in their success, harnessing their egos to resist the temptation of becoming "all powerful" and "all knowing":

> The good-to-great leaders never wanted to become larger than life heroes. They never aspired to be on a pedestal or become unreachable icons. They were seemingly ordinary people quietly producing extraordinary results. (p. 28)

Wise leaders reduce the opportunities for failure and increase the likelihood of innovation by listening to others, particularly those who question decisions or propose alternative strategies. Wise leaders guard against cultures lacking professional standards and insist on accountability for errors to ensure that people do not needlessly harm themselves and others.

In the previous chapter, two reporters, Blair and Kelley, plagiarized and wrote fictional news reports because the newsroom climate failed to enforce professional standards. A system of checks and balances may have warned them away from poor decisions and also protected the integrity of the system. Two million people become infected with life-threatening bacteria due to dirty hospital environments and failure to follow proper procedures. Plane crashes and needless accidents occur due to preventable human errors. Although the "demons" involved in human errors may cause havoc and sometimes needlessly claim lives, preventative actions reduce the frequency of these events. Sharing collective knowledge and using a team approach diminishes their occurrence.

Establishing routines and guidelines to diminish human errors, effective leaders insist on the consistent application of professional standards, diligently investigate failure events to learn from mistakes, implement changes, and impose consequences when appropriate. In some cases, the detrimental actions of individuals took place in politically charged environments in which individual actions were not questioned.

Less-than-accountable systems make it far too easy for individuals to make poor decisions and choose a self-destructive path. Failure events create opportunities to learn when the causes are investigated, and systems improve as a result of this effort. In the next chapter the importance of individual and organizational literacy and learning to increase the capacity of people to adapt to their environments and innovate are examined.

(9)

IT'S *NEVER* TOO LATE TO LEARN:
THE IMPORTANCE OF
LEARNING IN LEADERSHIP

No problem can be solved from the same level of consciousness that created it.

—Albert Einstein, (Quoteworld, n.d.)

Clarence Brazier's story reads like a movie script, complete with scenes of struggle, survival, and accomplishment. It also includes a surprise ending, even more fantastic because it happens during Brazier's ninety-fifth year of life. After a lifetime of illiteracy, Brazier learned to read. Roy MacGregor, a journalist for the national Canadian newspaper *The Globe and Mail*, introduced us to Brazier in the following excerpt:

> It is the tale of a young boy who took over the family farm by age 7, a youngster who survived the Spanish flu, became a logger and miner who survived various close brushes with death, a wood supplier who finally gave up his chain saw at age 99 and who, at 100, has perfect vision, a full head of hair and can get out of his easy chair so quickly he sometimes looks like a gymnast executing a kip-up. But none of this is remarkable. Not compared with what Clarence Brazier decided to do at age 93 and accomplished by the time he was 95. He learned to read. (2006, p. A1)

Brazier's father, George, lost his sight in a farm accident when Clarence was five years old. The accident left his spouse and six children destitute (MacGregor, 2006, p. A4). Unable to secure governmental support for George's injuries, the family survived on the income earned by Brazier's mother, Fanny Mae. Taking a position as a cook in a logging camp, Fanny Mae lived in the camp during the week and returned only on Sundays to be with her family. George enlisted Clarence's help on the farm, combining George's strength and know-how with Clarence's vision and hard work. Seven-year-old Clarence ran the farm, learning the "art of delivering calves, clipping sheep, dehorning cattle" (p. A4) and felling trees with a cross-cut saw, avoiding injury to his visually impaired father, who stood next to the tree and held the other end of the saw. The work on the farm kept Clarence from attending school and learning to read or write.

Functionally illiterate, Clarence relied on his spouse, Angela, to perform the duties needed for his survival, including shopping, paying the bills, reviewing documents, and reading the mail. Intellectually curious and politically active, Clarence headed the farmer's union and the local branch of the Democratic Party with the help of Angela, who took notes and read documents to him (MacGregor, 2006, p. A5). Only his wife and four daughters knew about his problem. Deeply ashamed of his inability to read, Clarence's strategy to survive lasted as long as his sixty-four-year marriage to his wife. When Angela died, Clarence, at age ninety-three, could not read his mail or the labels on food containers.

A survivor and self-taught man, Clarence cut off the labels from canned goods and boxes stored in the cupboard and matched them to the items stacks on the shelves of the grocery store. Determined to learn to read, he poured over the words and pictures in junk mail and advertisements, matching pictures of a tire, pizza, or hamburger to the printed word. Using this slow process, Clarence grew frustrated and discouraged with his unguided attempts to read.

Clarence accepted an offer from his daughter, Doris, to move to her home in Sprucedale, Ontario. Ironically, his daughter Doris was a literacy volunteer. After watching his feeble attempts to read, she asked Clarence if he wanted to learn how to read. Clarence agreed. "From junk mail he moved to primary readers, and from primary readers to children's books and then into youth novels" (MacGregor, 2006, p. A5). After a lifetime of deprivation, he now feeds his desire to learn with books on history, mining, logging, hockey, and Canada. At age 100, Clarence has become "the poster boy for the very thing he spent nearly a century avoiding" (p. A5). Proud of his accomplishments, Brazier learned to read only after admitting his problem to others and accepting their help. His accomplishment illustrates the importance of the old adage, "It's never too late to learn."

Leaders share stories of deep learning and transformation, encouraging us to learn and expand our individual and collective potential for creativity and growth. Describing how people admit gaps in their knowledge, overcome their resistance to change, seek help from others, and accomplish difficult goals, leaders offer hope to those who embark on difficult and challenging paths. Stories of transformation and accomplishment not only inspire us, they also offer clues about how to learn.

When we hear a story about how someone experimented, failed, and tried again, we see the importance of trial and error and persistence in innovation. A story about how an *ordinary* person attempts to figure something out and achieves a seemingly impossible goal emphasizes the importance of problem solving and individual effort in learning. We emphasize the importance of "ordinary" here because of the need for each of us to imagine ourselves in the story.

Sometimes an entire community learns as a result of a crisis, encouraging us to collaborate and share our collective wisdom. In most cases, learning stories tell about the experience of learning and its transformational effects, causing us to assess our own abilities and motivation to learn. Freeing our natural inclination to learn and experiment (sometimes lost in childhood), leaders cultivate the capacity of people to recognize and capitalize on their strengths, acknowledge gaps in learning, share approaches to novel and systemic problems, and learn together. Effective leaders model and promote lifelong learning.

Unfortunately, Brazier's story is all too familiar. Another Canadian, Jacques Demers, a famous coach and former general manager of the National Hockey League (NHL) Tampa Bay Lightning team, hid his illiteracy from the public and his four daughters until he was sixty-one years old. The details of his story are found in Demers's autobiography,

Jacques Demers En Toutes Lettres (Jacque Demers from A–Z), coauthored with Mario Le Clerc.

JACQUES DEMERS TELLS HIS SECRET

The victim of a troubled and violent home, Demers witnessed his father's physical abuse of his mother and also experienced his father's ridicule and verbal abuse about his poor school performance (Shelton, 2005). After his parents died, Demers enlisted the help of others to pass a driver's test and get his first job. Anxiety ridden and ashamed, Demers found inventive ways to fool people over the years. When asked to read, Demers would say he forgot his glasses. At restaurants, he ordered the nightly special described by the waitress or simply duplicated his companion's order. Eventually forced to admit his illiteracy to his wife, he enlisted her help after admitting he could not write a check. She kept his secret from their four daughters and the public.

Thrilled and terrified when he was promoted to general manager of the Lightning, Demers grew fearful that his inability to read would be exposed because of the increasing demands of a position that required reading. Asking his secretaries to save him time by reading and summarizing documents, Demers successfully hid his disability from the owners of the hockey team. At one point, Demers took the drug Paxil to control his anxiety over the constant threat of exposure (Shelton, 2005, p. 32). Reflecting on the cost of illiteracy, Demers said, "When you hide the truth, you suffer inside" (MacGregor, 2006, p. A4).

Brazier's and Demers's stories illustrate how their inability to read isolated them from others; created a life sentence of shame, fear, and dependency; and limited their opportunities for growth. Trapped by circumstances outside their control and unwilling to admit their deficiencies, both men deceived others, including family members, friends, employers, business associates, and members of their communities. Brazier lost his wife, his helpmate, and constant aide. Demers lost his job, growing weary of the charade and his constant fear of exposure as a public figure. Their lives changed dramatically only when they reached a crisis point. Each admitted his problem, releasing a tremendous burden and paving the way for a more productive and authentic life. Instead of expending their efforts in covering up their problems, they did something about them, finding freedom in their actions. Avoiding what we don't want does not help us get what we need.

The stories of Brazier and Demers mirror our experience in frozen or unhealthy organizations and offer us a model for working through our fears. Often the fear of change and the exposure of our deficiencies prevents us from acknowledging our problems and seeking help. In some ways we are all like Brazier and Demers: We may be quite capable individually and collectively in some aspects of our lives and illiterate in others.

Communities, organizations, and groups, like people, must avoid the trap of being bound by a limited capacity to learn. Leaders invest in learning organizations to signal the importance of lifelong learning regardless of our starting points. Rapid changes in technologies and careers may cause many of us to experience new types of illiteracy due to rapid change.

LEARNING ORGANIZATIONS

Increasingly, the metaphor of organizations as "think tanks" or "learning organizations" (as an extension of a college campus) reflects the need to stay abreast of change through continuous lifelong learning. Leaders champion individual and organizational learning to support growth and continuous improvement.

Mezirow and Associates (2000) describe four ways or strategies of learning: (1) "by elaborating existing frames of references, [2] by learning new frames of reference, [3] by transforming points of view, or [4] by transforming habits of mind" (p. 19). Using systems thinking, teams must "frame" and "reframe" (Bolman & Deal, 2003). Seeing an issue from a different perspective causes us to define a problem differently and yields a larger array of potential solutions. A recent example illustrating a shift in perspectives regarding the space program comes to mind.

Following the *Columbia* disaster, National Aeronautics and Space Administration (NASA) engineers attributed the accident to the failure of the heat shield tiles. Instead of trying to ensure that future space shuttles would never experience damage to the heat shield at launch, NASA engineers instead conceived of making a patch kit to repair heat shield tiles in the event of launch damage. Working collaboratively and imaginatively, NASA engineers "reframed" the problem, explored other alternatives, and increased the safety of future space travelers. Before taking off for reentry, astronauts make an inspection of the tiles before leaving the space station. We need more inventive thinking to expand our mental models and open new avenues of creativity.

Corporations build "campuses" or "academies" to help their organizations survive, adapt, and renew. The goal is continuous learning and improvement. Net meetings, conducted over the World Wide Web with a seemingly infinite number of participants, offer opportunities for transglobal, collaborative, and virtual learning. We were recently invited to a Net meeting to learn how technology applications might apply to our teaching. A computer, an Internet account, a website address, and a password allow virtually anyone to go to class.

Like Brazier and Demers, we must begin by freely admitting the gaps in our knowledge and enlisting the help of others. Their stories highlight the importance of accessing knowledge to survive and meaningfully participate in society and remind us of the ever-present need to develop literacy in all aspects of our lives.

Senge (1990) championed organizational learning as a strategy to fight against rigid mental models and encourage innovation and renewal within organizations. Sometimes the failure to adequately respond to an unexpected event, like a record snowstorm, damages even the best companies. However, the failure unfreezes mental models and opens opportunities for organizational learning.

JET "BLACK AND BLUE": A VALENTINE'S DAY HORROR STORY

Cheryl Chesner and her husband Seth left on Valentine's Day for Aruba. Instead of being "stranded" on an island for their honeymoon, they spent eleven hours on a runway in New York, waiting to get off a frozen JetBlue airplane scheduled for take off (*JetBlue Attempts to Calm Passenger Furor*, 2007). Entombed passengers complained about the excessive heat and lack of food and cleanliness on board the plane.

A passenger on a flight to Cancun described the primitive way airline personnel addressed the oppressive conditions on the plane. "They had to open the door every 20 minutes just so we could get air," said Sean Corrinet (p. 10).

Canceled flights, angry passengers, and total bedlam took over when at least 250 of the 500 JetBlue flights were canceled on the day of the storm. Passengers, stranded on the tarmac because gates were filled and personnel hoped the conditions would improve, became enraged over the total chaos that overwhelmed the popular "people-centered" airline. To make matters worse, the problem continued for days.

Overwhelmed by passenger demands, frozen planes, stranded crews in need of rest based on federal regulations, and limited staff to address the magnitude of the problem, ground operations imploded. Although the magnitude of this event seemed particularly adverse, the breakdown in communication and lack of a crisis plan startled even the most seasoned traveler.

A few months earlier, a fierce winter storm had prevented passengers from leaving Denver and flying home for the 2006 winter holiday season. Nightly news coverage of stranded passengers showed some people standing in long lines trying to rebook their flights while others slept on the floor, turning the airport into a makeshift hotel. Putting the New York failure into historical context, the lack of crisis planning seems even more surprising. A severe winter storm, an entirely predictable event, occurs quite often during the winter months. Errors in reasoning and false (foolish) hope sometimes prevent leaders from taking preventive action. The snow falls in Denver and New York.

Although many may understand a one-day, weather-related cancellation, 1,100 cancellations in a six-day period put red ink on JetBlue's bottom line and a red face on the company's chief executive officer, Neeleman:

> Neeleman called the fallout of the ice storm a "defining moment" for the airline and said the company is implementing new policies and adding management to improve operations. "We learned a huge lesson. That will never happen at JetBlue again," Neeleman said Tuesday on CNN's "American Morning." . . . Under its "Customer Bill of Rights," passengers hit by ground delays will now receive vouchers for free travel, and the airline will refund tickets for canceled flights. (*JetBlue CEO Pledges Last Week's Meltdown Won't Happen Again*, 2007, pp. 2–3, 4)

Applying mechanistic or technical models of thinking to solve problems in a dynamic environment has limited use (Wheatley, 1999). In the case of JetBlue, a qualitatively different kind of thinking is needed to go beyond the immediate crisis that emerged from a New York snowstorm to a more thoughtful and systemic approach to leadership. Despite the risks associated with significant change, Neeleman must take action to stabilize the organization and avoid further damage.

Systematic failure may lead to what Argyris (2004) describes as an opportunity for "double loop" learning. Defined as "the detection and correction of errors where the correction requires changes not only in action strategies but also in the values that govern the theory in use" (p. 10), double-loop learning requires people to investigate and reflect on what happened to identify root causes and systemic failures in systems and values. Following the failure, JetBlue announced changes in communication and their response to crisis events. CEO Neeleman led an inquiry into the systemic failure to determine its roots causes and guard against another failure. These changes in "action strategies" included cross-training personnel, improving communication, and compensating passengers for poor performance.

Promising a Passenger Bill of Rights with significant penalties to Jet-Blue for failure to deliver a high standard of customer service, Neeleman asked for trust and promised that the failure would never happen again (JetBlue's customer bill of rights, n.d.). Risking his reputation, Neeleman's attempt to save JetBlue from a Valentine's Day fiasco awaits the test of time. "We risk so many things when we act: taking a fall, failing to achieve a goal, appearing incompetent, evoking criticism or competition or resistance or anger, or simply being ignored" (Palmer, 1990, pp. 21–22). During a crisis, the failure to act and learn from it serves as a lost opportunity and a potentially fatal error.

As a *sense-making* activity, leaders cause members to reflect on experiences, discern their essence and effects, and learn. Emphasizing learning as a strategic response to *fluid, dynamic, and unknowable* circumstances, leaders capitalize on the intelligence and creativity of members to innovate and change.

Leaders practice and promote lifelong learning as a highly valued "core literacy" within themselves and their organizations. Effective leaders develop "learning organizations" (Senge, 1990) to continuously expand the productive and creative potential of people. Learning serves as a core technology, helping employees achieve increasingly higher levels of literacy as well as increasing the collective intelligence of the entire organization.

Literacy, defined as "the condition or quality of being knowledgeable in a particular subject or field" (Pickett, 2000, p. 1021), commonly refers to the ability to read or write. The capacity to read and communicate effectively through written language serves as a valuable life skill and source of continual renewal and growth. Those who enter the workplace functionally illiterate or fluent in a language other than the "dominant" language experience the same problem: They're unable to fully develop their capacities within the larger society.

To successfully manage the rapid changes in technology and culture, leaders must develop the capacity of people within their organization to make creative adaptations in response to a dynamic environment. Leaders guard against obsolescence caused by illiteracy and the inability to detect changes in the environment by encouraging continuous and lifelong learning. Basic communication literacies such as the ability to read and write, as well as emerging literacies such as cultural competence or technological literacy, serve a vital function in leadership, empowerment, and capitalizing on the collective intelligence of members. Dialogue serves as a process for knowledge sharing and relationship building.

DIALOGUE AND APPRECIATIVE INQUIRY

Burbules, author of *Dialogue in Teaching: Theory and Practice*, describes dialogue as "a spirit of tolerance and respect for a range of views, with the *intention* of addressing some sort of question or problem, and with the *hope* that these differences can be reconciled into an at least partial and provisional commonalities" (1993, p. 118). Participants in dialogue enter the relationship to seek consensus through the wide exploration of an issue or concern, as well as to gradually make a commitment to the relationship with others. They assume that knowledge results from the mutual exchange of information and views, and value many types of knowledge and experience.

Partners engaged in a dialogical conversation "proceed interactively, cooperatively, not toward a specific common goal, but in a *process* of mutual engagement directed toward shared understanding. I am drawn to *this* sort of dialogue with *this* person because in *this* process I see an opportunity to supplement and refigure my own understandings (and presumably my partner is motivated similarly" (Burbules, 1993, p. 115).

Staying open to diverse viewpoints and voices, dialogical partners create meaning through mutual sharing of viewpoint, resisting narrow views, and valuing many different types of knowledge and interpretations. Participants engage in dialogue by framing "life-giving" questions that focus dialogical inquiry using a strength rather than a deficit approach.

A process called appreciative inquiry (AI) offers promise in creating more generative and positive approaches to change on individual and global levels:

> Appreciative Inquiry is about a co-evolutionary search for the best in people, their organizations, and the relevant world around them. In its broadest focus, it involves systematic discovery of what gives 'life' to a living system when it is most alive, most effective, and most constructively capable in economic, ecological, and human terms. (Cooperrider, Sorensen, Whitney, & Yaeger, 2000, p. 5)

Appreciative inquiry assumes that talks about "achievements, assets, unexplored potentials, innovations, strengths, elevated thoughts, opportunities, benchmarks, high points, stories, expressions of wisdom, insights into the deeper corporate spirit or soul, and visions of valued and possible futures" will lead to positive change (p. 5). A strategy and an expression of faith in positive action, AI progresses in a cycle of inquiry through organizing questions: "What gives life? What might be? What is the world calling for? What should be the ideal? How to empower, learn, and adjust/improvise?" (p. 7).

As a *sense-making* activity, leadership causes us to reflect on our experiences, discern the essence and effects of them, and learn from them. Leaders must employ a variety of strategies to understand the situational and contextual challenges of leadership. This approach to thinking about leadership significantly broadens the ability of leaders to understand and function more effectively in their leadership environment. The changing context and environment for leadership require us to examine new models that emphasize leadership as a learning process in which we use wisdom, creativity, and intelligence to respond to *fluid, dynamic, and unknowable* circumstances.

This change from technical to adaptive challenges requires that we shift our perspective from viewing leadership as the skillful application of technical knowledge to viewing it as a thinking and learning process through which we become aware of future problems and potential solutions, but to which we have not yet developed routine ways of responding. Thus, we need to think differently, continuing to develop and expand our capacity to think analytically and creatively.

Reflective and generative processes help us identify reality and propel us into the *futuristic* work of leadership. As a result of what we understand from our experience and the meaning we attach to it, what do we now envision as the next step or action? Answers to this question propel us to act. Leadership, as an *action-oriented* activity, serves as a catalyst to change and a call to action. Ultimately, acts of leadership require our participation and engagement with others.

Handy (1989) encourages "upside-down" or discontinuous thinking, recommending that we engage in processes that cause us to change our thinking by looking at everything in a new way. The value of ideas may be more important than the mark of individuals in the scheme of things. "A mindful approach to any activity has three characteristics: the continuous creation of new categories; openness to new information; and an implicit awareness of more than one perspective" (Langer, 1997, p. 4). The power of thinking and new ideas may have a greater effect than a leader's influence at any one particular time:

> In the long perspective of history it may seem that the really influential people were not Hitler or Churchill, Stalin or Gorbachev, but Freud, Marx, and Einstein, men who changed nothing except the way we think, but that changed everything. (p. 24)

Our future may depend on our ability to develop and share our individual and collective wisdom.

During times of crisis and change, effective leaders and members stay open to double-loop learning, examining existing mental models, using different methods of knowing, locating alternative perspectives, and creating solutions to manage chaos and complexity. In the next chapter, "Change as a Metaphor for Life," the human and organizational aspects of change are explored through the power of story.

10

CHANGE AS A METAPHOR FOR LIFE: TRANSITIONS AND INNOVATIONS

It isn't the changes that do you in, it's the transitions.

—Bridges (1991, p. 3)

Change, a metaphor for life, occurs as a normal process in our personal, organizational, and community lives and transformations. Written by Bernard Ighner and recorded by Quincy Jones in 1974, the popular song "Everything Must Change" warns of the constant, unstoppable nature of change (*Second Hand Songs*, n.d.). The passage of time and seasonal changes in nature serve as the only constants amid life's uncertainty. A change story put to music, the song entreats us to face and accept the inevitability of change.

Sung as both a plea for reason and a prayer for acceptance, the lyrics lay down the phases of change, including loss, uncertainty, inner turmoil, and healing. A generational gift of wisdom, the song explains the nature of change and offers comfort in two simple phrases, "mysteries do unfold" (eventually the experience and its meaning become clear) and "a wounded heart will heal" (healing takes time). A song about suffering and change, the lyrics tell us what to do: Everyone who suffers must accept change to heal.

In the following story, Rob and Sally, a couple experiencing change, watch "winter turn to spring" through the picture window of Rob's "house-inside-a-barn," struggling with their own version of seasonal change in their relationship.

TABLE CREEP

Rob lives on the family farm, located fifty miles northeast of Minneapolis near the Minnesota–Wisconsin border. After finishing college and working briefly in an urban area, Rob returned home to farm the land and eventually build his home. Resourceful and inventive, Rob harvested a section of the barn (no longer used for livestock and storing hay), converting the space into a home. Designing and building his home, Rob captured three walls of the 1918 barn and constructed a fourth side, incorporating the existing beams and floor elevations into his design. Using authentic and affordable material to build his home, Rob nailed nearly every board into place. An enduring symbol of his creativity and a significant accomplishment, Rob's house represents him, his life history, and his personal signature. Rob is the house.

The house-inside-a-barn has three floors with unobstructed views of fields, woods, and a nature lake (that's a term for a lake you don't swim in because it hosts wildlife, vegetation, and fish, not people). A relatively modest size, the house uses only 1,500 square feet of space in the barn. When Rob walks out the back door of his house, he steps into a different century, where post and beam construction, hand-hewn beams, antique and salvage items, and years of accumulated history reside.

However, the inside of the house belongs to this century. The kitchen, bath, and dining area, located on the first floor (but really on the second floor of the barn), serve as the hub of family activity. A bay window and window seat immediately draw family members and visitors to the best view of the lake and surrounding woods. Two rarely vacant chairs hug the floor space next to the window seat. Newspapers stacked on the window seat and binoculars hanging on an adjacent wall offer hours of leisurely entertainment. The kitchen table occupies the space directly behind the chairs, sitting in close proximity to the window chairs to take advantage of the view.

Rob's kitchen arrangement served him and his two children well for many years until Sally, Rob's girlfriend and weekend companion, entered his life. Living together at the farm on weekends, Rob and Sally enjoyed being together and started making improvements to the house. Sally had a knack for decorating and took pride in the changes made in the house. Suffering only minor bruises and injuries, the couple managed to paint a room and remodel a third floor despite their differences in style and ownership of the now shared space. Making solid progress, things went well until a conflict developed over the placement of the kitchen table.

While Rob enjoyed the existing arrangement and objected to any change, Sally said the crowded arrangement disturbed her. She complained about the lack of space between the two viewing chairs and the table and four chairs residing next to them. On most days she claimed it required sideways walking to move between the two chairs at the window and the table set. Several feet of empty space directly behind the table provided an opportunity for a new arrangement. This move (in Sally's mind) would provide a more balanced furniture arrangement and improved traffic flow.

Assuming Rob would appreciate her homemaking skills, Sally moved the table one foot north to create more space between the chairs and the table crowding the window. She marveled at the improvement. Much to her surprise, however, Rob did not appreciate the move. What followed Sally now calls "table creep." After the first table move, Sally returned to her city home, pleased with the new location of the table. After Sally's departure and before the next visit, the table crept back to its original position. After a few weekends, Rob and Sally joked about the strange and inexplicable table moves. Not wishing to address their conflict, Sally and Rob avoided direct confrontation about the placement of the kitchen table and chairs. Instead a series of minor skirmishes ensued.

After the obvious repositioning of the table following each weekend, Sally decided to try a little change in Rob's perspective, hoping to hold her ground on the table move. Sally bought a rug and placed it under the table, wondering if Rob would notice the change. He noticed. Next Sally added a table leaf, thinking Rob might assume the change was the added length of the table, not the change in placement. Once again, Rob noticed. Sally even considered moving the center island (a large structure housing a microwave with base cupboards), but the weight of it and ludicrousness of her "night moves" finally caught up with her. Rob always detected her subterfuge and gradually inched the table back to its original position. What Sally thought was a simple change in table placement turned out to be a battle of the sexes.

Sally could not see that a move of one foot would compromise the view of the lake and wondered why Rob seemed stuck in the old arrangement.

Rob described the view as the most important element in the room and maintained that even one foot substantially altered his view of the lake, even drawing a diagram to illustrate the angular shift. Rob didn't understand why Sally wanted to change the one thing that was so important to him. Sally pushed back, listing many things that remained unchanged despite her suggestions. They found themselves at a standstill.

After many lengthy discussions, Rob and Sally discovered that they were both right about the "correct" placement of the table, but for different reasons. Although the old table arrangement provided the best view of the lake, the new way offered more space for Sally and family members to move freely in the room. Nothing changed until they began to see "table creep" as a metaphor for their adjustment to each other in a growing (and changing) relationship.

Sally and Rob discussed the problem and eventually compromised, moving the table far enough to provide a full frontal walk between the chairs at the window and the table. When visitors arrive, they make room for them by moving the table away from the window. When Sally returns to the city, the table magically "creeps" backs to its original position.

Sometimes on winter nights Rob and Sally (now engaged) place their chairs side-by-side, turn off the lights, sit together at the window, and hold hands in the moonlight, allowing the landscape to enfold them in its embrace. In these moments of utter stillness, peace, and love neither Rob nor Sally cares about the table or its placement in what is now becoming their future home. (Confidential, personal communication, 2007)

Sally's and Rob's battle over the table mirrors our experience with change. Moves and countermoves during a major change stir emotions, often creating conflict over the right direction or the value of the move. When faced with change, sometimes the price paid appears too high. Despite our best intentions to cooperate (even with a move one foot north), we can't resist returning to our old ways. Instances of "table creep" increase when the disputes take place within our sacred spaces. Although we make progress in inches, we sometimes fail to agree on whether the progress is forward or backward. Weathering these disputes challenges us to see the opportunities in the move as well as affirm the value found in each other, a lesson Sally and Rob eventually learned.

Most stories about conflict and change touch on the things within us that matter, disturbing our place in the universe and our identity. More often than not, it's not the change itself but rather the adjustment needed to adapt to the change that causes inner turmoil. Examining why a seemingly minor change evokes such a strong reaction from us opens a window for closely inspecting our core values, our routine ways of doing things, and the importance of relationships in our daily lives.

The couple's story draws attention to the disturbing and thrilling aspects of change and its effects. While there is opportunity in change, tensions around the answers to the following questions exist: "What values, norms, or traditions should stay in place because they still serve a valuable purpose? What changes are absolutely essential to adapt to an ever-changing environment? What are the human costs associated with change? Who pays the price for the change? Is it worth it?" The story of "table creep" captures the conflicted nature of change and our adjustment to it.

Revealing the inherent changes experienced by the couple as their relationship progresses, their story contains many themes, including identity, listening, learning, and core values. While the "cover" story describes their conflict about a kitchen table and its placement in a room, it also serves as a metaphor to describe their need to adjust (transition) to changes in their lives and relationships.

DISRUPTIVE EVENTS AND LIVES IN TRANSITION

Bridges (1980) lists several changes likely to be experienced as disruptive events occur, including (1) losses of relationships, (2) changes in home life (spouse or new baby), (3) personal changes (getting sick or well, experiencing success or failure), (4) work or financial changes (being fired, retiring,) and (5) inner changes (spiritual awakening, social and political awareness) (pp. 22–23). Some of these events result from shifts in life stages, while others may have completely unpredictable causes. Whether changes appear in the form of good events (like the couple's adjustment to each other) or bad events (divorce or death), they take their toll, often draining energy from other life tasks at work or home. Stress arises from the adjustment to change rather than the change itself:

> It isn't the changes that do you in, it's the transitions. . . . *Change* is situational: the new site, the new boss, the new team roles, the new policy.

Transition is the psychological process people go through to come to
terms with the new situation, Change is external, *transition* is internal.
(Bridges, 1991, p. 3)

Individual experiences with change often mirror on a small scale what
happens on a larger scale in organizational life. Because change takes
place in human, social, and cultural worlds, change leaders keep the human elements in the process foremost in their minds. Coping with
change requires people to work through the following phases identified
by Bridges (1991): letting go of something and recognizing the grief and
loss associated with this process; living in the chaotic "neutral zone" (in
between the old and new self or old and new way of doing things); and
the new beginning, a time when commitment to change occurs and begins to authentically take hold (pp. 5–6).

Leaders, aware of each of the stages, offer different types of support
during each phase. Bridges advises that each phase must be thoroughly
experienced before it becomes possible to move through it and make
change "work." This makes sense from a practical viewpoint. People
won't implement a new program without first experiencing some grief
regarding the price they have already paid to learn how to do something,
anticipating the price they're going to pay in learning a new program,
and calculating the considerable time and effort needed to gain profi-
ciency (1991, pp. 19–49).

Weary of past change initiatives, people often recognize that not all
changes are good or worth the effort. After working through losses of
identity and stability and losses in efficiency (effects of the first two of
Bridges's stages), leaders should help people accomplish the final stage,
the new beginning, by explaining the four "Ps." These include clarifying
the "purpose" of the proposed outcome, painting a "picture" regarding
how the outcome will look once achieved, offering a "plan" regarding its
implementation, and finally telling each person which "part" he or she
will play (1991, p. 52).

Many fail to anticipate the deep internal stress caused by changes in
assumptions or daily routines. When a transfer to another school or department or the elimination of a program occurs, "our world stops making sense; continuity is disrupted; our connections can no longer be
counted on. Virtually nothing is more painful or more threatening to our

basic security, our very ability to understand and cope with such things" (Evans, 1996, p. 29).

Experiencing considerable stress and a loss of identity when asked to change routine ways of doing things, many people feel change devalues their past success. The principal of a school who asks teachers to stop teaching in ways they were taught and have mastered, to instead adopt different methods, may not recognize the pain caused by the request:

> You [the principal] may see your recommendation as a gift, an addition to my repertoire, an opportunity for growth, and an answer to my own dis-satisfaction. But I may feel your suggestion to be a dagger in the heart. Even if you don't criticize me directly, I am likely to feel that you are de-valuing what I do and who I am. . . . You [the principal] may leave our con-versation [about the change] shaking your head, convinced I am too nar-row, rigid, and "resistant to change." Perhaps I am. But it may primarily be that I am bereaved. (Evans, 1996, p. 31)

A proposed change can be viewed in two ways. Those who advocate change see it positively, while those who are charged with making the change often view it negatively (Evans, 1996). The story of a failed bas-ketball design illustrates what can happen when two different view-points prevail about a proposed change and the concerns of the people implementing the change are ignored.

Spalding, a world famous manufacturer, held a press conference with National Basketball Association (NBA) officials to announce an exciting new change at the beginning of its 2006–2007 game season. Instead of using a leather basketball, players were introduced to and required to use the microfiber composite basketball. The advantages described by the manufacturer included the elimination of the break-in period re-quired for leather balls, moisture management, and a superior grip (Cheifetz, 2007).

According to columnist Cheifetz, players complained immediately, blamed the new basketball for leaving "small cuts and abrasions" on their hands, and also appeared on the court wearing bandages on their fingers (p. D8). Ignoring their concerns, league executives kept the ball in use until the players filed an "unfair practices complaint with the Na-tional Labor Relations Board over the imposition of the ball without player input" (Cheifetz, 2007). The new basketball, a spectacular flop, proved embarrassing for NBA Commissioner David Stern, who imposed his decision about the basketball without player input and then later ignored player concerns. Leather basketballs, viewed as a luxury item and indicative of "elite" status, were a symbol of player success (p. D8). This is one example of a "double-standard" change, one in which the persons advocating the change viewed it positively while those stuck with implementing the decision didn't see it the same way (Evans, 1996).

When people experience deep change, much of what they take for granted falls apart, disrupting their stability and the routine procedures reflected in their culture. Culture "represents the collective knowledge of our predecessors" and "shapes people's behavior, perception, and understating of events" (Evans, 1996, p. 44). The habit-bound ways of thinking and acting worked in some way, providing stability, allowing people to accomplish more or find leisure time. At some level all culture worked for a time. "The routines of any school [organization] provide a basic security, a framework within which people can come to count on one another and trust the world to be the way it is supposed to be" (p. 44). Why should anyone welcome change?

Leaders meet a "culture of resistance" in response to their directives and bemoan the rigidity of resistors (Evans, 1996). However, when closely examined, resistance makes sense. Much like other factors in change management, resistant cultures must be accounted for and *simultaneously respected* in the change process. Given the high costs of change, many people would appreciate providing input and being involved in decisions that affect them, whether it's using a new basketball or restructuring an organization.

CHANGE MYTHS

The following myths about change keep us from facing its demanding presence in our lives: (1) change is a temporary condition, (2) people experience change in the same way, (3) change progresses predictably and incrementally, (4) change can be mandated from above without enlisting the support of members, and (5) the nature and effects of planned change can be fully anticipated and managed.

It seems obvious, but *a period of stability is the temporary condition;* change is a more permanent and ongoing factor in our lives. When was the last time you remember an idyllic moment when all issues were satisfactorily addressed and no new challenges loomed on the horizon? *Many factors influence the way people react to change.* For example, change experienced simultaneously in both personal and work life more than doubles its impact because the opportunity to rest from stress is absent. General Mills, a worker- and family-friendly employer, recognized the loss of work productivity due to the demands of personal life and built a corporate campus to help people with their lives. Employees can visit a doctor, enjoy the services of a personal shopper, exercise, or get some help from employee assistance to finding nursing care for their families, all under the same roof (see www.gm.com).

Although many desire to experience change predictably and incrementally, real *change occurs unpredictably, with moderate to seismic effects,* causing the ground to move beneath us with little warning. Angry people want to know why leaders didn't see the change coming and warn them, ignoring the capricious and chaotic nature of change. No one can "see" change before it happens. But symptoms and signs of change eventually reach a level of awareness requiring capable leaders to detect and react to it strategically. It's not predicting change that matters, rather it is seeing a charging herd in front of you and being willing to join the herd or deflect it in another direction. Conversely, change leaders scan the environment and search for new ways to enable change before people and systems become overwhelmed by their static nature.

Change mandated from above using coercive power without enlisting the support of at least some members more often than not never really takes hold. The anticipated change produces plenty of discussion and complaint rather than action when a "power over" rather than a "power with" approach forces change. However, when external forces threaten survival, *conditions mandate change, not leaders.* When the ship sinks, everyone gets on board a lifeboat.

For example, numerous public school educators opposed school choice and state-supported charter schools, for many reasons. However, once students started choosing other schools and districts, public educators in local districts developed programs and used marketing strategies to retain their students and compete with private vendors. The school choice movement fueled competition and eliminated the company store.

Students and their families now participate in the education market as consumers and clients.

When people are involved in making change and their decisions affect their work, they become owners of the organization, at least metaphorically. In this case *purpose mandates change, not leaders.* Those committed to the mission or success of the organization become invested in change for a variety of reasons, including increased security, creativity, improved efficiency and effectiveness, and achieving a sense of control over their work. When leaders mandate change, it is likely to fail on many counts unless desire or desperation motivate others to get involved. When people or employees experience ownership in change, they can move mountains.

The final myth, that the nature and effects of "planned" change can be fully anticipated and managed, flies in the face of real change. *The unpredictable, explosive, and exponential effects of change operate outside of our control and experience.* If we could predict when change would occur or exactly how to respond to it, the effects would be minimized. On a personal level, people often say they lacked warning and could not have known how the change would affect them. Why do we expect to have increased understanding and predictability about change at the organizational, community, or global levels? This seems more like a wish to be fulfilled than a realistic expectation. Leaders rely on the capacity of others to detect and respond to change in environments where collective intelligence is shared, avoiding entropy and entering a fundamental state of leadership (Quinn, 2004).

"According to the second law of thermodynamics, all systems tend toward entropy" (Quinn, 2004, p. 18). Energy within a system is not available for use in a state of entropy. When systems grow, level off, become comfortable, and tend to stay in place, a normal state moves to stability and eventually entropy. Normal states, characterized by self-focused, internally closed, externally directed, and comfort-centered action (p. 20), support the human desire for comfort and stability. Many thwart efforts to change by responding in a "reactive state," attempting to solve problems with established systems and maintaining the status quo instead of embracing change (p. 20).

In contrast to this normal state, the "fundamental state of leadership" embraces changes, and the actions within this state involve support actions that are "other-focused, externally open, internally directed and purpose centered" (Quinn, 2004, p. 22). Now the interests of others are considered by seeking the common good, looking for honest feedback, following inner values, and focusing on the result or clear purpose desired (p. 22). In this state, excited people, energized by the work, attract others to their purpose because of their authenticity and passion about it.

Moving into this "state of leadership" causes fear, yet it is only in this state that real change occurs:

> The transition is painful, and we are often hesitant, fearing that we lack the courage and confidence to proceed. We uncover a great paradoxical truth. Change is hell. Yet not to change, to stay on the path of slow death, is also hell. The difference is that the hell of deep change is the hero's journey. The journey puts us on a path of exhilaration, growth, and progress. (Quinn, 1996, p. 78)

Despite the pain, individuals can and do make this transition, and when they do, a significant reality is realized. "When we take the necessary risks, we become self-empowered. . . . We become energized and slowly begin to recognize that we can make a difference. We begin to understand that one person really can change the system" (p. 219).

The human, social, or cultural factors associated with change influence the opportunities, challenges, alternatives, and limitations facing leaders and members during their experience of change. Leaders who fail to examine and account for the needs and likely responses of others put themselves and their organizations at risk. On the other hand, good leaders help people see the opportunities in change and can have a lasting impact on organizations.

In the next story, about the merger of two churches, lay and pastoral leadership and the good will of two congregations made the difference in accomplishing an unprecedented merger of the African American Border Church with a predominantly white Hennepin Avenue Methodist Church in 1957 (Carroll, 2007). Social changes on the horizon signaled the new direction and occurred during a time when merely sharing the same seat on a bus was forbidden in some parts of the country due to Jim Crow laws. The seeds for change within organizations ultimately allowed a group of people to make a giant leap of faith.

THE BORDER–HENNEPIN UNION

In November 1954, the Hennepin Avenue Methodist Church passed a resolution to welcome persons of all races into the church (Carroll, 2007, p. 19). The church posted a sign on its front lawn and also placed the resolution in its literature, becoming one of "the first churches in the area to adopt a policy that all races were welcome as members" (Davis, 2002, p. 130). Three years later the spirit of their intention was tested by a proposed merger between two racially segregated churches.

Unwelcome in white congregations and experiencing considerable discrimination in housing and employment, African Americans in Minneapolis formed their own churches in the early 1900s. A Sunday school for black children, founded in 1918, expanded into St. John's Methodist Episcopal Church, moved from South Minneapolis to Border Avenue in north Minneapolis, and was renamed The Border Avenue Methodist Episcopal Church (Carroll, 2007). A socially active church with about 150 members, "Border was counted among the churches that stood against racial injustice, poverty, and other social ills" (Davis, 2002, p. 128). A few miles south of Border Church, near downtown Minneapolis, The Hennepin Avenue Methodist Church, founded in 1875, enjoyed a large congregation and built a "large, cathedral-style church" to serve its growing congregation of white parishioners. "By the 1940s, Hennepin had 4,000 members, six pastors, a famous choir, a large Sunday night youth program called University of Life, and many clubs for men and women" (Carroll, 2007, p. 7).

An active civic life brought some of the church leaders of the Border and Hennepin churches together in supporting the work of the Phyllis Wheatley Settlement House. The mission of the Wheatley house was to keep young women out of prostitution and deter young people from crime. The Hennepin Church enjoyed considerable financial support, and when the Border Church was forced to move a few blocks again in 1937, the Border pastor, Damon Young, asked for and received help from the Hennepin Church to defray the costs of the move (Carroll, 2007).

Hard times fell on the Border Church during the 1950s. Reverend Charles Sexton, who took charge of the church in 1949, witnessed a decline in membership and received yet another relocation notice in 1955, when the city of Minneapolis decided on an urban development project. Harry Davis Jr., a lay leader in the congregation, advised against building a new church unless the church's membership could be dramatically increased. The church's future survival seemed doubtful.

Across town, members of the Hennepin Church learned about the problems in a discussion with Harry Davis. "Davis told them that Border had concluded that it was too small to rebuild. Mrs. Bennett [a board member of the Urban League] responded, 'Why don't we invite all of you to come to Hennepin?'" (Carroll, 2007, p. 11). The Reverend Chester Pennington, Senior Pastor at Hennepin Church, met with members of the Hennepin board. The church leaders supported Bennett's suggestion. Pennington and a delegation of Hennepin Church members went to the Border Church to formally invite them to join the Hennepin Church, "explaining it was 'simply a personalizing of the policy of Christian love to which we are committed'" (p. 2). Harry Davis recalled that, "Despite all the connections that had been built between Hennepin and Border, it was still a giant leap over a huge social and cultural chasm to think that we could be one congregation (Davis, 2002, p. 133). On December 23, 1956, Border members voted to accept Hennepin's invitation to merge. *The New York Times* published a story about the merger on Christmas Day, 1956, and Border church members were formally admitted on January 20, 1957. The fiftieth anniversary of the Border–Hennepin Union took place in 2007. The focus and religious life of the congregation shows the influence of the historic decision, including a strong tradition of social justice and a truly integrated congregation (see http://haumc.org).

Several factors shed light on how leaders and congregations agreed to merge despite a resistant culture of racism prevalent during the 1950s. Although the nation's history of racism was still a strong force, cultural changes were occurring, awakening people to injustice. Twenty years of contact between church leaders removed some racial barriers due to their participation in social service projects. The Border Church choir sang at the Hennepin Church, and members participated in service activities (Carroll, 2007, p. 9). Enlightened leaders such as Reverends Sexton and Pennington, Bennett, and Davis saw the opportunity for change and promoted the change within their organizations.

Harry Davis gave his word to the members of the Border Church that Hennepin people could be trusted. The members of Border Church were invited to join Hennepin Church *and* the invitation was issued in their church. After receiving the invitation, Border Church members attended a service at Hennepin Church before becoming formal members. Reverend Sexton chose personally not to join Hennepin. For several months after the merger, he served as a substitute pastor for area churches. In 1957, he was called as the permanent pastor for Champlin Methodist Church in Anoka. "Champlin was the first all-white congregation in the denomination's nine-state jurisdiction to be served by a black pastor" (Davis, 2002, p. 135). Enlightened leadership and healthy cultures in both churches helped members make a leap of faith when the opportunity presented itself. Change happens successfully as a result of positive human interaction and participation in the process of change. Davis fondly recalls the importance of this event and its legacy:

> We came to Hennepin as pioneers in American church integration. More than forty years later, many of us are still there, as are our children and grandchildren. Other black people have joined in the intervening years . . . as full participants in the life of a church that has become fully our own. (Davis, 2002, p. 136)

The Border–Hennepin merger shows the importance of leadership at all levels of organizational and community change. Often technical and goal-seeking processes associated with effective leadership emphasize rationality and control. However, wise leaders recognize the impact of change on people, including the day-to-day human messiness of living and working together as well as the importance of human contact and ownership of change. People make opportunities for others and end up reaping the benefits of their generosity. The spirit of social justice opened up opportunities for both white and black communities.

In the next story, a hospital laboratory supervisor and an employee at Northwestern Hospital in Minneapolis, Minnesota, had a hand in a series of events that eventually led to the accidental founding of Medtronic, Inc., the company that produced the world's first battery-operated pacemaker.

THE ACCIDENTAL FOUNDING OF MEDTRONIC, INC.

Marjorie Hawkinson served as the supervisor of a medical laboratory at Northwestern Hospital (now Abbott-Northwestern Hospital) in 1945.

She hired employees and supervised the work of technologists. Hawkinson was concerned about the state of disrepair of laboratory equipment. The equipment was vital to ensuring accurate and timely results from laboratory tests used for medical diagnosis. According to Hawkinson, the equipment never came with good instructions (or lacked any at all) and people did not know how to fix some of the machines. She was determined to figure out how to get the equipment repaired and made inquiries to see if anyone knew a qualified person to repair the equipment.

At the same time, a young woman, Connie Olson, applied for a position at the laboratory and Hawkinson hired her. Olson was dating Earl Bakken, a graduate student in engineering at the University of Minnesota. Hawkinson discussed her concerns about the laboratory equipment with Olson, aware that Bakken repaired electrical equipment. Hawkinson asked Olson if she would talk to Bakken about repairing the equipment; he agreed. Hawkinson recalls saying, "Maybe, if he does a good job, we can give him a referral to the University of Minnesota." Bakken repaired the equipment, developed the business, and gradually his interest evolved into what later became known as Medtronic, Inc., an internationally renowned, worldwide producer of medical technology. Bakken married Connie Olson and established the business with his brother-in-law, Palmer Hermundslie.

In *One Man's Full Life*, Bakken (1999) gives the following account of these events:

> While I was in grad school, I married a bright young woman named Connie Olson, who had been in my class back at Columbia Heights High. Connie had studied medical technology while I was in the service, and by the time I got home she was already working as a medical technologist at Northwestern Hospital in south Minneapolis. Often I'd run over to the hospital and wait for her to finish her shift. While I waited, I got to know several of the *doctors and technical personnel* [emphasis added] there. Knowing that I was studying electrical engineering, they'd sometimes ask me if I would take a look at this or that piece of equipment that was giving them trouble. If I could fix the equipment I would. It was a win-win situation. (p. 38)

Those named in Bakken's account were "doctors and technical personnel" who offered him work that eventually contributed to the discovery of his lifelong passion for saving lives with technology. Hawkinson's story provides interesting detail to the official account of Medtronic history. It doesn't include her name or contribution. However, her professional judgment and actions clearly contributed to Bakken's early career and success along with others who offered work and gave him referrals during those early years.

However, Bakken and his brother-in-law, inventive and risk-taking entrepreneurs, achieved their own success by recognizing the opportunity, offering a valuable service, and collaborating with medical personnel to create a life-giving worldwide corporation. Bakken guided Medtronic for an impressive fifty years. His famous collaboration with Dr. C. Walton Lillehei led to the development of the world's first battery-powered pacemaker (Bakken, 1999, pp. 45–51).

For many years, Bakken met personally with new employees to share the company's mission statement: "To contribute to human welfare by application of biomedical engineering in the research, design, manufacture, and sale of instruments or appliances that alleviate pain, restore health, and extend life" (1999, p. 86). Later Bakken retired in Hawaii and became involved in taking his corporate idea of healing to a community level, where a movement to establish "healing communities" is underway.

Many lessons can be drawn from the story of the accidental founding of Medtronic. There's always a backstory to every big story. When lives touch other lives through accidental meetings and fortuitous requests and intersect with innovative people like Bakken, a chain of events could produce a truly remarkable success. In all change stories, the relationships we have with each other, and the ones established by leaders to support the work, make the difference between success and failure and between chance and lost opportunities. Opportunity, vision, and effort sustain what people begin together.

Bakken described his theories of leadership in *One Man's Full Life*, emphasizing the importance of vision and strategic action: "Leaders have distinguished themselves by the length and breadth of their vision. They see farther than their contemporaries, in large part because they're looking down the road" (1999, p. 120).

Those willing to see change as a metaphor for life and live their lives courageously sometimes make lasting contributions to the world. The process of managing change and persisting in the effort despite the hard work and stress created by change must be supported with acknowledgments, celebrations, and sometimes, humor.

REWARDING SUCCESS AND FOLLY

Encouraging outstanding efforts, learning, taking chances, and occasionally failing in a risk-free environment, leaders celebrate the human aspects of change with a sense of humor. I (Noonan) attended an awards ceremony and observed Principal Pam Shea handing out "Tireless Leader Awards" to faculty members at Jackson Middle School in Jackson, Wyoming, to recognize staff effort above and beyond the call of duty. Names of faculty members and the dates of their recognition were "engraved" on an old black tire proudly displayed in front of the faculty during the "recognition" ceremony. Details of heroic efforts were shared, and staff applauded the recipients.

Each name "engraved" on an old tire told a story about someone's effort and its effects on others. When the old tire occasionally rested on the podium in front of the faculty, smiles broke out in anticipation of the surprise nomination. White chalk marks on the tire promoted staff morale more than a gold plaque. In another school, follies are celebrated with a special award.

Principal Bianchi of Paideia School shared the following story of the "Screw Up Hall of Fame," another ritual that served as a source of humor and enjoyment:

A number of years ago a few teachers and I began a tradition at Paideia. Once a year, usually in the privacy of the Board-Faculty Christmas party, we stage a pageant where ten finalists from the past twelve months are announced and, like a beauty contest, a winner is crowned. Throughout the year, nominations from faculty and staff pour into my office. I file in a box on my desk discreetly mislabeled "Faculty and Administrative Issues." Anyone who works for the school is eligible. I have won the award twice myself (and am nominated with discouraging frequency). . . . But we have kept the tradition going because it represents an attitude that acknowledges that our work is as complicated as life itself and that the potential for great folly and great achievement fills our days. (Binachi, as cited in Ackerman & Maslin-Ostrowski, 2002, pp. 121–22)

Leaders recognize the human effects of change on others, maintaining a spirit of camaraderie during change as well as helping people manage its stress-inducing effects. Change leaders understand the price people pay during transitions and support them in the process. Former superintendent of St. Paul Public Schools Dr. Patricia Harvey addressed the natural reluctance we all experience regarding change and its disturbing aspects when she remarked with a smile, "Change is good—you go first!" Perhaps those who are willing to go first may reap the greatest rewards. Whether we like it or not, change is here to stay, providing some of the most frightening and thrilling moments in our lives.

In the next chapter, the power of narrative healing helps leaders respond wisely and compassionately to grief and loss associated with wounds, illness, and suffering.

11

WOUNDS, ILLNESS, LOSS, AND SUFFERING: THE THERAPEUTIC NATURE OF STORY

Freedom may come not from being in control of life but rather from a willingness to move with the events of life, to hold onto our memories but let go of the past, to choose, when necessary, the inevitable. We can become free at any time.

—Remen (1996, p. 199)

Imagine creating a timeline of your life and marking all of the wounding events you have experienced, beginning with childhood and ending with yesterday. Whether a life or social history, the timeline serves as a story organizer to explain how tragic events and their effects cause changes within us. The timeline offers a perspective not usually present in the recall of a single event. When a series of events stack up, inflicting multiple blows to the spirit, a feeling of defenselessness emerges. Tragic moments shape our responses to other people and the environment. The nature of the wounds, when and how they were received, and their effects explain a lot about our attitudes and actions toward others. Blows delivered by loved ones seem to inflict even more pain.

Unfortunately, some children suffer their first wounds close to home. These may involve the absence of nurture and love, deprivation due to dysfunctional circumstances and poverty, or emotional or physical assaults. The wounds inflicted by family members cause injuries that may last a lifetime and never heal. Brooke Medicine Eagle, a Native American woman, tells the following story of childhood abuse and her response to the suffering she endured.

GOING INTO THE FIRE

Witnessing brutal beatings inflicted by her father on her mother, Eagle describes their pulverizing effect. "I could hear his fists connect with the flesh of her face as each blow landed. My older brother and I huddled together, shaking, so scared that our teeth chattered like dry bones on a desert" (Martin, 1999, p. 241–42). Although she was only four years old, Eagle felt compelled to respond, crawling between her parents' knees to separate them. Eagle recalled, "I cried and I screamed, hitting and kicking his legs, climbing up on him to intercept his blows" (p. 242). Eagle witnessed this abuse over many years, eventually making a choice about what to do with her suffering after a crucial incident. One day when she was eight years old, Eagle, her brother, and a neighborhood boy made a fire. Pouring gasoline on the fire caused the five-gallon can to explode and engulf Eagle:

> Death came close. I could see the flames around my face, knew my eyelashes were gone, smelled my hair melting. I screamed and ran. All the adults had just gotten in our old noisy jeep to drive up the hill. Dad later told me that his hand was on the ignition key when they heard me scream. Close, very close, death came, blowing its fiery breath up my nostrils. They heard my screams and came running. Mom put the fire out with her hands. Then, we drove forty-five miles over backcountry roads to a doctor. I was out of it for most of the ride, but I clearly remember my dad carrying me in his arms running into the hospital, crying out for help. (p. 242)

Eagle understood the meaning of this experience when, thirty years later, she heard Richard Pryor talk about his experience of being on fire. Pryor accidentally set himself on fire, experiencing third-degree burns on over 50 percent of his body (*Richard Pryor*, n.d.). Eagle reflected on the meaning of Pryor's statement, "'I used to be an angry man, but the fire burned all that up'" (p. 244), and recalled her choice to burn up her anger:

> And something deep inside me knew that I had made that choice, I had taken on that fire, to burn up the anger. I burned up the anger, not only

my dad's cruel anger and my mother's bitter anger, but mine: my anger that I had to save my family again and again; my anger that I didn't get to be a little girl safe in her parents' arms; my anger that no one was there to intercede, to help me. On some deep level, I had made a choice, to burn up the anger and change things, to wake up my parents or to leave life. Nothing else, not anything, not anywhere could be so bad as this. Something had to change. (Martin, 1999, p. 244)

Eagle understood how she had accomplished her own healing after listening to Pryor's story. When she was eight years old, she made the decision to choose life, becoming a respected healer, ceremonial leader, teacher, author, and songwriter. Eagle's story illustrates her creative response to suffering and its accompanying grief.

Tournier (1981) describes the effects of the relationship between bereavement, loss, and deprivation, and creativity.

The person matures, develops, becomes more creative, not because of the deprivation in itself but through his [her] own active response to misfortune, through the struggle to come to terms with it and morally to overcome it—even if in spite of everything there is no cure. (p. 28)

The scars borne by many are hidden within, invisible to others, despite their effects on their personae and outward actions. Those who suffer a loss must both experience it as well as decide what to do with their suffering—it can't be ignored. Choosing to either mitigate the pain with medication or end their lives, some become trapped in self-destructive paths while others develop a creative response to their pain. The choice about what to do with suffering helps to define us.

Suffering resides within us, influencing our worldview and responses to others. Painful stories of wounds and loss alert us to the blows delivered and the choices made in response to suffering. Stories offer a glimpse of the interior, revealing the depth and character of a life. Hearing stories about loss and suffering causes listeners to imagine how they would feel if the tragic event had happened to them. Identifying with the fellow traveler, the listener knows or imagines the journey. This exchange of story opens hearts in sympathy:

When we are seen by the heart, we are seen for who we are. We are valued in our uniqueness by those who are able to see us in this way and we become able to know and value ourselves. (Remen, 1996, p. 149)

An empathetic and compassionate response to suffering helps the afflicted and grieving loved ones accomplish healing through story as a therapeutic process. Sufferers and their survivors battle pain or work through grief in a blow-by-blow match against a formidable enemy, learning about its nature and experiencing its fierceness as a part of the healing and ending process. The depth of pain sometimes catches many by surprise because of its erratic and unpredictable nature. Didion experienced two blows during the course of two years, losing both her husband and daughter, turning a family of three into a family of one. She made sense of her grief in her memoir, *A Year of Magical Thinking* (2005).

LIFE CHANGES IN AN INSTANT

Capturing the unexpected changes caused by the loss of her beloved husband, Didion said, "Life changes in an instant. The ordinary instant" (2005, p. 3). These eight words convey a warning: When your life changes, there's no going back, no warning, no predictability, no control, no sense to it. The most dramatic moments in life, she warns, occur "in the ordinary instant."

Taking the reader on her sense-making journey, Didion examines what happened to her in all of its painful detail. Establishing a detailed chronological record, Didion gets control of the events by reconstructing in nearly day-by-day order the details of her husband's death and her daughter's life-threatening illness. The story moves back and forth, told by either the voice of the grieving widow or the despairing and determined mother, who valiantly supports her gravely ill thirty-eight-year-old daughter's fight against a life-threatening illness.

Plagued by grief and guilt, Didion studies her husband's death to answer her questions about how it happened and why. Reconstructing his death in exact detail, she reads the building log to note the exact time the ambulance arrived and requests medical records to determine if anything might have prevented her husband's death. She even considered attending the autopsy until she realized this request took things too far. Recognizing her moments of irrationality regarding her husband's death, Didion resists looking at some of her husband's things until she can figure out the meaning of his death and manage the loss. Unwilling to give away her husband's shoes after his death, Didion realizes that she can't give them away because her husband will need them *when he comes back*. She yearns for his return.

Recalling her husband's physical and emotional state weeks and months preceding his death, Didion uses knowledge to get a sense of control over the dreadful outcome. Using her considerable investigative skills as an author, Didion examines all possible angles of his death, searching for answers in poetry, medical books, and personal reflection. Noting the human tendency to make order out of chaos, Mahoney observed, "We seem to be neurologically 'wired' to classify our experience and to transform the 'buzzing booming confusion' of sensation into some codified and dynamic representation of the world" (cited in Carlsen, 1988, p. 5).

The ordering and reconstruction process draws Didion back to her memories, triggering what Didion describes as the "vortex" effect. Seeing familiar wallpaper, driving on a particular street, or remembering a family vacation engulf her in a sea of unmanageable emotions, causing waves of grief. Didion cautions, "The way you get sideswiped is by going back" (2005, p. 112). Once aware of the "vortex effect," Didion shrewdly avoids it:

> I saw immediately in Los Angeles that its potential for triggering this vortex effect could be controlled only by avoiding any venue I might associate with either Quintana [daughter] or John [husband]. This would require ingenuity . . . . I plotted my routes. I remained on guard. (pp. 113–114)

The vortex effect may renew the cycle of suffering and all-encompassing grief. "Grief is nothing we expect it to be. . . . Grief is different. Grief has no distance. Grief comes in waves, paroxysms, sudden apprehensions that weaken the knees and blind the eyes and obliterate the dailiness of life" (2005, pp. 26–27). Unavoidable, grief keeps the emotions and experience raw, while time passes.

The anniversary of a painful event changes a temporary event (he just died) into a more permanent one. Noting changes near the passing of a year, Didion buys a new set of Christmas lights and struggles to find faith:

> This [buying lights] served as a symbol . . . as a profession of faith in the future. I take the opportunity for such profession where and whenever I can invent them, since I do not yet actually feel this faith in the future. (2005, p. 212)

In the closing pages of her book, she reveals an important insight, one meant to be shared with others experiencing loss and suffering:

> I know why we try to keep the dead alive: we try to keep them alive in order to keep them with us. I also know that if we are to live there comes a point at which we must relinquish the dead, let them go, keep them dead. (pp. 225–226)

In her memoir, Didion unmasks her inner pain, exploring and experiencing it to accomplish the healing process. Although no one can be expected to fully recover from wounds, the meaning-making process helps people find healthy responses to suffering.

Didion's memoir shows the power of externalizing deeply personal events, discussing them as if they have happened to someone else, to see their effects. A painful life event, shared and interpreted through story, causes narrative healing to occur. The wounded take control of the experience by distancing themselves from the problem or event and closely inspecting it with a clinical eye, reducing the chance of successive woundings by looking at the experience from an intellectual perspective. Emotions overwhelm and crowd thinking, while taking charge of the incident through thought enables some to heal.

Tolman describes process and dialectical tensions in the struggle to find meaning in the narrative process of healing (quite often a significant aspect of personal story):

> [I]t [meaning making] involves the following essential elements: movement from one state (ignorance, uncertainty, error) to a qualitatively different state (knowledge, certainty, truth) by means of a process (conversation, dialogue, debate) that is characterized by opposition (contradiction, refutation, and negotiation) and governed by an internal necessity (logic, deduction). (cited in Carlsen, 1988, p. 5)

Because the wound brings continuous and unacceptable pain, those in battle with pain must manage suffering or succumb to its power. Replacing uncertainty with truth, the sufferer makes sense of a disturbing and painful life event by engaging in an internal dialogue with self or perhaps participating in a therapeutic conversation with another. Examining contradictions (this wasn't supposed to happen to me) and negotiating with the unchangeable nature of the event (despite this loss, I must continue to live), the wounded person rewrites his or her story with a palatable ending and begins to heal.

Storytellers bring their wounding experience to our attention. Relating the details and the totality of their experience, they locate where they were in their lives when something happened and how it stopped them dead in their tracks to experience their grief. Recalling the nature and extent of their wounds, the walking wounded and bereaved name the damage and its effects, often using the experience to explain their current state of desolation or perhaps to call us to action. Initially, story aids in healing by helping the sufferer make sense of his or her experience. Later, story may help survivors figure out what to do with all the pain.

Sometimes storylines must be closely examined and contradicted. For example, healing may happen when the victim of abuse realizes that the abuser caused the violence, not the action of the victim who suffered from it. Through interpretation and negotiation, a new story emerges with its own logic and truth.

THE STAGES OF GRIEF AND THE NATURE OF COURAGE

An international scholar on the subject of death and dying, Elizabeth Kübler-Ross talked to patients about their experiences with terminal illness to learn about the stages of their grief (Maciejewski, Zang, Block, & Pirereson, 2007). Kübler-Ross's model, "a 5-stage response of terminally ill patients to awareness of their impending death: denial-dissociation-isolation, anger, bargaining, depression, and acceptance" (p. 7), approximates the typical stages of grief encountered by loved ones all too familiar with loss.

Kübler-Ross started her research by talking to terminal patients about their feelings. Initially reluctant to talk about death with her patients, she postponed her first planned interview by one day and learned the next day that the patient had died. Tournier (1982) describes Kübler-Ross's experience: "By then, of course, the man had died, and she [Kübler-Ross] realized that she had first to overcome her own fear of the emotion involved in dialogue. She shows us that it is we, who are well, who lack the courage to enter into such conversations" (1982, p. 97).

According to Tournier, people often attempt to boost patient morale by false optimism, denying the existence of a terminal illness and ignoring the reality of a patient's life and final days. Instead, he recommends facing the situation with courage, recognizing that sometimes fear, rather than denial, drives our response to the patient's suffering. Tournier asks, "Is it not really we ourselves who lack the courage, when we are more afraid than our patient of facing the truth?" (1982, p. 96). Courageous patients teach us how to accept the reality of their condition. The decision to live courageously during struggle often serves as a loving example to others. The sufferer tells us how to live with pain and what to do when he or she departs.

Deb, a vibrant woman diagnosed with terminal cancer at age forty-one, showed her family the face of courage through a strong will to engage life until illness finally claimed her. Struggling to get out of bed and get dressed, fighting chemotherapy and radiation-induced nausea, and aided by a wheelchair, Deb mustered the energy to faithfully attend her children's school events. Continuing to experience and contribute to the lives of others, Deb also volunteered to serve on a church fund-raising committee during the last months of her life. Meetings were held in her bedroom, with committee members arrayed around her bed. She maintained her work with the committee until her weakened condition rendered her unable to speak.

Her husband Tom, dismayed by the drain on her energy and wishing to reduce the added stress of her commitment, asked why she volunteered for this service to her church during the precious remaining days of her life. Deb's response answered his question and offered a message of how to live after her departure: "I'm doing this because this is what I can do right now." Until her last breath, she resisted the raven's call, instead finding meaning by contributing to her family, church, and community.

Deb's example inspired her daughter to become a medical doctor, enabling her to battle illness and suffering in the world. Adopting his mother's commitment to social justice, Deb's son applied to and was accepted by a law school with an emphasis on ethical practice and community work. Both children learned a second language, allowing them to successfully communicate in diverse communities. Deb, like others who have courageously faced their illness with a constructive response, leaves a legacy of contribution and service. Radiating courage and joy in living, sufferers'

> lives demand permanent courage, a constant expenditure of courage; and since courage belongs to the spiritual economy, the more one spends it, the more one has. It is like a current flowing through them and producing joy, the joy of victory over one's fate. (Tournier, 1982, p. 98)

The gift of their example demands our creative response to their permanent courage. Because they chose "life," we must do so as well:

> One of the most surprising lessons our teachers offer is that life doesn't end with the diagnosis of a life-challenging experience—that's when it truly begins. It begins at this point because when you acknowledge the reality of your death, you also have to acknowledge the reality of your life. You realize that you are still alive, that you have to live your life now, and that you only have this life now. The primary lesson the dying teach us is to live every day to its fullest. (Kübler-Ross & Kessler, 2000, pp. 223–224)

Even after someone close has died, lessons about life and love continue. Mike Klein agreed to share his story about coming to terms with grief and loss.

THE CEDAR STRIP CANOE

> My dad died after a six-month battle with malignant melanoma. He was diagnosed with the disease just after he retired, and 16 years after he had recovered from its first occurrence. His love for me was deep and so was my grief after his death. I tried to deal with it through projects, realizing later this is very common to males. I organized a hundred-mile hike to raise funds for cancer research. I spent long weekends renovating an old family cabin. And I tried to finish a cedar strip canoe someone else had started.
>
> That canoe became a symbol of both grief and hope, although not as I anticipated. I worked hard to grieve through these projects, but never really let myself *feel* the loss of my dad. Working on the canoe kept the pain present but at arm's length. Yet grief has a way of working through all our attempts to hold it off. The poem (see page 178) seeped out of me while

I cut cedar strips and fitted them onto curved forms. It was the first indication of overwhelming feelings to come.

Nearly two years after my dad's death, I finally and deeply felt his absence in the midst of other losses. My spiritual mentor died, so did my godmother, even our two dogs. It also became apparent that our daughter would be our only biological child due to secondary infertility. When all that grief finally washed over me, it came fast and hard like a storm across the lake. I felt swamped and the anguish continued for days; a feeling of cold, damp wool pulled tight and dark around my face. I was so overwhelmed I couldn't think; couldn't do anything about it. I could only feel all that intense accumulated grief. I wrapped up my cedar strip canoe for the winter but in a raw, unfinished state. During those cold months it cracked right down the middle, making it a pretty useless boat. And my heart felt cracked and useless, too. Now it seemed the end of my poem—the resolution of my grief—couldn't happen. There would be no quiet wake of passing.

By springtime, I had a new idea about the canoe, but it was a radical change from my initial project. With more than a little trepidation, I took hold of a circular saw and with a deep breath, cut the canoe into three pieces. The middle section was just big enough for a coffee table, leaving two ends for bookshelves. Eventually, I realized the canoe was a symbol of my healing, not the healing itself. I was also coming to understand grief as a story—one that becomes a part of us—that we are changed by loss. I gave up trying to get back to who I was, and started discovering who I was becoming. My canoe would never carry me across Forest Lake and I couldn't work on it anymore. Now it works on me. It stands in my office holding the authors and poets that influence and shape me, just as grief and loss continue to influence and shape me.

My canoe-bookshelf holds some hard but precious lessons about transformation, too. I will always feel the loss of my dad, but now that grief comes less like a storm and more like recollections of his love. He is a part of me. I carry his story with me as I continue to become a new person. All those other losses exist there, too, like bookends that prop up ideas about who I am. No longer a canoe, my bookshelf is a reminder that hope is found in grief transformed. (unpublished manuscript, 2007)

Cedar Strip Canoe
I am building a cedar strip canoe.
Dad and I talked about projects like this now and then:
A wooden boat; a roadster from a kit

that beckoned from the display.
Now with every cut,
with curls that drop from the plane
I work with him on that project
that we never quite started
until now.
He is a partner
who stands aloof when my attention
is too focused on the keel-line
instead of the real project:
I am shaping grief,
and cutting through loss.
The saw through cedar balks against the grain
if the cut is too fine, the strip too narrow and pointed.
This canoe will cut too,
through water someday soon.
Perhaps that slicing will hurt less, even heal.
Forest Lake will part around the bow
and flow together after the stern,
holding fast to this vessel
even as it slips through,
even as he did.
The eddies and swirls
will follow behind
To fade gently,
though not without notice,
into the quiet wake of passing.
We are building a cedar strip canoe,
Dad and I.

Mike Klein

THE GIFT OF A LOVING RESPONSE

Leaders recognize grief's effects on others and invite stories that promote healing and constructive responses to suffering. Being fully present to those suffering in companionate love might be all we have to offer. Showing respect to terminal patients means slowing down, facing
the reality of the patient's condition, and offering a caring response to

his or her suffering. Johyne, a medical doctor, learned the importance of being in relationship with her patients during a patient's final days:

> She remembers "the moment" when she suddenly understood "the essence of respect" . . . . She discovered that respect was expressed by *doing very little* when there is little to do . . . . For the first time she saw clearly that respect can also be carried through "a certain stillness," simply by being present, attentive, and loving (Lawrence-Lightfoot, 1999, p. 88)

A "normal" period of bereavement due to the loss of a loved one from natural causes (94 percent of all deaths) lasts at least six months and generally can extend to eighteen months (Maciejewski, Zang, Block, & Pirereson, 2007). However, an unnatural death, death by violence, an accident, an illness, or suicide produces a prolonged pattern of grief, affecting the bereaved differently. Survivors take longer to accept this loss and often experience substantial yearning for the loved one.

The survivor often experiences depression simultaneously with "complicated grief," a term that describes an inability to accept the loss and recover resiliency (Maciejewski, Zang, Block, & Pirereson, 2007). Death can sometimes steal life from the living unless survivors "break the hard crust of our [their] physical and mental habits" (Tournier, 1982, p. 138) and create a new ending to their story. Compassionate leaders, aware of suffering and its residual effects, recognize that their response to others during difficult moments either aids healing or contributes to their pain. Many feel helpless about how to respond to suffering without the benefit of professional training and experience.

"The tendency to avoid problems and the emotional suffering inherent in them is the primary basis of all human mental illness" (Peck, 1978, p. 17). Dr. Peck, a psychiatrist, attempted to treat Helen, a patient who resisted his best efforts to help her, despite twice-weekly visits over a nine-month period. In frustration, he told Helen it seemed that he was unable to help her:

> "Helen," I replied, "it seems to be frustrating to both of us. I don't know how this will make you feel, but you are the single most frustrating case I have ever had in a decade of practicing psychotherapy. I have never met anyone with whom I have made less headway in so long a time." . . . A glowing smile came over Helen's face. "You really do care for me after all," she

said. "Huh?" I asked. "If you didn't really care for me you wouldn't feel so frustrated," she replied, as if it were all perfectly obvious. (pp. 172–173)

According to Peck, the therapy progressed at a rapid rate and soon he knew what was really going on in the mind of his patient. In the process Peck learned a valuable lesson: "the essential ingredient of successful deep and meaningful psychotherapy is love" (1978, p. 173). Whether described as compassion, empathy, caring, or love, the importance of "truly involving oneself at an emotional level in the relationship, to actually struggle with the patient and with oneself" (p. 173) as an aspect of healing can't be overestimated.

In the next story, a young woman struggles over a terrorizing day with a stranger, experiencing a loss of freedom and safety. Her illness and recovery cause us to think about how vulnerable people are cared for in our society.

JOHANNA'S STORY: THE KINDNESS AND TERROR OF STRANGERS

After losing her sight at age thirteen from a traumatic brain injury, Johanna started life over, learning rudimentary skills of navigation using a cane as well as how to meet such personal needs as eating, dressing, and attending school. After several years of success, Johanna enrolled in a special program offered by Blind, Inc., in Minneapolis, Minnesota, to learn how to expand her independent living skills. Things went smoothly until a series of incidents and their effects robbed Johanna of her hard-won independence. Johanna tells part of the story in the following excerpt.

> During the summer of 1997 I attended a program offered by Blind, Inc., in Minneapolis, a nonprofit organization that assists people with visual impairments in independent living and vocational coaching. I lived in a student apartment located several miles away from the Center. Students were expected to travel between the school and the apartment independently after their first few days in the program.
>
> The incident that I'm about to describe took place on a rainy day in August. Blind, Inc., has a policy that requires instructors to go to the student apartments if a student is absent and determine why the student did not

come to class. Unless seriously ill, all students are expected to come to class.

It was actually Blind, Inc.'s policy of not allowing students to remain in their apartments during the day that created the situation. I went back to the student apartments with my travel instructor, Russell, to bring another student back to the Center. Russell is totally blind and was not qualified to serve as a certified Orientation and Mobility Instructor. In order to be a certified Orientation and Mobility Instructor individuals must be sighted and possess a driver's license.

Russell and I went over to the student apartments without any difficulties. It was on the way back to the Center that I separated from Russell and the other student a few blocks away from the apartment. Travel was difficult because it was raining, making it hard to hear anything or anyone. Russell didn't realize what had happened because he couldn't see. If he had been able to see me, he would have realized I was missing right away.

I spent the next three hours trying to get back to Blind, Inc. Along the way, two people stopped and asked if they could help me. The first person was a woman in a car. I think I asked her for verbal directions. I somehow managed to find my way back to the bus stop and board a bus to the area near Blind, Inc. By this time I was quite hungry. I decided to walk to SuperAmerica just a few blocks away to buy something for lunch.

One of the instructors from Blind, Inc., saw me and tried to give me directions to cross the street and come into the Center. I told her I was going to walk to SuperAmerica. It was on the way back from SuperAmerica that I got lost. I was obviously uncertain and confused, and a man stopped and asked me if I needed some help. I told him no but asked for directions, and he gave me an umbrella.

Shortly after he walked away, a second man walked up to me and asked me if I wanted a ride. I said no and asked for directions. He told me he knew exactly where Blind, Inc., was located. He said it was only about three blocks away from our location. I asked him if he would walk me back to Blind, Inc. He insisted we take his car. I said no. He persisted and badgered me by saying, "Why didn't I trust him? Didn't I need help?" By this time, I was willing to accept help from anyone.

I got in the car and my nightmare started once I closed the door. Over the next few hours, he molested me, trying to touch me in the car. I tried to get out of the car and he locked the door. He kept driving around. I tried to get him to take me to the Center. In an attempt to get rid of him I finally asked him to take me to my apartment. I tried to push him away at the outside door before entering the building. He followed me up the stairs to my apartment door, forcing himself into the apartment.

Once inside he kept asking me to take off my wet clothes. He got me to take some of my clothes off and tried to make advances. I said no but he kept insisting, trying to fondle me and pushing me onto the bed. At one point I got away from him and called Blind, Inc., to see if I could get some help from an instructor. I was afraid to say too much with the strange man in my apartment.

The instructor said she had to stay at the Center because she had to wait for another student to return from a route to the airport. After what seemed like hours, I finally got rid of the man by offering him some money. No one from Blind, Inc., came over to my apartment until later that night.

At some point I called my mom to tell her what had happened to me. My sister answered the phone because my mother was at work. She told my mom what had happened when she got home later that night. My dad and sister came over to Minneapolis to pick me up while my mom called the police. My parents took me into the emergency room at Hennepin County Medical Center. I talked to a police officer and described the incident. I also had a pelvic exam, medication for sexually transmitted diseases, and the "Morning After Pill." I was assigned to a counselor, who gave me some support over the phone.

Shortly after this incident, I became depressed and was later diagnosed with Post Traumatic Stress Disorder. I was suddenly afraid to be alone even when I was in the shower. Sensitive to touch, I pulled away from my mother if she walked by me in the hall and touched me. I did not want to leave the house or get into a car with a man, even my father. I remember one incident that took place with my sister several months after the incident. We were in a gas station. My sister reached into my pocket to pull out some money. I yelled at her to get her hand out of my pocket.

PSTD affected all of my relationships. I had to leave a residential school for the blind in Faribault, Minnesota, because of my emotional trauma. It took about a year and a half for me to return to a relatively "normal" emotional state. I lost a year of school because I couldn't cope with the emotional strain. I entered therapy, took medication, and gradually overcame my fears. I also had to switch schools, which put me behind my class.

I think people should realize that bad experiences build resilient people. Although I am sometimes vulnerable because I am blind, I had to take my life back and continue to live independently. I currently live alone in my own apartment and travel independently in my community. (Johanna Smith, personal communication, March 27, 2007)

Johanna's story, like those of others who experience a loss of freedom and safety at the cruel hands of others, causes us to reflect on how society treats its most vulnerable people. When people experience trauma, the whole family system falls apart, temporarily lost in grief, shock, and outrage. As Johanna's mother and the author of this book (Sarah Noonan), I know this painful truth from my direct experience. When I first saw Johanna after the incident, she was curled up into a fetal position, unable to explain exactly what had happened. Without much to go on, we took her to the hospital and reported the incident to the police. We also had several heated conversations with the director of the school.

Her recovery took some time and, as family members, we fear a repeat of a similar incident in the future. I think of this event periodically and wonder how to protect my daughter even ten years later. Her nightmare became mine. I found consolation in remembering that there were three strangers who offered my daughter help on that fateful day, two of whom were decent human beings, while the third lives in my dreams. I battle him for her survival in an occasional nightmare, and so far I'm winning. Despite our best efforts, we can't always protect the people we love because excessive protection denies them an opportunity to lead a rich and full life. Johanna challenges us to consider the importance of agency in facing a disability as well as surviving a crisis. Survivors overcome their grief and emerge more resilient in the process by sharing their stories and writing new endings.

White and Epston (1990) offer guidance to therapists who use "storied therapy" as a means to help clients accomplish healing in *Narrative Means to Therapeutic Ends*. This includes honoring the "person's lived experience," valuing the individual's interpretation of experience, and encouraging "a sense of authorship and re-authorship of one's life and relationships in the telling and retelling of one's story" (p. 83). While leaders should avoid becoming therapists, they should recognize the importance of an empathetic and compassionate response to suffering through narrative modes.

FIGHTING AGAINST LOSS

Unwilling to accept the destructive or senseless nature of loss, some survivors decide to make sure the suffering doesn't happen to someone else or that the loss did not occur in vain. Foundations, scholarship funds, memorials, and new laws created in response to tragedy reflect this desire. For example, Mothers Against Drunk Drivers (MADD), established to prevent further loss of life due to the lethal combination of drinking and driving, represents a creative response to suffering. Designed to mitigate at least some of the paralyzing and damaging effects of tragedy through concerted action, the bereaved declare that something good must come from tragedy and take action.

The Jacob Wetterling Foundation, established after a kidnapper took Jacob Wetterling away from his loving parents, "educates families and communities to prevent the exploitation of children." The sad tale of his disappearance haunts his parents and others to this day:

> Jacob Wetterling was born on February 17, 1978. He grew up in St. Joseph, Minnesota, with his parents, Patty and Jerry Wetterling, and his three siblings. On the evening of October 22, 1989, Jacob, his brother Trevor, and his friend Aaron rode their bikes to a local convenience store to pick up a movie and snack. On the way back home, a man wearing a mask and carrying a gun stopped the boys. The gunman told the boys to throw their bikes into a nearby ditch and lie face down on the ground. He then asked each of the boys their age. After the boys responded, he instructed Trevor to run into the woods and told him not to look back or he would shoot him. Next, the gunman turned Aaron over, looked into his face, and told him to run into the woods without looking back or he would shoot him. As Trevor and Aaron were running away, they glanced back to see the gunman grab Jacob's arm. When Aaron and Trevor reached the wooded area they turned around again and the gunman and Jacob were gone.
>
> The local police were called to the scene of the abduction only minutes later and a search ensued that involved hundreds of volunteers, local law enforcement, FBI agents, and others. Jacob's case has resulted in over 50,000 leads and has been studied by staff and trainees at the FBI academy in Quantico, Virginia. The case is highly unusual in a number of ways. Rarely are children abducted, especially by non-family members or while playing in groups. There are only 115 cases of long-term, non-family abduction, called stereotypical kidnappings, each year. To date, law enforcement and Jacob's family still do not know what happened to Jacob or his abductor or where they are now. (*The Jacob Wetterling Story*, n.d., pp. 2–4)

A tragic story often propels us to action. The Wetterling kidnapping complicates grief because of its insidious nature—the name of his kidnapper and the story regarding what happened to him after his abduction remain a mystery. Denied this knowledge and robbed of their peace of mind, Wetterling's parents fought against the loss by helping other parents protect their children. Loss shakes the ground underneath us and demands a response.

The tragic murder of Jimmy Magnus in Minneapolis attracted the instant attention of Minneapolis City Council members, who got involved in the investigation and eventually passed a new law. Jimmy Magnus lost his life on November 30, 1995, during a robbery in which thieves took $200 and cigarettes and shot him execution-style in the back of the head after forcing him to lie face down on the ground (Mary Carlson, personal statement [SN], February 16, 2007). No camera recorded the murder.

Investigators hypothesized that Magnus left a bulletproof kiosk to take out the garbage and met his killers when he returned (O'Connor, 1995, December 1, p. A19). The Magnus law, passed by the Minneapolis City Council after Magnus's death, requires that video cameras be installed in all convenience stores. Although Magnus's killers were eventually caught and convicted, the presence of the camera may deter crime as well as warn others—beware, a camera records your every move.

Grief stricken, the family found some relief in the possibility that the new law would prevent another person suffering Magnus's fate (Mary Carlson, personal statement [SN], February 16, 2007). Robbed of the chance to say good-bye, family members consider the law at least some kind of memorial to Magnus's death.

The two tragedies, the loss of Wetterling and Magnus, create an underlying sadness in what should generally be an ordinary life. Children should return to their parents after a bicycle ride with their friends, and sons and brothers should end their shifts in a convenience store without losing their lives over a few hundred dollars.

Acts of personal violence belong in a category all by themselves. Shifting from personal loss to the violence of war, the *loss of life, innocence, and ideals* extracts a terrible price from men and women engaged in warfare. In the next story, a quilt artist living in the Kentucky hills just outside of Elliottville protests the ravages of war by creating a "baby war quilt" to express her "public shout" against the Iraq War and also the effects of the Vietnam War on her beloved husband Cecil (Cec).

BABY, BABY, WE ARE GOING TO WAR

Now displayed on a national art exhibit, Ison's quilt, "Baby, Baby, We Are Going to War," expresses what Bet Ison calls her "public shout" about war and the suffering it causes (www.womanmade.org/show_pics.cgi?type=group&gallery=shamtoshame2007&pic=22). Revealing her private thoughts and creative process, Ison describes her thinking and the quilt design from start to finish. Her story illustrates how art is both a deeply personal reflection of character as well as a cultural product accessible to all for interpretation and meaning. Ison's story gives us a glimpse of her interior, telling us how the process of making a quilt relates to her life and experiences:

> I believe that we sew ourselves into our quilts. I'm careful what I think on while I sew. Mostly I sew in hope and happiness and power and serenity. Sometimes I sew in questions, sometimes I sew in the answers. I sew in comfort. I sew in religion and I'm at my most religious when I'm working on a quilt. When a quilt is gone, given away, I miss it like a piece of myself. I long for it. Think of it and on it. If I get to see it again, I feel a sense of relief like the return of a child. I feel each quilt like it has its own presence. It feels like a part of me. Sometimes I think I will never be whole again, so many pieces of me have gone away.
>
> For the first time—this quilt is different. Still a piece of me and maybe I'll miss it if it goes. I'll think on it, but maybe I'll not long for it. It doesn't seem right to long for anger, for pain, for sorrow. 2003 was a hard year and this quilt is the result. Sewn into this quilt are the dismay, the sense of betrayal, helplessness and grief I've felt during the last year. I've been pretty quiet though it all. So this quilt is my public Shout. This is me—standing in this public place and shouting "THIS IS WRONG."
>
> I tried to write down how I felt about the war in this essay, but I just keep deleting it. Nothing I write seems to explain it as well as the quilt itself. My own feelings about this war are complicated and deepened by what's happened with my husband. The day after Bush declared war— Cec, a Vietnam vet was pushed straight over an edge into major post-traumatic stress disorder symptoms. So dismay over a distant war has been a time of personal distress, too; an example every day of what war does— even years later. For me, this war is a betrayal of our country, our flag, of the ideas of "liberty and justice for all." I believe this war has been a corruption of our flag and our country, an evil thing.

Into this quilt, I've sewed my husband, along with myself; and all the complicated and complex feelings of 2003 and 2004. Some of the symbolism is too secret to tell, but they are his doll pictures, it is stars from his shirt quilted into the squares; his gun in the picture; scraps of his clothing make up the army green. I haven't even told him how much of him is in this quilt. But he knows. One evening when it was almost done, I found him standing—looking at it. He said "this is what war is like." Afterward, he had one of his bad PTSD [Post Traumatic Stress Syndrome] "episodes" where he could barely move or speak. He says that he thinks he could have handled it if it weren't for the size (baby size). So this quilt will have to go because it can't stay in the house. It's just too painful.

Every quilt has its origins, its beginnings—the stories that go into it and materials from which it is made. I don't think I ever think up anything all on my own—I just end up quilting the different pieces of my life into my quilts.

I used the traditional symbol of a country gone wrong—the reversed flag, and added a black border around it in mourning and a sense of betrayal.

I need to pause here and say something about the baby doll pictures on this quilt. I live in the Home for Wayward Baby Dolls. Abandoned and abused baby dolls are a common item around our house. People send us pictures and the baby dolls themselves. I've been thinking about how they could be used as symbols and examples of abuse. I've been thinking about using them for a long time for some quilts that talk about things that bother me (abuse, war). These dolls were photographed as "found"—not created for this quilt.

I used iron-on photo transfer on this quilt. It was the first time I'd used it for a quilt—and it seemed to work all right this time. The pictures are printed on special paper with my inkjet printer, then they are ironed onto cotton cloth and the paper is peeled away, leaving the picture—just like on a t-shirt. The pictures are then sewn into the blocks using a technique called "reverse appliqué"—which I use a lot (but usually to make flowers). That's all done by hand, as is the quilting, but the blocks are sewn together with a sewing machine. The words were done the same way. The resulting process looked alright, but especially with the words, it photographs badly.

As to the words, a long time ago, I was reading the book, *The Jade Peony* and little boys in Vancouver during WWII take a doll, douse it in lighter fluid, light it on fire and watch it melt. "That's what bombs do" says one of them. I don't know where the line comes from—"every mother's son was born to die"—I know I've heard it somewhere. Don't know if I made up the rest or if I've used someone else's words. Just seemed to have that "cowboy" feel to it—"Baby Baby we are going to war."

I was listening to gospel music while I was making this quilt and along came the song Lazarus—"he once was so fair, he once was so young; he was some mother's darling, some mother's son; she rocked him to sleep . . . left there to die like a tramp on the street." And I'm not just thinking of babies here—but soldiers and grown men and women—their lives destroyed by war. Each of them was some mother's child. This is women's experience of war—loss and grief.

So I used traditional baby quilt materials and methods and size, those things that make for comfort and love and caring and then changed it all with dead baby doll pictures and words and symbolism. It seems to me that's what war does to people on the ground—it takes your home and your comfort and the things you depend to be safe and it twists them all to horror.

I can't decide what I think of my quilt. I went to visit it while it was in an art exhibit a few weeks ago. (I missed it after all.) I stood and looked it. I straightened a star or two. I picked off a stray thread. Smoothed out a thread in the flag. I felt like a mother straightening up her kid for Sunday school. Tweaking a collar, tucking in a strand of hair. I stood and looked and tried to decide—do I like it? Is it OK? It's so hard to judge because usually I would ask, "Is it beautiful?" And it's not. Sometimes I think it's my best work and sometimes I think I don't like it at all. (Ison, 2005)

Finding a creative response to her suffering, Ison issued a public shout to warn of the wounds of war and to memorialize suffering in her baby war quilt. Ison and other quilt artists tell stories about the past and provide social commentary on current conditions. Those who deny the occurrence and effects of tragic loss denigrate the suffering of others and inflict more wounds on survivors and the bereaved. Holding a place in community memory, the baby war quilt challenges viewers to squarely face the violence and hidden costs of war and its lasting effects on others.

Recognizing the complexities of grief and suffering, leaders honor the stories of those who experience loss as a result of tragedy through authentic expressions of grief and visible presence, with others as companions in grief and at commemorative visits to public sites of mourning. The public display of art, particularly the artistic expressions of those who directly experience suffering, hold an important value for seeing tragedy and loss as wounds in need of respect and healing. Beyond the immediate expression of sorrow and grief, leaders preserve the importance of these events in public memory to honor human suffering and loss as well as to learn from it.

REMEMBRANCE

Standing in protest outside Iran's mission to the United Nations in New York, Frances Irwin, a Holocaust survivor, pushed up the left sleeve of her coat to reveal the permanent mark of the concentration camp, and photographer Emmert (2006, p. AA5) captured her pain. Irwin's face, filled with determination and outrage, drew attention to her cause. Protesting the subject of an international conference held in Tehran, the denial that the Holocaust actually existed, Irwin stood as a living memory of its existence. Current Iranian President Mahmoud Ahmadinejad preferred his "personal interpretation of history" (Applebaum, 2006, p. AA5), ignoring the vast literature and documentation of the Holocaust's existence.

Although scholars were not invited, Ku Klux Klan members attended the two-day conference, where participants met and attempted to revise history. In an opinion piece, Applebaum stressed the importance of paying serious attention to the ludicrous position of the Iranian president:

> [This] particular brand of historical revisionism is no joke, and we shouldn't be tempted to treat it that way. Yes, we think we know this story already; we think we've institutionalized this memory; we think this particular European horror has been put to rest, and it is time to move on. I've sometimes thought that myself. . . . And yet—the near-destruction of the European Jews . . . requires constant re-explanation. . . . [T]he endless rebuttals will go on being necessary, long beyond the lifetime of the last survivor. (2006, p. AA5)

Langer (in Keshgegian, 2000) interviewed survivors and created a "typology of memory that includes common memory, deep memory, anguished memory, humiliated memory, tainted memory, and unheroic memory" (p. 74). Langer challenges the belief that memories of survivors help them to "establish meaning, purpose, and connection, to integrate the sequence of the events in their lives, [rather] most memories function in the opposite way: remembering witnesses to the persistence of disruption and injury and loss" (p. 75). Still, the voices of victims and survivors must be heard without an expectation of closure or meaning. These anguished memories, held simultaneously by victims and survivors, run parallel with their normal lives: "survivors inhabit two worlds simultaneously" (p. 75).

Preserving memory as well as the act of remembering "is both a problem and a resource for those struggling with life" (Keshgegian, 2000, p. 16). As a problem, it requires survivors and descendants to preserve and recall highly traumatic events, serving as witnesses to the oppression of their members. As a resource, survivor stories offer hope and proof of the power of human agency, momentarily lifting us out of the brutal events that took place to learn how the human spirit overcomes adversity. These dual purposes capture the survivor's dilemma: Should the story be primarily about the oppression or the will to live? Keshgegian (2000) says both aspects must be incorporated into survivor stories:

> Jews ask whether their remembrance should focus on their victimization in history with its ultimate climax in the Holocaust, or on contribution to civilization and methods of survival. African Americans also question whether slave narratives witness to a history of brutalization and torture or are memoirs of resistance and the resilience of the human spirit or both. People who are displaced and denied their histories seek to retrieve their past and assess what is the "true story." (p. 16)

Social memory carries the lived experience to successive generations. African American descendants of slaves experience the wounding effects of slavery through social memory despite the absence of a direct, personal experience of it. Maya Angelou (2002) told a story of her experience with depression and her emergence from it after a night spent swapping tales and jokes with a friend. Her companion, Jimmy, related her individual struggle to the experience of African Americans who have survived the effects of slavery and its aftermath.

As a resource, the story serves to remind descendants of their power to overcome adversity. Jimmy showed Angelou how to survive her current condition:

> We put surviving into our poems and into our songs. We put it into our folk tales. We danced surviving in Congo Square in New Orleans and put it in our pots when we cooked pinto beans. We wore surviving on our backs when we clothed ourselves in the colors of the rainbow. We were pulled down so low we could hardly lift our eyes, so we knew, if we wanted to survive, we had better lift our own spirits. So we laughed whenever we got the chance. (2002, p. 197)

The brief story, preserved in social memory, stresses the importance of human agency as shown by the determination of African Americans to survive. Failure to preserve the memory and recall it potentially contributes to the loss of cultural identity. Whether individual or collective, the purposes and effects of narrative schemes "fill our cultural and social environments" (Zerubavel, 2003, p. 3). These environments place us in a world where cultural traditions, beliefs, and practice influence the opportunities for leadership. Sites of public mourning offer a healing experience, documenting loss and dedicating holy ground to its memory for generations of survivors.

SITES OF MOURNING AND MEMORY

Violent and public deaths draw mourners to the symbolic or actual site of the tragedy, serving as a place to express sorrow over the loss of life as well as preserving what happened in public memory. For example, Thomas Watt Hamilton walked into an elementary school and took the lives of sixteen children and their teacher in Dunblane, Scotland, in 1996. Long before a memorial garden replaced the gymnasium where the tragedy occurred "townspeople and visitors were drawn to the site, bringing flowers, toys and messages to place reverently on the sidewalk or tie to the railing in front of the school" (Jorgensen-Earp & Lanzilotti, 1998, p. 150).

At the site of the Oklahoma City bombing of the Murrah Federal Office Building, "a spontaneous shrine of flowers, teddy bears, and others objects began to form in front of the rubble where eighty people still lay buried" (Jorgensen-Earp & Lanzilotti, 1998, p. 150). The tragic events of 9/11 at the World Trade Center and the controversy over how to memorialize the deaths at the site show its significance to survivors and public memory.

Visiting the site of the tragedy allows mourners contact with the victims as well as putting them in proximity to holy or sacred ground (Jorgensen-Earp & Lanzilotti, 1998, p. 159):

> With sudden and violent death, the site of the tragedy is also the deathbed of its victims. In one sense, the presence of mourners at the site is a deathbed vigil after the fact. Survivors face the guilt that they were not in attendance at the death, that the victims were ripped and not eased from this world. (p. 159)

Public shrines memorialize the loss and also continue to serve as places where private grief is expressed. Daily visitors leave tokens of love and mementos at the Vietnam Wall, creating an individual response to a public tragedy. "Although these deaths [caused by the Oklahoma bombing, Vietnam War, and Dunblane school shootings] were public and the mourning collective, the individuality of offerings seeks a personal understanding of the loss and blurs the line between public and private grief" (Jorgensen-Earp & Lanzilotti, 1998, p. 163).

Because of the high incidence and damaging effects of violence on others, leaders should be aware of the real possibility that there may be many "walking wounded" in their midst, still trying to manage their pain and heal from its consequences. Going beyond healing to a constructive response to suffering, compassionate leaders engage in a grieving process with members and also resolve to change what they can, knowing that many wounds result from unjust and violent acts committed against persons and humanity.

Courageous leaders recognize the impact of tragic events and social suffering on people and encourage people to share their stories to accomplish healing. Suffering causes us to look within for the sources of stories and also to respond courageously to oppression and challenge it. A sense of personal agency as well as constructive response to suffering assists healing and fights against loss. Social suffering awakens leaders to change, sometimes signaling a drift away from important cultural values while at other times calling for a shift in cultural values and a call to action.

What causes some to portray the enemy, the stranger, the foreigner, as unfailingly evil and inhuman and unworthy of our compassion, while others respond to cultural difference with loving action toward others, standing in love and offering compassion to them by granting membership in their moral community? Stories of moral courage prepare and pave the way for social and cultural transformation, telling us what happened to others when they faced a defining moment of conscience and how their actions changed the world.

12

STORIES OF MORAL COURAGE: SEEING INJUSTICE, HEARING THE CALL, TAKING ACTION

What should move us to action is human dignity; the inalienable dignity of the oppressed, but also the dignity of each of us. We lose dignity if we tolerate the intolerable.

—Dominique de Menil, (Quoteworld, n.d.)

People only see what they are prepared to see.

—Ralph Waldo Emerson, (Quote DB, n.d.)

Five years before Rosa Parks refused to give her up her seat on a bus to a white person, ten-year-old African American Jerome Smith took a stand against oppression. Boarding a streetcar in New Orleans, Smith removed the screen that served as a visible barrier to separate seating for blacks and whites and sat down in the white section, drawing hostility from white passengers (*A Young Boy's Stand on a New Orleans Streetcar*, 2006). Much to his surprise, Smith's actions evoked an angry response from a black woman passenger, who approached Smith to deliver her own message about his protest:

Smith says that as he sat in the white section of the streetcar in Louisiana, an older black woman from the rear of the car descended on him, hitting him so hard that "it felt like there was a bell ringing in my head." The woman loudly said she'd teach the boy a lesson, telling him, "You should never do that, disrespect white people. You have no business trying to sit with them." She forced Smith off the streetcar, and around the back of an auto store. But once they were behind the building, the woman's tone changed. "Never, ever stop," the woman told Smith as she began to cry. "I'm proud of you," she said. "Don't you ever quit." Smith, who went on to help found the New Orleans chapter of CORE, The Congress of Racial Equality, says it was that moment that made him who he is today. "Even though I didn't know the words 'civil rights' then," Smith says, "that opened up the door." (¶ 3–7)

The woman on the bus who rescued Smith from a potentially dangerous situation practiced what Horton called the "two-eyed theory of teaching": The teacher "keeps one eye on where people are, and one eye on where they can be" (1998, p. xx). In this case, Smith needed loving guidance to protect him from harm while at the same time he needed support for taking a stand against injustice—essentially the only way available to change an inhumane system. When Smith took a stand against Jim Crow laws on a streetcar, he experienced it as a young black man. Another man, John Howard Griffin, also encountered racism on a New Orleans bus, riding it first as a white man and later as a black man.

Griffin decided to experience racism firsthand by changing from his position as a privileged white male to a position as a poor black man in the South. Altering the pigment of his skin color from white to black by ingesting high doses of powerful medication, Griffin changed the color of his skin, dyed his hair, left the safety of his friend's home, and boarded a bus as a black man, going into the night to experience what no other white man had experienced previously. The story of his encounter with oppression and racism changed him and the world.

THE STORY OF JOHN HOWARD GRIFFIN

John Howard Griffin traveled to New Orleans on November 1, 1959, to gain an insider's perspective on racism in the South (Griffin, 1960). Describing his experience in *Black Like Me*, Griffin changed his skin color from white to black by ingesting medication and exposing his skin to ultraviolet rays. Griffin's goal, to "pass" as a "Negro" person and objectively compare his experience as a white and a black person in the same environment, was achieved using an accelerated dosage of medication taken in the span of one week. Determined to waste no time in conducting his "experiment," Griffin shaved his head, applied black dye to enhance his already coffee-colored skin, and changed his identity. Becoming someone he did not recognize, Griffin looked into the mirror for the first time and reflected on his transformation: "The completeness of this transformation appalled me. It was unlike anything I had imagined. I became two men, the observing one and the one who panicked, who felt Negroid even into the depths of his entrails" (Griffin, 1960, p. 11).

Beginning his dangerous experiment at midnight on November 7, 1959, Griffin traveled into the night as a "colored" person subject to the Jim Crow rules in effect in Southern states. Griffin boarded his first bus late that evening after being followed by harassing white males. Learning quickly to wait at the end of the line and seek invisibility from the hateful stares of whites, Griffin followed the unwritten laws of being black in America in the 1960s. Finding lodging, Griffin settled into the "best" hotel in the poorest section of the city, beginning his education as an African American.

Griffin noted the ways blacks treated each other with great courtesy, as if making up for the poor treatment by whites. Looking for a job and finding lodging and a place to eat were the major occupations of his first week, despite his considerable financial resources. Looking through the windows of Brennan's, New Orleans most famous restaurant, he realized the only entrance for him was through the back door as kitchen help (1960, p. 42).

Returning to a shoe stand that he had previously patronized as a white man, Griffin succeeded in convincing Sterling Williams, the shoeshine man, of his change in identity. Sharing the goals of his "research" project and winning a promise of secrecy, Williams warned Griffin about how to survive (1960, pp. 22–29). His advice included planning ahead by locating stores and cafes where he might buy food, learning the location of restrooms marked "colored" in advance, and never loitering. The advice continued: keep walking, lower your eyes, and stay out of areas of the city where blacks aren't welcome.

Griffin felt the oppressiveness of the Jim Crow laws, growing weary after just one week, discouraged by indignities encountered on a daily basis:

> All the courtesies in the world do not cover up the one vital and massive discourtesy—that the Negro is not treated not even as a second-class citizen, but as a tenth-class one. His day-to-day living is a reminder of his inferior status. He does not become calloused to these things—the polite rebuffs when he seeks better employment; hearing himself referred to as nigger, coon, jigaboo; having to bypass available rest-room facilities or eating facilities to find one specified for him. Each new reminder strikes at the raw post, deepens the wound. (Griffin, 1960, p. 45)

Throughout *Black Like Me*, Griffin addresses the rationalizations offered by whites in defense of racist acts and debunks each one. Daring to write about these views and say the unspeakable, Griffin's book was published in November 1961, selling an initial 100,000 copies and later selling millions worldwide.

Although Griffin's story is remarkable, it becomes even more remarkable when what preceded it is added to the story of his fascinating life. Just ten years earlier, Griffin had walked through the same streets of New Orleans as a blind person. After sustaining a head injury during World War II, Griffin lost his sight, experiencing a different kind of otherness. In his memoir, *Shattered Shadows: A Memoir of Blindness and Vision*, Griffin describes his struggle and adaptation to his loss of sight, published posthumously in 2004.

During the first few years, Griffin learned to read Braille, skillfully traveled with a cane, and managed the daily challenges of eating, dressing, grooming himself, and maintaining his home. He even became a sheep farmer and award-winning breeder for several years. Realizing this occupation did not tap all of his capacity and considerable scholarly interests in music and other intellectual pursuits, Griffin discovered writing with the encouragement of a friend. He devoted himself to writing and eventually authored several best-selling works prior to *Black Like Me*. After marrying his piano student, Elizabeth, he later fathered two children.

Yet tragedy struck again. Five years after losing his sight, Griffin lost the mobility in his legs, in 1954. Suffering terribly, Griffin was confined to a wheelchair. Now "sightless and legless," Griffin reflected on his condition and the necessary adjustments to it:

[A]ll persons, gravely handicapped through lost[s] of eyesight or limbs, when left completely alone at the very outset begin to compensate for the loss. Only when the adjustment involves the sighted does the element of pity and the idea of tragedy enter. The opposite, of course, is even worse, when those who attempt not to treat the sightless person as an object of pity make him an object of contempt and brutality. The middle route of encouragement and tranquility and love minimizes the difficulties of the adjustment. (Griffin, 2004, p. 172)

After months of severe pain, Griffin tried an experimental treatment for the infection attacking his nervous system and gradually recovered his mobility, just in time for the birth of his first child, Susan. The gift of mobility returned, and Griffin spent the next few years writing at his farm in Mansfield, Texas.

But the remarkable tale doesn't end here. One day Griffin began to see again. Griffin described the return of his vision on January 9, 1957:

[A]s I was walking from the barn studio to my parents' house to prepare lunch—redness swirled in front of my eyes. Then I thought I saw the back door, cut in portions, dancing at crazy angles. I stood dumbfounded. Elements continued to dance and there was pain in my eyes and head. (2004, p. 213)

Griffin fully regained his sight a month later and wrote about his new-found joy in the following excerpt, dated June 28, 1957:

I live each moment as though I could not believe it, as though all of it were new. Each time I take a bath, shave, lie down to rest, it is new, and it is seen and felt vividly, every discomfort, that too is strange and interesting to a man given a new vision of the world. (2004, p. 227)

After suffering ten years of pain, loss, recovery, and joy, Griffin chose to place himself in grave danger because of his desire to seek an answer to the question that "haunted" him: "If a white man became a Negro in the Deep South, what adjustments would he have to make? What is it like to experience discrimination based on skin color, something over which one has no control?" (Griffin, 1960, p. 1).

After reading a report about the rise in suicide rates among Southern "Negroes," Griffin wondered, "How else except by becoming a Negro could a white man learn the truth?" (1960, p. 1). Convincing an editor to provide financial support and publish the results of this experiment, Griffin traveled to New Orleans in search of the answer. The answer to his question is found in his international best seller, *Black Like Me*.

Comparing Griffin's memoirs *Black Like Me* and *Scattered Shadows*, Robert Bonazzi, an authorized biographer of Griffin, states:

> Both experiences concern the same man, misperceived as a stereotype and reduced to the "inferior status" of the *Other*, who discovers a greater humanity in otherness. Griffin realized that blindness was judged by the sighted to be a tragic handicap, an intrinsically different condition that had no relation to the inner life of the blind—exactly as whites prejudged black people as intrinsically Other based entirely on skin color, with no consideration of their qualities as individual. (Griffin, 2004, p. 10)

A close reading of both memoirs also reveals differences between Griffin's perception of each experience of otherness and his adjustment to it. Despite the debilitating personal struggles of a sighted, healthy twenty-seven-year-old person who was severely disabled for a decade, Griffin adjusted remarkably, growing in capacity, character, and wisdom. When threatened with the loss of mobility, he became depressed but began to accept some aspects of his new condition. He worried primarily about others, not himself. Yet six weeks of living as a black person in the South shocked him to his very core and changed his life forever. Becoming a human rights activist during the 1960s and 1970s, Griffin placed himself and his family in peril. He could not do otherwise.

In both situations, Griffin adjusted to his condition and sustained himself with the support of family, mentors, and moral strangers who saw his need and met it. In Griffin's memoir of blackness, he describes the most encouraging aspect of his struggle: the community bond of friendship and help found among the members of oppressed groups for each other. The hatred expressed by his oppressors stands out as the most discouraging element. In contrast, Griffin's memoir of darkness glowingly describes the love he received from family and mentors. However, he becomes discouraged by his encounters with others who express pity or impose limitations on him due to their insensitivity or lack of knowledge about his condition. Griffin's experience of *otherness* sensitizes us to the needs of the oppressed and disabled.

In each story, the importance of love, respect, dignity, and freedom are paramount. Cultural differences affect how he is treated and his response to others and the environment. Griffin's experience convinced him that racial hatred primarily explained the poor living conditions of African Americans. His finding caused him to speak openly about what he experienced and join the civil rights movement as an advocate for change. Socially just leaders understand how cultural difference may adversely affect conditions of fairness as well as exclude others in democratic processes. An understanding of the psychology of hate offers many insights into what causes oppression and how its sources may be diminished.

THE PSYCHOLOGY OF HATE

Sternberg (2005) proposed a theory of hate, based on the following three components: (1) negation of intimacy (distancing): repulsion and disgust, (2) passion in hate: anger-fear, and (3) decision—commitment in hate: devaluation—diminution through contempt (p. 39). The first component, distancing, occurs as a result of real or perceived disgust with the hated person's characteristics or actions. Distancing can even occur without direct contact when people learn to hate others through propaganda stories. A second component involves emotion—a negative and destructive passion expressed as either anger or fear. Hatred takes on an added dimension when emotion combines with an attitude of disgust or revulsion. Finally, a third component relates to the way in which hated people are viewed as "barely human or subhuman" (p. 39). When this dimension joins the other components, hatred accelerates because the filters that work against failing to see another person as a fellow human being disappear as reference points.

Thus, each component adds to the experience of hate, increasing in intensity as more aspects of hatred are adopted, ranging from "cool hate" (disgust for a targeted group) to "burning anger" (a need for annihilation) (Sternberg, 2005, pp. 39–40). These elements explain what happens when "good people" participate in acts of oppression and physical violence. Distancing removes others from consideration, objectifying them by eliminating their positive attributes. Boiling emotions expressed as rage remove all remnants of empathy, compassion, and fairness from consideration. A frenzy of hatred justifies the elimination of people and targeted groups because they threaten physical survival and a way of life.

The level of hatred determines the response of combatants. In suicide bombings, the level of hatred reveals a burning anger, characterized by the highest level of sacrifice: To win one must lose a life. Acts of discrimination require oppressors to dehumanize individuals and groups, viewing them as unworthy of respect, or in the extreme as "savages" or property.

> How can people who hate live with themselves? They may very well establish separate identities for themselves for different roles they enact (Suleiman, 2002). That is, the person who is a hater at a violent rally may go home and become a loving husband or wife. The roles are bifurcated from each other, so that the hater may see him- or herself as a loving and caring person in the roles in which loving and caring seem relevant. Or he or she may engage in moral disengagement by generating excuses or hating or inflicting suffering on others while maintaining a clear conscience. (Grusendorf, McAlister, Sandstrom, Udd, & Morrison, 2002) (in Sternberg, 2005, p. 41)

Hatred stories have common themes and sequences. The main characters, the perpetrator and victim, play predictable roles (Sternberg, 2005). The perpetrator portrays himself or herself as the victim of violence, justifying attacks and crimes against others. In propaganda stories, the hated person is portrayed as "a stranger, as impure and contaminated, as a controller, as an enemy of god, as morally bankrupt, as a purveyor of death, as a barbarian, as a criminal, as a torturer, as a murderer, as a seducer, an animal pest, a power monger, a subtle infiltrator, a comic character, and/or a thwarter or destroyer of destiny" (Sternberg, 2005, p. 43).

Counterstories fight hatred and oppression by negating distancing images and dehumanizing portraits and replacing hateful propaganda stories with human interest and personal stories to reveal the humanity of others. Often hate propaganda is disguised as a factual account, "selling truth" with cultural stereotypes and creating distancing among cultures and societies. The effects of these "constructions" of truth told as cultural stories offer accounts of otherness based in fiction, not fact, and justify unearned advantage as well as unfair access to privilege, power, and position:

> Class, race, and gender are not natural or essential attributes of who we are as human beings. Contrary to dominant assumptions, they are not like hair or eye color or blood type. Rather, class, race, and gender distinctions are artificial constructions that mutually condition one another. They have been created historically by the most powerful social groups to serve their interests as these interests change over time. (Hobgood, 2000, p. 3)

Moral and cultural leaders challenge stories containing negative cultural stereotypes and instead replace distancing actions and stories with direct and personal contact and experiences. Human contact and dialogue work against rigid views and actions. Allen (2004) comments on the state of cultural diversity in America and the reasons why racial and ethic divides are so difficult to close:

> A lot of people are understandably reluctant to take on the risks of intimacy outside their own groups for fear of being perceived as traitors. Another reason is a lack of trust in the Other. They are afraid of cruel and thoughtless barbs. They are not sure intimacy with people of other groups can ultimately nourish and sustain their particular ethnoracial identities. They lack basic trust in people of other backgrounds. . . . As we look across racial and ethnic divides, we Americans are not enemies, but we are not exactly friends. Ambivalence and distrust in relationships with people of other ethnoracial groups is the unfortunate fact of the matter. It is not as bad as it once was, but it is not over. (2004, pp. 236–237)

Seeing the injustice in "social justice" means examining how unequal power and acts of oppression preserve a social order that benefits some and disadvantages others. The way we talk about race may distance people from one another. Applebaum (2006) describes three discourses that ignore the reality of race and its influence on people of color and their experience: (1) the discourse of "colour-blindness" (2) the discourse of meritocracy, and (3) the discourse of individual choice (pp. 282–286).

Color-blindness essentially denies the influence of racial differences in relationships. This perspective "obscures the positive cultural contributions of race to individual identity," "ignores the positive contributions of racialized groups," and "denies the systemic harms that people of colour experience" (pp. 282–284). Applebaum prefers the term "color ignore-ance" to describe the lack of knowledge regarding how color influences social relations (p. 288).

Referring to the discourse of meritocracy, Applebaum states, "Meritocracy assumes that one's social location can and should be ignored" (2006, p. 285). This perspective promotes the myth that the American dream is equally available to all citizens, ignoring the influence of white privilege on education and occupational success.

The third perspective, the discourse of individual choice, allows individuals to avoid moral responsibility for social and institutional racism, as if saying, " Because I [as a privileged White person] did not participate in racism, I am not morally responsible for its effects on others." A focus on individual choice functions to obscure the full understanding of how systemic privilege contributes to the marginalization of "Others" (2006, p. 287). Moral leaders guard against these distancing discourses (perspectives) that deny the reality of racism in America. Instead leaders encourage members to share their experiences, whether privileged or marginalized, and examine how social location, race, and cultural differences influence individual and group access to power and resources.

Injustice varies by culture, community, and nation-state, ranging from failure to provide equal access to resources to acts of violence committed against others. People who are disadvantaged frequently experience low wages and poor conditions in employment, unequal health care and educational experiences, and generational poverty.

Race, class, and gender influence employment opportunities and financial success. In the next story Barbara Ehrenreich (2001) goes undercover as an investigative journalist to experience work at the lowest rungs of the ladder. She reflects on this experience in her best-selling *Nickel and Dimed: On (Not) Getting by in America.*

WOMEN WORKING IN AMERICA

Applying for the best possible job with limited qualifications, Ehrenreich (2001) accepts various low-paying jobs to earn a living. She learns how poverty disadvantages people in the way they conduct their lives. Ordinary tasks, such as finding a place to live, making food, and accessing health care are quite complicated without resources.

There are no secret economies that nourish the poor; on the contrary, there are a host of special costs. If you can't put up the two month's rent you need to secure an apartment, you end up paying through the nose for a room by the week. If you have only a room, with a hotel plate at best, you can't save by cooking up huge lentil stews that can be frozen for the week ahead. You east fast food or the hot dogs and Styrofoam cups of soup that can be microwaved in a convenience store. If you have no money for health insurance . . . [,] you go without routine care or prescription drugs and end up paying the price. (p. 27)

Cleaning motel rooms, working as a waitress, and serving as a Wal-Mart sales associate, Ehrenreich discovers the hazards of living on the margin. Job uncertainty, mindless bureaucracy, limited opportunities for promotion, and low wages sink her optimism. Because the lowest-paying jobs are held by women, particularly women of color, the penalties of race, class, and gender appear as primary characters and culprits in maintaining the adverse conditions experienced by the working power and unemployed. Women and children in America and the world suffer the highest levels of poverty (Miller, n.d.). On a global scale, the picture is even more disturbing.

Stories of moral courage call us to see the effects of injustice and do something about it based on our willingness and ability to engage in the struggle. Challenging stories that portray the stranger as the enemy, leaders and members *stand for and with others* to oppose harmful constructions of otherness that create distance, hatred, and oppression. Hobgood (2000) advises moral leaders: *"to act justly in the world, we need to know how the world works"* (p. 14). Looking deeper for the root causes of inequities plays an important role in replacing naive views with informed ones.

KATRINA STORIES

The struggle for decency and justice in New Orleans continues long after Griffin walked the streets of New Orleans. Collectively the stories of Katrina survivors and emergency workers present a picture of the different ways people experienced the hurricane: as survivors, victims, witnesses, volunteers, and emergency management personnel. They all share one common theme: utter shock at the failure of government and enormous grief about the loss of people and a way of life. Many personal stories of struggle, loss, and survival, collected as oral history projects, can be located online at www.storycorps.net. Visiting this site provides an opportunity to hear the voices of those who suffered and participate in their stories as empathetic and often shocked listeners.

Questions regarding how race, class, and ethnicity contributed to the failure of the government to respond to Katrina erupted into national consciousness during the crisis and its aftermath. Widely believed to be at least some part of the reason why an uncaring government failed to respond to the dire circumstances of the people of New Orleans, poverty and prejudice clearly played a role in emergency preparedness and rescue efforts. Over 100,000 people in New Orleans did not own a car, and when the hurricane pounded New Orleans, inadequate evacuation plans resulted in many deaths (Hsu, 2006).

The poor gathered at the Superdome. The influence of race and class differentially affected how people experienced the hurricane and now plays a role in how people manage their recovery:

> Overall, according to Richard Campanella, a Tulane University geographer, the storm flooded 51% of the white- occupied homes and 67% of the black-occupied homes in the three-parish area—a disparity, but not an overwhelming one. "Those terrible photographs of African Americans crowded into the Superdome showed who couldn't evacuate, not who had their home destroyed," Campanella says. When the storm hit, Louisiana health authorities tallied up the dead. In the three parishes, people of color comprised 52% of the pre-Katrina population and 53% of the dead; in Orleans Parish alone, the numbers were 66% and 62%, respectively. But if race and class did not play a dominant role in the storm, they have dominated its aftermath, both because Katrina's poor and African American victims are disproportionately affected by the economic burden of rebuilding and because political disputes inflamed by race and class are paralyzing the city government. (Mann, 2006, pp. 41–43)

Government ineptitude also contributed to the horror of the events. The Select Bipartisan Committee to Investigate the Preparation for and Response to Hurricane Katrina found a myriad of problems, including failure to recognize the scale of the event, lack of preparedness, breakdowns in communication, bureaucratic roadblocks, and overall, "a failure to initiate" (*A Failure of Initiative*, 2006).

The lack of "situational context" regarding Katrina's likely impact on people and the environment before and during the crisis led to an inadequate response. However, the conditions of poverty, prevalent in the daily lives of the homeless, unemployed, and working poor, added dimension to the situation. Many simply lacked the resources to evacuate, perhaps pinning their hopes on being able to wait out the storm in their homes or taking shelter in public evacuation sites. Not only was there a *failure to initiate* but also a *failure to understand* the conditions faced by the impoverished citizens of New Orleans.

Fluker (2005) challenges us to dig deeper into the real roots of this tragedy:

> There is a failure of ethical leadership in American society that crosses racial, political, social and cultural lines . . . far more dangerous and costly, and in the end, more damaging than even the worst hurricanes that wreak devastation on our shores. . . . Questions of race, ethnicity, and class must be addressed. But most importantly, it will be the critical task of leadership to infuse the ethical dimension into any inquiry so that objective, historical and subjective questions are systematically explored. (2005, pp. 3–5)

Feelings of helplessness, despair, and rage followed in the aftermath of the hurricane after the desperate struggle to survive receded with the floodwater. A new kind of struggle emerged: the struggle to deal with loss and figure out how to build a life on meager resources. Maddening conditions caused by oppression may produce what bell hooks (1996) calls "a killing rage": the desire to strike back at others for attacks on personal dignity, marginal living conditions, and other racialized incidents. *When the moment comes, moral courage requires us to stand with and for other people because a just cause demands action.*

The importance of challenging unjust authority, themes in Smith's removal of a sign on a New Orleans streetcar and Griffin's decision to darken his skin and gain the perspective of oppressed people, inspires others to take moral action. Ehrenreich's study of marginal work and Hobgood's exposé of the effects of class, race, and gender on life choices and opportunities serve as additional examples of moral courage. They offer indirect leadership as investigators of injustice and witnesses to oppression, changing our minds based on the power of their ideas (Gardner, 2004). Moral courage can be expressed in many ways.

Collectively, stories of moral courage do more for the development of moral character of young and old alike than stories about "slaying dragons" in ancient and modern tales:

> So many of the models of courage we've had, ones that are still taught to boys and girls are about going out to slay the dragon, to kill . . . . It's a courage that's born out of fear, anger, and hate. But there's this other kind of courage. It's the courage to risk your life, not in war, not in battle, not out of fear . . . but out of love and a sense of injustice that has to be challenged. It takes far more courage to challenge unjust authority without violence then it takes to kill all the monsters in all the stories told to children about the meaning of bravery. (Martin, 1999, pp. xii–xiii)

To overcome hatred created by distancing thoughts, passionate anger and fear, and devaluing acts, leaders and members must recognize the sources of distrust and hatred and use story and dialogue to counter oppression.

A couple facing prejudice and hate crimes due to their sexual preference needed both a coat of Teflon and courage to challenge intolerance and cope with hate crimes. Gerriann shares the following story:

> I think any time we are in a situation where our orientation is obvious or revealed we have "wounded readiness"—a Teflon coating that is readied at the moment in case of a potential wounding. The woundings can be harsh words, like the time a teenager yelled at me "Lesbian Bitch," my mother chiding me that I wasn't feminine enough, a work colleague telling me I would go to hell, or physical acts when the windshield of our car was smashed, or the eggs thrown at the house, the latter two classified as hate crimes by the police. But the potential of a wounding vividly brings back all those past experiences, refreshes the pain and discomfort, but also provides a basis of strength and ability to cope, no matter what happens.
>
> Our last notable experience with this was one year ago when Barb's mother died. Her mother had gone to great lengths to never reveal her daughter's sexual orientation, including avoiding eating at her favorite restaurant with her daughter. Someone might stop over and ask how Barbara was, and that might lead to questions. So when her mother died Barb proudly put in the obituary that her mother was survived by her daughter Barbara and Barbara's partner Gerriann. Nothing like coming out to the entire town!
>
> At the funeral we showed our solidarity as a couple. We endured stares, a lot of questions, and were rudely ignored by some as a couple, especially

by the presiding minister. I took Barb's hand and walked up the aisle of the
Missouri Lutheran Synod Church, my daughter by our side, proud, solid,
and together. I said to myself, "My partner lost her mother, she needs me,
and I am here for her, whether you like it or not." (Confidential submission, personal communication [SN], March 18, 2007)

The couple's story alerts us to the cumulative pain associated with cultural difference. Serving as conscious objectors and allies to others, leaders must refuse to participate in exclusionary acts as well as speak for the rights of others to make decisions about their lives.

The next story about a hate crime, powerfully told with the moral authority only a mother can claim, transforms us because of its meaning and tragic effects. It describes one mother's response to her suffering as a result of a hate crime committed against her beloved son and the loss she experienced with his death.

THE MATTHEW SHEPARD STORY

Standing in front of a packed audience at the University of St. Thomas, Judy Shepard delivered a speech to students about the brutal death of her son, Matthew Shepard (Shepard, 2006). In October 1998, Aaron McKinney and Russell Henderson had driven the twenty-one-year-old gay college student into a remote area after luring him into the car by claiming to be gay. They tied Shepard to a fence, terrorized him with repeated beatings, and left him to die on an isolated road near Laramie, Wyoming. Eighteen hours later, a morning jogger found Matthew Shepard in near-death condition and called for help. The savage beating left Shepard so disfigured that even his own mother didn't recognize him at first sight. He died five days later, on October 12, 1998.

Responding to the horror of her loss, Judy Shepard turned her pain into a national campaign against hate crimes. Shepard's personal campaign began the moment she realized that her son was not going to recover from his injuries. She said, "I realized that he wasn't going to recover, that we were losing him. I knew in that moment that his life and mine had changed forever" (Shepard, 2006). Determined to make something positive out of a terrible loss, Judy Shepard became a public spokesperson for gay rights.

Shepard's family started a foundation (www.matthewshepard.org) to stop hate crimes and gain recognition for the civil rights of gay, lesbian, bisexual, and transgender people (GLBT). In the victim impact statement Judy Shepard delivered during the sentencing portion of her son's murder trial, she described her pain to the audience and the devastating effects of his loss on her family and friends.

She emphasized two key themes in her speech in the form of questions: "Why did he have to die?" "What crime did he commit?" (Shepard, 2006). Then she passionately answered her questions. First, she said, Matthew didn't have to die. Gay people, as American citizens, should enjoy the same civil rights as heterosexuals. Shepard challenged the audience to think about why only some citizens are entitled to exercise their freedom and be protected from harm.

Describing civil rights as the basis for American citizenship, Mrs. Shepard drew on American history and the Constitution as authority for her position. What was Matthew's crime? According to Mrs. Shepard, his only crime was to seek love in a society where GLBT people are shunned, terrorized, and discriminated against. Simplifying her son's sexual preference and his choice to be a gay male to a single truth, Mrs. Shepard said, "You are who you are, you love who you love, and that's just the way it is" (Shepard, 2006).

Exhorting the audience to look more closely at Matthew's death and the moral responsibility to defend vulnerable others, Judy Shepard said American citizens are members of a "SIC" society—a society in which the majority of people are "silent, indifferent, and complacent." In her call to action, Shepard described many ways to organize and support the civil rights of anyone who loses his or her freedom because of difference. In an effort to make sense out of Matthew's senseless death, Shepard decided to share her story with others as a change leader so that others might be spared a similar tragedy.

Even though we know of the Matthew Shepard story, many people want to hear the story directly and intimately from Matthew's mother to understand its meaning for her and to indirectly become involved in the tragedy. Her story transforms us, awakening our sense of injustice and calling us to see another's tragedy and respond. Determined to find some meaning in the senseless death of Matthew, the Shepard family established a foundation and a national campaign to "replace hate with understanding, compassion, and acceptance" (Matthew Shepard Foundation, n.d., p. 3). When one of us suffers a savage death, some of our humanity disappears down a desolate Wyoming road.

UNPOPULAR CAUSES AND DANGEROUS STANDS

A little more than nine years after Matthew Shepard's death, Republican State Representative Dan Zwonitzer expressed his willingness to risk his seat in the Wyoming legislature over the issue of same-sex marriage (Associated Press, 2007). Delivering a speech in a legislative committee meeting, Zwonitzer spoke against a bill that would have banned recognition of legal same-sex unions (p. 2). The following excerpt of Zwonitzer's remarks reveals his courage in standing up for his beliefs and addressing the wounds left by the legacy of Matthew Shepard's death:

> Thank you Mr. Speaker and Members of the Committee. I am not going to speak of specifics regarding this bill, but rather talk about history and philosophy in regards to this issue. It is an exciting time to be in the legislature while this issue is being debated. I believe this is the Civil Rights struggle of my generation.
>
> Being a student of history, as many of you are, and going back through history, most of history has been driven by the struggle of man against government to endow him with more rights, privileges and liberties to be bestowed upon him. . . . It is wrong for one segment of society to restrict rights and freedoms from another segment of society. I believe many of you have had this conversation with your children.
>
> And children have listened, my generation, the twenty-somethings, and those younger than I understand this message of tolerance. And in 20 years, when they take the reigns of this government and all governments, society will see this issue overturned, and people will wonder why it took so long. My kids and grandkids will ask me, why did it take so long? And I can say, hey, I was there, I discussed these issues, and I stood up for basic rights for all people.
>
> I echo Representative Childers [sic] concerns, that testifying against this bill may cost me my seat. I have two of my precinct committee persons behind me today who are in favor of this bill, as I stand here opposed, and I understand that I may very well lose my election. It cost 4 moderate

Republican Senators in Kansas their election last year for standing up on this same issue. But I tell myself that there are some issues that are greater than me, and I believe this is one of them. And if standing up for equal rights costs me my seat so be it. I will let history be my judge, and I can go back to my constituents and say I stood up for basic rights. I will tell my children that when this debate went on, I stood up for basic rights for people.

I can debate the specifics of this bill back and forth as everyone in this room can, but I won't because the overall theme is fairness, and you know it. I hope you will all let history be your judge with this vote. You all know in your hearts where this issue is going, that it will come to pass in the next 30 years. For that, I ask you to vote no today on the bill. Thank you. (Spaulding, 2007, pp. 5–15)

Zwonitzer's remarks drew a flurry of responses, eliciting hate mail as well as notes of congratulations. In response to a note of thanks from a gay rights supporter, Zwonitzer described his thoughts twenty-four hours later:

I have obviously thought about this issue a great deal in the last 24 hours, and have truly come to realize that marriage in any form is greater than allowing a group of our citizens to continually be persecuted; and I've come to understand that many of the reasons they are vilified in our society is directly related to the fact there is not an opportunity to form recognized, committed long-term relationships.

It is my sincere hope that the outside world does not continue to believe Wyoming to be an intolerant and bigoted state. We have a low population which does not allow a lot of room for intolerance here as everyone knows everyone. When people come to know others who are different and accept them, their attitudes change.

Luckily, I have not had significant negative feedback today from people in my District. Yes, there has certainly been some comment from citizens from the "deep red" portions of my state. I am hoping that the silent majority of Wyoming understands and agrees with me, as I am fairly confident they do. It was greatly controversial right up until it was killed in committee, and within a day things have settled back down. (Spaulding, 2007, pp. 18–20)

The legislature voted not to go on record banning same-sex marriages, killing the issue in committee. Zwonitzer listened to diverse

voices and showed his willingness to learn and act on his beliefs, overcoming his desire for political support and reelection. Taking a tough
stand and participating in social change requires patience as well as a
willingness to risk public ridicule and, unfortunately, threats of personal
violence. Whether operating within the system or standing outside of it,
presenting the "adaptive challenge" to others makes leadership dangerous (Heifetz, 1994).

Adaptive challenges require leaders to learn new ways of thinking to
uncover root problems, examine underlying assumptions, question existing ways of operating, and discover new strategies to address challenges in highly unpredictable environments. Leaders who address conflicts in the values people hold or diminish the gap between the values
people stand for and the reality they face put themselves in danger of
being rejected by others or even physically harmed. Because adaptive
work requires a change in values, beliefs, or behavior, those who offer
leadership during dangerous times put themselves at considerable risk
(Heifetz, 1994). Leading from outside the system increases this risk because of the limited access to resources and the lack of political power
associated with positional authority. What happens to people who take a
stand against the prevailing view or challenge the president of the
United States?

President Bush's refusal to talk to Cindy Sheehan about her son, who
died in the Iraq War, attracted national attention. Determined to meet
with President Bush, Sheehan camped outside President Bush's ranch
in Crawford, Texas on August 6, 2005. She wanted to speak to the president about why her son had to die. Soon others joined her outside the
ranch. Her individual protest energized the national debate, giving others permission to express their doubts and opposition to the war. Bush
refused to meet with her, fueling more acts of protest. Fame followed
along with attacks against her character.

Columnist Doug Grow (2007) briefly summarizes her story and describes the impact taking a stand has had on her life:

Sheehan can barely remember her life before April 4, 2004. On that
Palm Sunday, her son Casey, an Army specialist, was killed in Iraq. A few
months later she became the most recognizable face in the antiwar
movement. This was a lonely place to be. And when, in August 2005, she

set up camp outside President Bush's Texas ranch, she became a target of many who didn't think she was doing what a bereaved mother should do.

For example, conservative author-columnist Ann Coulter had this to say: "To expiate the pain of losing her firstborn son in the Iraq war, Cindy Sheehan decided to cheer herself up by engaging in Stalinist agitprop outside President Bush's Crawford ranch. It's the strangest method of grieving I've seen since Paul Wellstone's funeral. Someone needs to teach these liberals how to mourn."

Such attacks on her pain, her family, her motives were shocking at first. "I didn't expect it, but it didn't intimidate me," she said. "After a while, I even understood I must be having an impact if I was making some people so angry." (Grow, 2007, pp. 5–11)

Coulter's deeply disturbing remark lacks empathy for Sheehan's loss, refusing to see the personal effects of war on others. Bemoaning apathy about the war in Iraq, Sheehan challenges a system that sends poor and disadvantaged men and women to war and the elites to college. Tracing the sources of apathy to class differences, Sheehan says that those serving in Iraq are not the sons and daughters of elites. "I don't want to disparage college students, because many are wonderful," she said. "But I think one of the reasons campuses haven't been more active is that college is so expensive that the campuses are filled with the elites. They'll never have to serve" (Grow, 2007, p. 16).

Others stand with Sheehan in her protest. At the Lake Street Bridge in Minneapolis, Minnesota, people assemble to protest the wounds of war, as peacemakers in a violent world.

PROTEST AT THE LAKE STREET BRIDGE

The drive over the Lake Street Bridge in Minneapolis, Minnesota, offers a spectacular view of the Mississippi River—the same legendary river of Native Americans, Lewis and Clark, and Tom Sawyer. River boat captains navigate the channels of the river, maneuvering football-field-length containers filled with prairie grain headed to the Port of New Orleans and from there, all over the world. Every Wednesday, protesters against the war in Iraq take their positions on the Lake Street Bridge, serving as witnesses for peace.

Some protestors carry signs that say, "Stop the Killing," drawing attention to their cause and receiving the welcome honk, wave, or peace sign from passersby signaling their agreement. Not everyone supports the group's vigil on the Lake Street Bridge. One day, a driver expressed his reaction to their protest by shouting angrily out his window, "Get a job!" (Coleman, 2006, p. B1). Columnist Nick Coleman observed the event and wrote an article about Sister Brigid McDonald, a seventy-three-year-old member of a religious order, who opposes the war in Iraq along with her colleagues on the Lake Street Bridge:

> There was a small huddle of dissenters on the east end of the bridge yesterday, waving signs saying Stop The Killing. A surprising number of passing drivers honked in support. A few glared. An occasional twerp shouted, "Get a job!" which was funny in a stupid way, because these peace workers have labored hard all their lives and are dedicated now to trying to leave a better world than the one they found. (p. B1)

Depositing his rage in a drive-by wounding, the driver stereotypically implies that the protestors are lazy, shiftless, noncontributors to American society. His logic leads him to one possible conclusion, "I don't need to listen to them—they're not like me." Another frequent protestor who participates in the peace demonstration on the bridge, Michael Klein, instructor in justice and peace studies, shared the following description of the many "forms" in which people who support the Iraq War respond to the protestors:

> In this repressive political climate, anything to the left of far right is seen as "Communist." So that label is regularly applied as a "drive-by wounding." Drivers have yelled: "°uckin' Hippies!" We appropriate this expletive by describing ourselves as "huckin' fippies."
>
> We also appropriate another common response as the "one-fingered peace sign" or the consolation that "at least we got half a peace sign." At other protests, the suggestions have also been made that we: don't support/disgrace our troops and/or soldiers who gave their lives; should love or leave America; are one of those °ucking _____ (fill in the blank: Taliban, terrorists, etc.); lend comfort to our enemy; should thank our soldiers for defending our freedom to protest; or are generally unpatriotic or cowards.
>
> At some major protests (like the annual School of Americas/WHISC Vigil at Fort Benning, GA) a well-organized counterprotest called "Rolling Thunder" tries to disrupt protest activities by driving by with loud motorcycles

blaring patriotic music from boom boxes strapped to the back and draped in American flag paraphernalia.

Even for all of these "drive-by woundings" as you call them, the response from passersby has typically been overwhelmingly positive and more so in recent months with many honks, waves, and two-fingered peace signs. Protests like these are essential to our democracy. Such democratic action challenges the rationale for war, attempts to transform violence and anger, and seeks peace by peaceful means. (Michael Klein, personal communication [SN], March 19, 2007)

Protestors, inspired by history and examples of social change, maintain hope that their protests may make a difference. "'But we have hope,' said Maried Braun of Minneapolis . . . . The Berlin Wall fell, Nelson Mandela was released. We've seen things that were unexpected. The unexpected can come again" (Coleman, 2006, p. B3).

Whether standing alone or joining others in solidarity, acts of protest serve as a creative response to suffering and also have the potential to produce social change as a result of changing values expressed in "critical communities" (Rochon, 1998). Differences in cultural values cause people to join together in "critical communities" to express alternative viewpoints and create conditions for social change:

The creation of new values begins with the generation of new ideas or perspectives among small groups of critical thinkers: people whose experiences, reading, and interaction with each other help them to develop a set of cultural values that is out of step with the larger society. The dissemination of those values occurs through social and political movements in which the critical thinkers may participate, but whose success is determined to a far greater degree by the course of collective action in support of the new values. Together, critical communities and movements are sometimes able to initiate changes in cultural values that represent a truly original break from past ways of thinking about a subject. (Rochon, 1998, pp. 8–9)

People share their stories and stand alone or with others against enormously powerful people and institutions. Eventually, if enough people experience a change in cultural values, a critical mass forms and the weight of public opinion causes a shift in thought and future direction. Cultural change occurs when a crisis point ignites action.

For example, the televised beatings of African American citizens on "Bloody Sunday" during the March 7, 1965, march from Selma to Montgomery in Alabama shocked the nation and changed the course of history:

> On "Bloody Sunday," March 7, 1965, some 600 civil rights marchers headed east out of Selma on U.S. Route 80. They got only as far as the Edmund Pettus Bridge six blocks away, where state and local lawmen attacked them with billy clubs and tear gas and drove them back into Selma. Two days later on March 9, Martin Luther King, Jr., led a "symbolic" march to the bridge. Then civil rights leaders sought court protection for a third, full-scale march from Selma to the state capitol in Montgomery. . . . On Sunday, March 21, about 3,200 marchers set out for Montgomery, walking 12 miles a day and sleeping in fields. By the time they reached the capitol on Thursday, March 25, they were 25,000-strong. Less than five months after the last of the three marches, President Lyndon Johnson signed the Voting Rights Act of 1965—the best possible redress of grievances. (Selma to Montgomery March, n.d., p. 1)

Bringing the brutality of violence to the television screen, the images of oppression reached a crisis point, causing a swift change in federal law. Rochon (1998) explains the rapid change in policy:

> What causes tidal forces to sweep periodically through the political system, disrupting long-standing policy networks and widely accepted understanding of policy issues? What are the circumstances that enable public demands for reform to gain the momentum of a runaway freight train? The one-word explanation for these events is "crisis." Public recognition of a crisis generates demand for a political response. . . . For political leaders, crisis loosens the normal constraints on action by creating expectations of the kind of leadership that is normally hemmed in by institutional routines. (pp. 7–8)

Once a critical mass of support is achieved, a dramatic change seems to happen overnight. It takes a crisis to wake us up and take a stand. Courageous leaders like Nelson Mandela raise awareness of issues, radicalize members, and move issues from the sidelines to the center of public discourse and eventually political action.

NELSON MANDELA

Nelson Mandela's lifetime commitment to social justice and his refusal to abandon the cause of civil rights despite years of imprisonment serves as an international model of moral courage. The seriousness of his intent and his refusal to cooperate in an unjust system inspired millions to join the struggle. The following story reveals how Mandela's awakening serves as a model for our development as moral leaders.

In his autobiography *The Long Walk to Freedom*, Nelson Mandela describes his awakening to injustice and development as a freedom fighter (1994). Describing his family, tribal origins, and customs, Mandela takes us on joyful excursions into the woods near his home. From his childhood mastery of "warrior" games with his peers to his passage to manhood, we see Mandela moving through the thrilling, uncertain and painful moments of childhood and eventually gaining a fragile foothold of his adulthood. Sharing deeply disturbing stories of his oppression in painstaking detail, we learn about the gradual and increasingly more brutal assaults on his dignity and personhood. . . .

As he grows older, the assassins of his dignity are more skilled and brutal. Resorting to withdrawal of privileges and opportunities, deception, forced menial work, banning and "house" arrest, threats against his peace of mind and body, and periodic imprisonment, his oppressors motivate him to rise up against them. We know what he will do, what he must do, what we would do—become a freedom fighter! . . .

Because we know him through his "coming of age" story, we feel his powerlessness and rage. He becomes increasingly more human to us through story. Mandela becomes a freedom fighter when he knows who he is, what he stands for and what he must do. . . .

An awareness regarding how culture shapes identity, colors perceptions, and forms an invisible boundary in our thinking and interactions, allows us to detect its insidious effects on our perceptions, judgments, and life opportunities. The change within us moves us to think about how institutions (family, government, economic system, education, religion) and dominant cultures preserve the status quo advantaging some "tribes" over others. Gradually Mandela sees the solution to apartheid in dialogue, engagement, negotiation, understanding perspectives, and eventually forging relationships with his oppressors (Mandela, 1994). He is unwilling to move from prisoner to victor to oppressor. He sees the beauty of a vibrant, engaged, and "non-racial" Africa that embraces all of its citizens. . . .

Mandela's prison experience mirrors his life: he resists the psychic and physical boundaries of his circumstances, holds firmly to his personal and cultural identities and "sees" his interactions and exchanges with others (including their ideologies) as his primary opportunity to continue his struggle for social justice and evolve as a human being. Embodying the role of scholar, teacher, and leader, his approach to diversity and learning must be ours. Beginning with the self as a subject worthy of study while continuously exploring difference, we must go back and forth to look inward while at the same time, going beyond ourselves. (Noonan, 2007, pp. 9–10)

Displaying a passionate and personal commitment to people and justice, morally courageous people leave a legacy of moral action for all to follow because of their ethical ambition. Defined by Allen (2004) as "a keen desire to do what is right, is normal, healthy and admirable" (Allen, 2004, pp. xviii–xix), ethical ambition calls us to moral action.

Krishnamurti (1994) advises us to look within ourselves first for the sources of suffering, recognizing that the capacity for both love and hatred exists within us:

Humanity does not need more suffering to make it understand, what is needed is that you should be aware of your own actions, that you should awaken to your own ignorance and sorrow and so bring about in yourself compassion and tolerance. You should not be concerned with punishment and reward but with the eradication in yourself of those causes that manifest themselves in violence and in hate, in antagonism and ill will. (1994, p. 2)

Combining moral courage with ethical ambition, moral leaders see injustice, hear its call, and take action, fighting against hatred, oppression, and unnecessary acts of violence in the world. Mandela's call to action should inform ours:

The twentieth century will be remembered as a century marked by violence. It burdens us with its legacy of mass destruction, of violence inflicted on a scale never seen and never possible before in human history. But this legacy—the result of new technology in service of ideologies of hate—is not only the one we carry, not that we must face up to.

Less visible, but even more widespread, is the legacy of day-to-day individual suffering. It is the pain of children who are abused by people who should protect them, women injured or humiliated by violent partners, elderly persons maltreated by their caregivers, youth who are bullied by other youths and people of all ages who inflict violence on themselves. This suffering—and there are many more examples that I could give—is a legacy that reproduces itself, as new generations learn from the violence of generations past, as victims learn from victimizers, and as the social conditions that nurture violence are allowed to continue. . . . We must address the roots of violence. Only then will we transform the past century's legacy from a crushing burden into a cautionary lesson. (Krug, Dahlberg, Mercy, Zwi, & Lozano, 2002, p. ix)

Mandela's call to action inspires us to address the roots of violence through concerted action. Embracing diverse voices in dialogue, ethical leaders seek alternative perspectives to gain wisdom and make decisions for the common good. This work is carried out in communities where listening to all members (including Wolf and Wolf's brother) contributes to their well-being and ensures the survival of communities.

13

WOLF AND WOLF'S BROTHER SPEAK: LISTENING TO DIVERSE VOICES

Listening to diverse voices and locating turning points in dialogue—places where we are influenced and changed by others—inspires moral imagination and commitment to find a different way to be together.

Long ago members of an ancient tribe searched for a new place to live in the forest. Drawing on the knowledge of tribal members, the People consulted "experts" on a proposed new site for their future home. The tribe was growing and their home could no longer sustain them. While some understood the "flow of waters," others knew of the "storms of winters" (Spencer, 1983, p. 23). Tribal members assembled to choose a new place to live.

> They listened closely to each of the young men
> as they spoke of hills and trees
> of clearings and running water
> of deer and squirrel and berries
> They listened to hear which place
> might be drier in rain
> more protected in winter and where our Three Sisters
> Corn, Beans, and Squash

might find a place to their liking
They listened
and they chose

(Spencer, 1983, p. 22)

The Eldest member pronounced the final decision. Unfortunately Wolf's Brother was missing when the discussion took place and no one spoke for Wolf. When Wolf's Brother returned, he advised against the move to the "New Place" because it was the "Center Place" for the "great Community of Wolf" (Spencer, 1983, p. 25). Wolf's Brother warned that the new place would be too small for the Wolf community and the tribe. He knew Wolf so well that sometimes their "young followed him through the forest" (p.18). Already committed to their decision, tribal members refused to listen. The new place was ideal except for the presence of "Wolf Watching from the Shadows" (p. 27).

After the move to the new place, tribal members soon found fresh meat disappearing from their camp. Faced with Wolf's challenge to the tribe, a silent bargain was struck: Tribal members left food for Wolf in exchange for a place to live, eventually taming the Wolf. Unfortunately, Wolf grew bold enough to walk through camp, scrounging for food and causing alarm in the women and children (Spencer, 1983, p. 28). Eventually a plan was devised to drive off Wolf, guard the camp, and cause Wolf to return to a natural state. The battle with Wolf consumed so much effort that tribal members lacked energy to make winter preparations. The situation grew worse and the tribe held a meeting. Deeply troubled by the conflict and opposed to becoming Wolf killers, they decided to move to a new place where they would not be in conflict with Wolf. After the long winter passed, the tribe moved to a new place, learning a lesson about listening to and respecting Wolf.

AND SO IT WAS
That the People devised among themselves a way of asking each
    other questions
whenever a decision was to be made
on a New Place or a New Way
We sought to perceive the flow of energy
through each new possibility
and how much was enough

and how much was too much
UNTIL AT LAST
Someone would rise and ask the old, old question
to remind us of things
we do not yet see clearly enough to remember
"TELL ME NOW MY BROTHERS
TELL ME NOW MY SISTERS
WHO SPEAKS FOR WOLF?"

(Spencer, 1983, pp. 36–37)

A Native American story passed down through generations, *Who Speaks for Wolf: A Native American Learning Story as Told to Turtle Woman Singing by Her Father, Sharp-eyed Hawk*, warns us that unless all perspectives are considered, we may make unwise and costly decisions. The author of this story, Paula Underwood Spencer (1983) originally heard it from her father. At the end of each successive retelling, her father asked her, "And what may we learn from this?" (p. 9). The story contains many powerful lessons on decision making, listening, and inviting the lone voice, even when absent from the discussion, to speak his or her truth.

In this story Wolf might represent the marginalized, those with opposing views, messengers with news of an impending crisis, or even the silent co-inhabitants of the natural environment in need of our stewardship:

"We Indians think of the earth and the whole universe as a never-ending circle, and in this circle, man is just another animal," explains Jenny Leading Cloud of the Rosebud Indian Reservation. "The buffalo and the coyote are our brothers: the birds, our cousins. We end our prayers with the words—and that includes everything that grows, crawls, runs, creeps, hops, and flies." (*The Way of the Spirit*, 1997, p. 11)

The voices we refuse to hear, like Wolf's Brother, Wolf and his brothers, sisters, and cousins, may save us from foolishness, self-indulgence, complacency, contentedness, or our reluctance to believe and heed a doomsday message. Natural human tendencies explain our resistance to invite and listen to others, particularly those who offer a counterview to our reality. In part, this automatic resistance is based on the desire to satisfy human needs.

Maslow devised a "Hierarchy of Needs" to describe and explain human needs and behavior (Bolman & Deal, 2003, p. 117). Physiological needs include the basic need to maintain our bodily or biological functions that are the most basic to our survival. Moving up the hierarchy, safety needs include the things needed for stability, having a job, being safe in one's family, and being free from violence or harm. Loving and belonging needs include the desire for acceptance and the experience of affection, intimacy, and love from a partner, friend, or family member. Humans seek approval from others as support for their status and "esteem" needs, including feeling important, being visible to others, and being recognized for our accomplishments. Finally, the highest level is actualization, where individuals achieve self-actualization (Johnson & Johnson, 2000).

Advancing yet another (and somewhat complementary) theory of human needs, Glasser (1998) describes the following basic needs: (1) survival; (2) love, love and sex, and belonging; (3) power; and (4) freedom (pp. 31–41). The first two basic needs are well described in Maslow's theory. However, Glasser's ideas related to power go beyond Maslow's need for esteem and status, emphasizing the drive to accumulate power among humans. "Power for the sake of power is unique to our species" (Glasser, 1998, p. 37). This "powerful" drive explains the tendency to ignore the voice of the lone "Wolf."

If we hear Wolf, we may have to change or share power "with others." Admittedly, power helps us to provide for our families, access resources, and feel safe. Yet at the same time, an excess accumulation of power or privilege at the expense of others allows us to enjoy "unearned advantage" as both a cause and effect of oppression (Hobgood, 2000). Seeking to enjoy privilege and maintain power, the powerful often attempt to frame and control reality. Although we are not always aware of the drive to get and maintain our power, we are often subconsciously guided by this desire and may not inspect our desires unless confronted by those we seek to marginalize.

Neither evil nor good, power is an element in human behavior, and as such it serves as an important motivation for our behavior. Sometimes in our desire to maintain power, we lose it by not sharing it, listening to those who threaten us, or increasing power through the empowerment of others. Although this seems counterintuitive, we may have to share power in order to keep it, requiring us to work against the natural desire to protect our self-interests (sometimes at the expense of others) and instead provide for the common good.

Oppression occurs when power is tightly held by the privileged few and limits our freedom. Glasser (1998) defines freedom as "evolution's attempt to provide the correct balance between your need to try to force me to live my life the way you want and my need to be free of that force" (pp. 39–40). The absence of freedom causes great pain because it limits our opportunity to express ourselves and be creative. "Whenever we lose freedom, we reduce or lose what may be a defining human characteristic: our ability to be constructively creative" (p. 40). Threats to human needs are negatively viewed and opposed. While Wolf may offer us wisdom, perspective, and information, we need to see his or her voice as an opportunity for learning and a necessary ingredient of a free and democratic life.

Ethical leaders listen with the intent to include others, gain perspective and wisdom, and expand the opportunities for freedom within us. As group members, we often work against the voice of Wolf for similar reasons, but this time based on the survival needs of the group. Sometimes we even refuse to listen to the unimaginable.

Elie Wiesel, in *Night,* tells the true story of Moshe the Beadle, a devout Hasidic Jewish resident of Sighet, Transylvania. Moshe survived a Nazi death camp by escaping his captors after pretending to be dead and later returned to warn fellow Jews of their impending doom. Finding the twelve-year-old Wiesel on a bench near the synagogue, Moshe (as told by Wiesel) describes his deportation and near-death experience:

> The train full of deportees had crossed the Hungarian frontier and on Polish territory had been taken in charge by the Gestapo. There it had stopped. The Jews had to get out and climb into lorries. The lorries drove toward a forest. The Jews were made to get out. They were made to dig huge graves. And when they had finished their work, the Gestapo began theirs. Without passion, without haste, they slaughtered the prisoners. Each one had to walk up to the hole and present his neck. Babies were thrown into the air and machine gunners used them as targets. This was in the forest of Galicia, near Kolomaye. How had Moshe the Beadle escaped? Miraculously. He was wounded in the leg and taken for dead. (Wiesel, 1960, p. 4)

Traveling from one Jewish home to another, Moshe told his story, describing in painful detail the horrible deaths of people known to those he talked to. Ignoring his story and choosing instead to believe that Moshe was motivated by a desire for pity, no one listened to him at the end of 1942. "The Jews of Sighet were waiting for better days" (Wiesel, 1960, p. 5), falsely believing things would improve despite the steady advance of the German army. In 1944, the Jews of Sighet were ordered to make room for German soldiers in their homes; they were now residents of an occupied city. Later, they were forcibly moved to a ghetto established to control and quarantine Jews. Wiesel's father passed up a chance to escape from the ghetto, still not believing the worst and ignoring Moshe the Beadle's dire warning, reissued in 1944 (p. 6). The Jews of Sighet could not imagine the fate that awaited them, even when the evidence of their impending demise appeared irrefutable. Wiesel lost his entire family, including his mother, two sisters, and father, between 1944 and 1945 in Nazi concentration camps. Cautioning us against complacency, Wiesel warns, "to remain silent and indifferent is the greatest sin of all" (DePaul University, 1997, p. 1).

GROUPTHINK, MENTAL TRAPS, AND AVOIDANCE STRATEGIES

When individual human desires to avoid change are combined with the "concurrence seeking" behaviors of group members determined to maintain their current reality (Johnson & Johnson, 2000, p. 302), the early stages of a crisis are often ignored. In the case of the Sighet Jews, individuals resisted the idea of losing their lives and the group collectively "agreed" that there was nothing to worry about, silencing the voice of Moshe the Beadle. Surely the Germans would be stopped, and they would be saved. The phenomenon of "groupthink," a term coined by Irving Janis, explains the tendency of group members to avoid conflict and maintain a more favorable point of view by ignoring alternative viewpoints.

Janis defined groupthink as

> the collective striving for unanimity that overrides group members' motivation to realistically appraise alternative courses of action and thereby

leads to (a) a deterioration of mental efficiency, reality testing, and moral judgment, and (b) the ignoring of external information inconsistent with the favored alternative course of action. (Johnson & Johnson, 2000, p. 302)

Groupthink threatens survival, masking the appearance of danger by minimizing or denying its existence. After studying a number of historical fiascoes (for example, Pearl Harbor and the Bay of Pigs invasion), Janis identified the following eight factors that contribute to the likelihood of groupthink:

1. *Self-censorship* (members fail to voice their doubts)
2. *Illusion of unanimity* (members assume everyone else agrees with the common viewpoint except themselves)
3. *Direct pressure on dissenters* (members pressure others to conform)
4. *Mind guard* (members prevent others from raising objections)
5. *Illusion of invulnerability* (members believe the group can't be wrong)
6. *Rationalization* (members justify actions, blocking misgivings)
7. *Illusion of morality* (members assume the group's actions are moral)
8. *Stereotyping* (members cast critics and opponents as weak, stupid, or evil)

(Johnson & Johnson, 2000, pp. 302–303)

Many elements of groupthink were present in the ancient story of Wolf and the modern story of the Jews of Sighet. After the Elder announced the decision, tribal members were invested in it and failed to listen to Wolf Brother's objections. Justifying their move, tribal members rationalized their decision by claiming that Wolf would live in peace with the tribe despite their awareness that the new place was in the center of the Wolf community. The Jews of Sighet reassured each other that their viewpoint was correct by regularly meeting and reassuring each other. Because everyone agreed, the group suffered from the illusion of invulnerability. Stereotyping Moshe the Beadle, the group both pitied and ridiculed him, describing him as mentally ill or in desperate need of attention. Eventually Moshe fell silent. Whether in matters of life and death, organizational health or failure, or individual survival or tragedy, listening to all voices and avoiding groupthink help us to see the current reality.

Leaders must work through linguistic or cultural barriers that interfere with effective communication. Barriers refer to the physical or psychological "noise" that gets in the way of effective communication (Johnson & Johnson, 2000). The following factors increase the presence of "noise" in interpersonal and group communication:

(1) how a group member is perceived; (2) how much information a group member thinks each of the others has; 3) how trustworthy a member has been in the past; (4) how the messages are formulated and sent; (5) what receiving skills are used; (6) how cooperative the group is, and (7) whether the member believe his or her information will contribute to the group's efforts. (pp. 156–157)

Each interaction sets the stage for the next exchange. The "noise" experienced in communication may be a result of our previous negative interactions, creating a dynamic situation in which the previous experience causes us to avoid contact or discount the viewpoints of others. A positive outcome yields the opposite effect, creating a deposit in the "bank account of trust" (Covey, 1989, pp. 188–190).

Positive and negative interactions create a communication history, predisposing our attitudes before the communication event. Racism, sexism, and ethnic differences influence "speech events" by operating under the surface as undetected "psychological noise" (Johnson & Johnson, 2000), often interfering with our ability to authentically listen to and engage with others. Historical and cultural barriers get in the way of seeing, interacting, and understanding the experiences of diverse others.

Effective listeners and speakers, sensitive to the potential cultural and psychological barriers that exist in one-to-one or group communication, use this awareness to be patient and adjust their communication strategies to encourage participation. A teacher's story about José, an "elective mute," draws our attention to the importance of a creating a welcoming environment; accepting others; and being patient, loving, and caring in relationships to achieve understanding.

JOSÉ FINDS HIS VOICE

Years ago, when I was teaching in a small school in central Mexico, I met José Manuel, one of the many young heroes who have inspired me. I like to tell the story of this little boy because my experience with him profoundly moved me, and our experience together as teacher and student was transformational. An important lesson I learned about leadership and followership and how we stay connected to one another in and through [words] both [sic] came in the form of my struggle to help José Manuel find his voice.

From the day in September when I met this tiny kindergartner until the following spring, he spoke not a single word at school. After consulting with a child psychologist, my colleagues, my mother, a number of books and research articles, I found that there was a name for José Manuel's condition— Elective Mute. The advice that I was consistently given was to continue talking, talking, talking to him as though I thoroughly expected at any time for him to join me, or anyone for that matter, in conversation. My job at the school was to immerse the young students in English. I laugh now when I think of the countless one-way conversations I conducted in a language that he didn't speak and I was sure he didn't understand! I told him several times a day in as many ways as I could that I was sure that one day he would talk to me.

Acting as both a leader (teacher) and a follower (a learner of this new methodology) I made a leap of faith in what the experts reassured would eventually be the key to breaking his silence. I remember the day when I resorted to song, rather than my endless chit-chat. While dancing a lively jig to an American classic, I heard a tiny giggle. My heart leapt!

José never did talk to, or even make eye contact with, me or any other person at the school during his kindergarten year. On the last day of school, at an all-school assembly, the Director announced that I would be returning to the United States. Traditional songs and dances of farewell followed her announcement as I snapped one photo after another in an attempt to capture this memorable moment in a tidy little photo essay that I could share with friends and family upon my return to "the States."

Suddenly, I was looking through the viewer of my camera straight into José Manuel's eyes, which were filled with tears. Later that day as I walked home from school, a car pulled up next to me. José Manuel and his mother, seated in the back seat of a taxi, both smiled nervously. "Dile (Tell her)!" she told him. After ducking for cover and being pulled up from the floor of the cab several times, finally he spoke. It was the first and only time that I would ever hear his voice.

In broken English, he repeated a phrase that I had said to him at least a thousand times, "That's O.K. honey, I know you be alright." His mother beamed with pride, "¡Ya sabe Ingles (He speaks English)!" Giggling, José retreated quickly back to the floor of the cab as they pulled away. (Hoy, 2006, pp. 1–2)

José's story reminds us of those who can't speak for themselves or lack the ability to fully participate because of cultural differences and limited access to language. Waiting patiently and continuing to issue the invitation helps others eventually overcome the barriers to listening and being heard. Hosting a welcoming environment, Hoy models inclusive leadership—she's committed to engaging with others to break through the often-distancing barriers of language or cultural difference.

In the next story, Tom Whelihan shows the importance of speaking on behalf of others when their requests fall on deaf ears.

BECOMING A VOICE FOR OTHERS: THE SILENT AGREEMENT

I attended a little league baseball game last summer. It was the last game of the season, bottom of the 6th, and my son's team was behind 21–2. There was no hope. One of the kids on the team who had a severe learning disability and wasn't particularly coordinated at baseball, expressed an interest in pitching the last inning. His mother happened to be an auxiliary coach.

She approached the head coach and asked if her son could pitch the rest of the game. Without hesitation, he said "No." She asked again and this time expressed her rationale for the request. She stated that this would mean so much to her son and it would be his capstone experience for the whole season. And it would make him so happy. Again, with a somewhat irritated demeanor, the head coach denied the request and began to provide his rationale for the denial. He stated, "John would not even be able to get the ball across the plate. It would be a humiliating experience for him and it would be too embarrassing."

The mother finally walked quietly out of the dugout in despair. Throughout this whole dialogue another father and I were standing a few feet away, listening. Without saying a word, we exchanged glances. In that exchange, we developed a strategy without having to say a word to each other. We had agreed to do everything we could to convince the coach to let John pitch, and not a word was spoken. It was really an amazing experience. I began by encouraging the coach to take the risk. I said, "What would it matter, we're getting our butts kicked anyway?" The coach folded his arms in defiance and started to respond to my request. Immediately, the other father reinforced my request and we began a verbal volley intended to wear the coach down.

Several minutes passed and the ump walked over and told us to start the game. Reluctantly, the coach finally acquiesced and walked John to the pitcher's mound. The first pitch made it halfway to the plate and the second pitch fell a few inches short of the plate. Of course, it didn't really matter if the pitch hit the catcher's glove. He had the biggest smile on his face and the crowd was cheering him on. It was a great moment! I had chills going down my spine. On the third pitch, the ball made it across the plate and the batter hit the ball into the infield. I thought John was going to explode with joy. The crowd went wild.

In a small way, this story exemplifies my notion of what it means to lead a good life. You try to serve others in some way every day, and you assume responsibility to give voice to those whose voices have been silenced. For me, this is the essence of leadership. In the end analysis, living a good life involves working for a world that I will never see. It means that I will commit my life to being a voice for those who, for whatever reason, don't have a voice. (Whelihan, 2005, pp. 22–23)

In this story, listening (and overhearing) alerted a bystander to the presence of injustice, calling him and the other parent to serve as advocates. Objecting to the coach's decision and cajoling him to change his view, the two men prevented an ill-considered and painful decision from harming a mother and son, increasing their integrity by taking action. "The road to integrity is paved with speaking up about and acting on small corruptions of principles as we encounter them; left unchecked, these moral pot holes can become sink holes that swallow the common purpose" (Chaleff, 2003, p. 104). Physical and cultural distance poses challenges in communication, limiting our experience of *otherness* and our understanding of diverse viewpoints, and sometimes preventing a sensitive response to a legitimate request.

Barriers to communication require us to negotiate meaning and create hospitable environments for all aspects of diversity, including race, ethnicity, gender, sexual orientation, socioeconomic status, religion, and lifestyle preferences, to name a few. As communication "hosts," leaders invite diverse voices to the table, where all are welcome to participate in dialogue. The importance of listening with an open mind and being fully inclusive of others, regardless of their positions, viewpoints, cultural differences, or lack of "expertise," should not be underestimated.

Cultural leaders show considerable skill and knowledge in communicating across cultures. Using effective interpersonal skills and drawing on

aspects of their cultural competence, cultural leaders successfully interact with diverse people and groups. Competent intercultural communicators exhibit the following skills: (1) intercultural sensitivity (readiness
to understand and appreciate cultural differences), (2) intercultural
awareness (understanding of cultural convention and behavior), and (3)
intercultural adroitness (detecting cultural cues and using knowledge to
respond appropriately in cultural interactions) (Chen & Starosta, 2006, p.
357). They value democratic and inclusive processes and serve as communication hosts in their organizations and communities.

Ancient and emerging human technologies invite people to enter into
dialogue by establishing a place, process, and practice for the exchange
of stories. Making a place for stories in organizational and community
life may be literal, symbolic, or both. On the site of the Anasazi tribal
homeland, archaeologists speculate that men and boys as early as AD
750 held religious ceremonies and tribal meetings in a unique structure
called a kiva:

> Usually a pueblo [cluster of homes in Southwestern United States] had at
> least one special subterranean community pithouse—a kiva, sometimes up
> to 60 feet in diameter. Most were entered through a hole in the roof. A
> stone bench for sitting lined the perimeter. There was a hole in the floor—
> now called a sipapu—symbolizing the people's connection from birth with
> Mother Earth. Near the center was a fireplace. Ventilator shafts on the
> sides made the kiva more livable. . . . Today, the Hopi and other descen-
> dants still use kivas (square and above ground in the case of the Hopi) for
> ceremonial, religious and celebratory purposes. (*Anasazi*, n.d., pp. 1, 3)

Women and children, excluded from entering the kiva, were left out
of these discussions. While men gathered to smoke, tell stories, discuss
matters of importance, hold spiritual ceremonies, and participate in celebrations, women and children stayed outside. Some archaeologists believe town hall–type meetings were held in these sacred spaces. Visitors
may tour kivas located in Colorado and New Mexico to experience a sacred space reserved for community rituals and discussion. Today, people
hold a kiva to discuss important matters in the spirit of dialogue. Arranging a room in circular or square fashion, members discuss important
issues to understand diverse perspectives, following guidelines established by a facilitator.

Adopting ground rules for dialogue developed by the facilitator or group, participants receive a topic for discussion, guiding questions, and a warning: Tell the truth from your perspective, listen with no interruptions, prepare your statements with care, limit your remarks and keep them on the topic, fill the space with your story, and avoid sharp words and judgments. The facilitator provides an opening topic, sometimes in the form of a question, and dialogue begins. A designated recorder takes notes and later summarizes and shares the key points of the discussion with the entire group. Everyone else listens and only speaks when the space and rules allow.

Individual viewpoints emerge in dialogue, offering visibility to both diverse perspectives and people. Participants explore issues, not their resolution. Debate polarizes discussion and should be avoided. Individuals speak their piece, avoiding a direct response to comments made by previous speakers, and often turn the dialogue in a different direction. Speakers add to the collective knowledge by offering their experience in story form and sharing its meaning to them and the discussion topic. Facilitators steer the group away from the premature exploration of solutions because it reduces the opportunity to hear diverse perspectives and narrows the range of available solutions. Solutions often emerge in the debriefing activity following the kiva experience or after days or months of dialogue.

The selection of issues for discussion must be undertaken with considerable care. Trust among members develops through dialogue and cannot be rushed. Speaking about personal matters before the group matures and proves itself trustworthy guards against exposing members to potential harm. Voluntary participation and self-disclosure offer some protection from others.

Different arrangements change the nature of the dialogue. Sometimes constituent groups sit together in rows facing the center, representing collectively different views based on roles or experience. For example, men might sit opposite women and discuss the way gender influences power or opportunities in their organization. Parents, students, administrators, and community members might be arranged in groups to discuss school rules or discipline. Often constituent groups discuss their concerns first in small groups before entering the space arranged for the kiva discussion. This allows the safe exploration of viewpoints and increases the likelihood that more people voluntarily participate in the kiva discussion.

Borrowing from Native American tradition, a talking stick may be passed to each speaker, providing order and giving him or her permission to proceed. Once the speaker receives the talking stick, he or she holds the floor for as long as he or she possesses the stick. Speakers take turns sharing their perspectives with others, talk slows down, listening sharpens, interruptions cease, and competition to speak ends.

Although viewpoints may not change, attitudes about the participants may undergo substantial change as participants examine viewpoints from alternative perspectives. The practice of holding a kiva establishes a culture of listening, encouraging full exploration of issues without penalty to individual members. Wheatley, author of *Leadership and the New Science* (1999), hosted an international conference called "From the Four Directions" (Baldwin, 2005, p. 186). Many international hosts and guests attended the conference, exchanging and exploring viewpoints to promote healing. Toke, an expert in facilitating dialogue, helped Baldwin and others learn the "Art of Hosting" (p. 187). Hosting, both a calling and vision for healing, emerges out of a commitment to use the generative processes of story to expand collective wisdom:

> Someone puts a staff in the ground and calls for a team of hosts to volunteer to hold the space for the three levels of story: the individual, the organizational, and the species. We bring people together of diverse nations and backgrounds, both those who call and those who answer the call. And what we create is a community of people who are practicing the power of conversation to change the world. (p. 187)

Leaders place faith in the power of story and host discussions, using story to share collective wisdom and accomplish global change. We tell our stories to claim identity, reach across boundaries, and seek opportunities in expressing on three levels: personal, community, and global (species). Stories intersect with lives, creating a consciousness that draws us in as fellow travelers on our journey. Conflict in the world and breakdowns in communication require us "to shift to a new level of consciousness, to reach a higher moral ground . . . to shed our fear and give hope to each other" (Maathai, 2004, pp. 26–27).

Intercultural leaders strive for new levels of consciousness and reduce barriers to authentic and respectful communication. What happens when dialogue fails and trust evaporates?

DIALOGUE FAILURE AND BREAKDOWNS

Dialogue failure occurs when relationships and the quality of communicative exchanges deteriorate. This becomes evident when the "failure of dialogue pertains primarily to damage done to the fabric of the dialogical relation itself: what cuts the discussion short, what pre-empts certain areas of investigation, or what silences or overwhelms certain points of view within it" (Burbules, 1993, p. 144). Control of the discussion, excessively long speeches, manipulation of others, and aggressive insistence on a single and dominant perspective contribute to dialogue breakdowns.

Caused by failures of spirit as well as a lack of communicative virtues, dialogue breakdowns resist repair. Participants who shout, exclude, embarrass others, talk *at* rather than to people, or operate from hidden motives and agenda destroy trust and limit the possibility of dialogue.

A few years ago, I (Sarah Noonan) worked with a small group of teachers who were experiencing a complete breakdown in communication. Conflict, tears, arguments, and requests for transfers revealed the depth of the problem. I worked with them as a consultant in "team building" to see what I could do to help the situation. I decided to ignore the looming problem and instead ask each person to describe the aspects of his or her work that were most rewarding and also describe the experience during the early years of working together as a team (approximately ten years). Group members listened to colleagues without interruption (a guideline adopted by the group) until all stories were expressed. The process took about four hours.

The teachers discovered several things: (1) They all felt passionately committed to the mission of the school and students, (2) they missed having meaningful discussions about the students, (3) the nature of their program demanded more from them than was reasonable to expect with declining resources and reduced staff, and (4) they remembered that they actually liked and respected each other. Laughter, tears, stories, and heartfelt emotion emerged from dialogue. They made a commitment to repair their relationships by reducing paperwork and scheduling discussions at their weekly meetings about students and important aspects of their program.

As the facilitator of the group I simply established the ground rules for respectful dialogue and listened. They did the rest. *Listening to diverse voices and locating turning points in dialogue—places where we are influenced and changed by others—inspires moral imagination and commitment to find a different way to be together.* In this way, dialogue serves as a foundation for personal and social transformation as well as cultural survivance in human communities.

⑭

CULTURAL IDENTITY AND SURVIVANCE: THE POWER AND GIFT OF CULTURAL STORY

There are always strangers, people with their own cultural memories, with voices aching to be heard.

—Greene (1988, p. 87)

Stories, ancient as life itself and deeply embedded within family and cultural traditions, transmit knowledge and shared meaning, linking people together in a human chain of history and memory. Drawing from human experience, cultural knowledge, traditions, beliefs, values, and history, leaders and members use story to facilitate the work of leadership in diverse communities. Leaders and members strive to ensure the survival and long-term stability of their families, social groups, and communities.

If families or social groups ignore threats to their survival, people and cultures may eventually become extinct. However, imposing rigid boundaries on membership and cultural practices and adaptations also creates conditions leading to decline and extinction. It turns out people and cultures need change to survive, yet must struggle to preserve identities in highly diverse environments. Individuals need autonomy to find meaning and leave their personal imprint on life as well as communities to embrace and shelter them.

The concept of survivance relates to the way people attempt to preserve cultural identity and heritage in the face of extinction. Exploring survivance from both dominant and marginalized viewpoints reveals the dialectical tensions in adaptation due to the accelerated rate of cultural change experienced by many in increasingly diverse environments. Many marginalized group members struggle to survive due to exclusionary practices by dominant groups and unequal access to power resources. Members of dominant groups feel the ground shaking and struggle with demands for cultural adaptation and change. Challenged by these tensions, democratic leaders affirm individual and cultural differences while simultaneously promoting social unity.

SURVIVANCE

Survivalists place their "personal and group survival as a primary goal in the face of difficulty, opposition, and especially the threat of natural catastrophe, nuclear threat or social collapse" (Pickett, 2000, p. 1743). Assuming a hostile environment, cultural survivalists fight to preserve their beliefs, values, and ways of living. A contemporary definition of survivance refers to the struggle of marginalized people to preserve their cultural identities and traditions due to the threats of extinction encountered in their environment or loss as a result of assimilation. Essentially, survivance seeks to ensure that people remain fundamentally true to themselves and their culture, fighting against cultural adaptation and assimilation. Yet "culture keeps on cooking," changing us despite our attempts to stay the same.

> Culture moves and expands through the same process as demographic growth, through seduction. Hear my music, eat my food, you are mine, you are me. Politics shakes its angry fist, theorists polemicize. Culture keeps on cooking. Culture just happens, and it happens more suavely when it tastes good. (Fernandez, 1994, p. 1)

The tensions in staying true to cultural values and traditions, yet thriving through cultural change and adaptation, are obvious. Internal threats to survivance occur when cultural values, traditions, stories, and language slowly fade from use. When competing people and cultures "colonize" others through coercive control or dominance, the external threat often weakens cultures, damaging existing cultural values and ultimately extinguishing them altogether. Cultures attract and change us.

Actively describing and engaging in expressions of culture (through storytelling, celebrations, and community meetings) keep culture alive and valued. Like an endangered species, thriving cultures lose ground and ultimately disappear when community members lose their vigilance. To counter this effect, many ethnic or tribal groups tell a creation story to identify the cultural distinctiveness and uniqueness of their group, building group identity and ownership in the community. These stories create a sense of belonging and group cohesion. They also divide us.

The following Ute creation story illustrates how a creation story works. As the story unfolds, listeners learn about the "birth" of the Utes as the chosen people as well as the "birth" of their enemies. Two characters, Sinawav the creator and Coyote, play lead roles in the story:

> In the days even before the ancient times, only Sinawav, the creator, and Coyote inhabited the earth. . . . The earth was young and the time had now come to increase the people. Sinawav gave a bag of sticks to Coyote and said, "Carry these over the far hills to the valleys beyond." He gave specific directions Coyote was to follow and told him what to do when he got there. "You must remember, this is a great responsibility. The bag must not be opened under any circumstances until you reach the sacred ground," he told him. (Wroth, Bates, Ellis, Fowler & Goss, 2000, p. 7)

You can guess what happens next. Coyote didn't get very far before his curiosity overcomes him. Out of sight and hoping to sneak a peek, Coyote opened the bag:

> Just as he untied the bag and opened a small slit, they rushed for the opening. They were people. These people yelled and hollered in strange languages of all kinds. He tried to catch them and get them back into the bag. But they ran away in all directions. (Wroth et al., 2000, p. 7)

Only a few sticks remained in the bag, and when Coyote reached the sacred ground, he dumped the remaining people out of the bag— the "real" Utes. Sinawav explained the effects of Coyote's foolishness,

"Those you let escape will forever war with the chosen ones. They will be the tribes which will always be a thorn in the sides of the Utes" (Wroth et al., 2000, p. 8). Unfortunately, Coyote, banished from the sacred grounds, was left to "wander this earth on all fours forever as a night crawler" (p. 8).

The Ute story contains many valuable cultural lessons. Affirming their significance as a tribal group, the "real" Utes, the "chosen ones," lived on sacred ground (the site of their ancestral home). In contrast, those who were prematurely released and spoke in strange languages would always be dangerous to them, threatening their very existence. Finally, a moral lesson completes the story: Those who fail to follow the lead of the Creator will be banished and left to crawl on the earth on all fours.

The underlying message of the tale is a "plausible" explanation for its origin and the portrayal of the stranger as the enemy. Cultural preservation sometimes comes at the cost of failing to see the humanity of others, particularly those most unlike us, who may be viewed as a potential threat to our existence. For example, the Ute creation story does not promote good will toward all humankind. The "sticks," the people who escaped prematurely and failed to make it to the sacred place, will always be a thorn in the side of the tribe. However, the story affirms the value of the Ute people and cultures, offering a way for Native Americans to claim and affirm their tribal identities.

Creation stories trace lineage, mark cultural identity, instill pride, and identify members and enemies. Drawing distinctive lines between in- and out-group members, some cultural stories emphasize distinctiveness and difference. In these stories "foreigners" threaten the tribe by their cultural differences; however, legitimate or "real" members are deemed worthy of protection and love. Stories of pioneers following the trail of westward expansion in colonial days portray European settlers as enlightened people and Native Americans as savages. Justifying the colonization of Native people and land, the story serves the teller, but is not an accurate or ethical accounting of what actually happened. Essentially all cultures need creation stories to preserve identity and culture. However, a literal interpretation of the creation story may justify exclusion, perhaps even violence toward others, because of ethnocentric views.

SEEING HUMANITY IN THE STRANGER

William Sumner coined the term "ethnocentrism" early in the twentieth century to describe the relationship and attitudes of group members who oppose each other during warfare (Forbes, 1985). According to Sumner, warfare causes ethnocentric members to develop "loyalty and approval of the distinctive customs and beliefs" of in-group members and display "hatred and contempt for outsiders" (p. 22). In the 1950s, the meaning of ethnocentrism expanded, and it now refers to "an ordinary person's unsophisticated reaction to cultural differences—[his or her] unthinking defense of familiar ways as absolutely right, and unqualified rejection of alien ways as simply wrong" (p. 22).

This group phenomenon influences individual responses to "otherness" based on group norms. People with ethnocentric views make generalizations about those perceived to be culturally different, often maintaining rigid, negative characterizations of individuals based on their membership in groups. Failing to use a critical eye to see deficiencies in in-groups, those with ethnocentric views assign only positive attributes to the members of their group. Extreme positions reveal the presence of ethnocentrism. During times of struggle and threatened extinction, stories told by warring groups exaggerate differences, often assigning negative traits to the outsiders to justify treating them poorly. Working against violence and exclusion, leaders resist rigid stereotypes and boundaries.

To see humanity in the stranger, foreigner, or enemy, the lines between cultural and social groups must be blurred to promote the mutual recognition of shared humanity, but must be distinctly maintained to preserve cultural values and people. Story helps us see the face of the stranger and know his or her life. The divisions diminish and the possibility of seeing others as fellow human beings increases. The tensions between preserving cultural identities yet seeing ourselves as members of the larger community must be negotiated, equally valued, and taught through the exchange of our cultural stories. Stories help us see how difference and commonality are interdependent and integral to achieving social unity. We must resist the temptation to harbor negative feelings and cultural hatred based on social norms of prejudice and bias and instead choose to value both unique and common aspects of our humanity. What brings forth pride can also promote exclusion and prejudice.

Members guard again the extinction of their culture because it ultimately causes the extinction of the "People." Recognizing the threat to
their cultural identity and way of life, marginalized people struggle to
maintain their culture and sense of community while simultaneously
claiming their rights and responsibilities of membership and agency in
the community at large. When we seek "an understanding of cultural
phenomena, people do not deal with the world event by event or with
text sentence by sentence," rather they "frame" events and experiences
in larger structures to provide an interpretive context (Bruner, 1990, p.
64). An understanding and application of social and cultural history help
people understand the context and meaning of cultural stories.

Survivance requires a kind of doggedness to withstand threats from
the external environment as well as a lapse of cultural knowledge and
sharing needed to provide continuity to its members.

The goals of survivance may exclude and marginalize others, imposing rigid instead of fluid boundaries. The rigidity leads to the demise of
dominant groups as well as co-cultural groups. Affirming the value in
our multiple identities while simultaneously recognizing the challenge
of overcoming our divisions, Said (1993) offers this perspective:

> No one today is purely one thing. Labels like Indian, or woman, or Mus-
> lim, or American are not more than starting-points, which if followed into
> actual experience for only a moment are quickly left behind. Imperialism
> consolidated the mixture of cultures and identities on a global scale. But its
> worst and most paradoxical gift was to allow people to believe that they
> were only, mainly, exclusively, white, or Black or Western, or Oriental. . . .
> No one can deny the persisting continuities of long traditions, sustained
> habitations, national languages, and cultural geographies, but there seems
> little reason except fear and prejudice to keep insisting on separation and
> distinctiveness, as if that was all human life was about. . . . It is more re-
> warding—and more difficult—to think concretely and sympathetically,
> contrapuntally, about others than only about "us." (p. 336)

When cultures lack good stories and break down, the culprit may be the
absence of cultural cohesion and purpose or an unwillingness to think
"concretely and sympathetically, contrapuntally" about others.

When cultural breakdown exists, stories or narratives reveal it. "To be
in a viable culture is to be bound in a set of connecting stories, connect-

ing even though the stories may not represent a consensus" (Bruner, 1990, p. 96). Bruner warns of three conditions in which dominant narratives reveal the breakdown of culture.

In the first condition, the narrative describes a breakdown in agreement regarding something viewed as "ordinary" compared to something considered "divergent" (he calls it the "battle of lifestyles"). These stories portray intergenerational (and perhaps now intercultural) conflict (Bruner, 1990, p. 96). Conflict represents the contrasting views of right or wrong, acceptable or unacceptable.

The next type of cultural breakdown reveals itself when "official stories" by the government appear "so ideologically or self-servingly motivated that distrust displaces interpretation and "what happened" is discounted as fabrication" (Bruner, 1990, p. 96). We find this in closed and restrictive societies or totalitarian regimes. Bruner also places "official" bureaucratic stories in this same category, where all "except the official story is silenced or stonewalled" (p. 96). We see cultural breakdown through our doubt regarding the story and distrust of the storyteller and the institution he or she represents.

Finally, the third condition occurs when the culture is bankrupt of stories—"a sheer impoverishment of narrative resources"—due to extreme conditions of hopelessness in which "worst scenario" stories reflect limited opportunities and experiences (for example, refugee camps, impoverished rural or urban areas, etc.) (pp. 96–97). We need stories to renew culture and sustain faith in the American dream.

Stories help us figure out our identity and, when shared with others, reveal our ongoing development and struggle as human beings. Some of the most powerful stories remain hidden because of the reluctance of first generation immigrants to trust others and share their struggle to make it in America. They have often endured considerable hardship and showed courage and perseverance in seemingly impossible circumstances to support themselves, their families, and quite often, their extended families.

For example, my friend Carol waited ten years to receive her paperwork to leave South Vietnam and enter the United States with her eleven-year-old daughter after the Vietnam War. Carol's husband left during the closing days of the war, granted asylum because he fought with the Americans against the North Vietnamese. Arriving in

San Francisco without any money or knowledge of the English language, Carol soon learned that her husband had divorced her during their ten-year separation and a new wife and family now lived with him. Carol exclaimed, "No home. No money. No English!" Homeless and terrified, Carol worked as a seamstress for low wages and lived in her brother's home with her daughter. Working long hours and saving money, she finally earned enough to rent a small apartment and live in relative poverty with her daughter.

Carol said she cried silently every night after her daughter fell asleep so as not to worry her. Because of strict Vietnamese conventions even in the United States, Carol was not allowed to go out after 9:00 P.M. or date anyone without her daughter present as a chaperone. When her boyfriend asked her to marry him, she asked her daughter for her approval. Her daughter said yes, and she married him, went back to school, and later opened a nail salon. Now a successful businesswoman, she earns a good living and no longer cries with fear in the night.

Carol described the difference in freedom for women in America. In Vietnam, a young woman marries a man and immediately moves into her husband's home, becoming more like a servant to the family than a real member. Women are not allowed to disagree with their husbands or their families. The men often adjust to a different way in America, where women enjoy more freedom. Carol's daughter grew up, married, and gave birth to a boy.

Now a grandmother, Carol dotes on her grandson, who speaks fluent English, Vietnamese, Chinese, and some French. *He's six years old*. The next generation lives globally and multiculturally, crossing many boundaries and fluidly blending and remaking American culture. Immigrant stories attract our attention because, as a nation of pioneers, we love an adventure story.

Immigrant stories also offer hope to people who have fled their countries under difficult circumstances, leaving despair behind them, surviving a perilous journey, and adapting to a new life miles from home. The following story about a young man who walked for three months across his country to survive shows how resourcefulness, courage, and adaptability helped him escape terror and claim a new life.

FLEEING ETHIOPIA: GORSE'S STORY

When Ethiopian Emperor Haile Selassie was overthrown in 1974, a military committee, known as the Dergue, governed the country (*The Dergue (1974–1991)*, n.d.). The Dergue initiated socialist reforms to distribute land to peasants and nationalize industries and services. Conflict emerged over the next few years about changes in social policy (redistribution of lands, nationalizing industries and services), disputes over the Eritrean border, and the struggle for power among the leaders of the Dergue. Opposition groups formed against the Dergue, creating conditions for a civil war. The Western Somali Liberation Front (WSLF) and the Eritrean rebels (EPLF) were the two main vanguards to secede from Ethiopia in the 1970s and oppose the Dergue.

Mengistu Hailemariam, who eventually emerged as the sole leader of the Dergue, initiated a reign of terror, ordering mass executions. Those suspected of supporting opposition groups were imprisoned, tortured, or executed. Bodies were left in the streets and across the countryside for several days to serve as a warning to others. Only the government was allowed to collect the bodies (*The Dergue (1974–1991)*, n.d).

In 1977, Somalia invaded Ethiopia and occupied the Western Somali Region, now called Somali Region State. In desperate need of forces to fight the rebels, Mengisut asked the Soviet Union and Cuba for support. "Thousands of Cuban and Russian personnel and armed forces came to the aid of the Mengistu regime and were involved in military planning and fighting against Somalia" (*The Dergue (1974–1991)*, n.d., p. 5).

Caught in the middle of a foreign invasion and civil war, Ismail Gorse, a fifteen-year-old living in Dire Dawa, Ethiopia, fled for his life, leaving his family and home behind. The following account describes the next thirty years of his life, including his experience fleeing Ethiopia, living in a refugee camp and going to school in Djibouti, immigrating to Canada to attend college, and later marrying and raising a family in the United States. [Gorse, personal communication, March 25, 2007]

When rebel troops arrived at the outskirts of Dire Dawa around 11:00 A.M. in July 1977, many residents stayed calm because the rebels had considerable support in the city. As the rebels entered the city, people assumed the Ethiopian military soldiers would flee. The calm lasted only a few hours. By 6:00 P.M., helicopters overhead bombed the city while soldiers fought in hand-to-hand combat in the streets with rebel forces. When the bombs went off, people fled for their lives. Young Gorse, caught in the crossfire, fled into the countryside, leaving behind his family and home. He left with nothing but the clothes on his back, lacking money, food, or provisions of any kind.

On the outskirts of the city, Gorse jubilantly found six boyhood friends who had played soccer and attended school together. They formed a group of seven who fled in terror, wandering for nine days in the countryside trying to escape the war and avoid all the dead bodies. "For nine days all we saw were dead bodies. No matter what direction we took, dead bodies," Gorse said. They were lost and living on food provided by generous people who lived in the countryside. On the ninth day, the young men saw the lights of the city at night and realized that despite their days of wandering, they had returned back to where they had started, the outskirts of Dire Dawa. Fortunately, that night they met some rebel fighters, who transported them out of the conflict zone. They rode a "lorry" (a wagon attached to an animal to transport people) into their first refugee camp, stayed the night, and learned their fate for the next three months.

After receiving meager provisions, the seven men (perhaps no longer young after surviving in the woods) were told what to do. Anyone who could walk should begin immediately and try to make it to Djibouti, a neighboring country with many Somali tribal members sympathetic to the rebels and willing to accept refugees. The boys, now men, set out to walk across 300 kilometers of wooded and hazardous terrain. The journey to Djibouti took three months to complete. They soon adjusted to the terrain, stopping at night to avoid wild animals, receiving help from strangers, walking alone, and sometimes encountering refugee groups for a part of their journey. One of the men had to stop because he simply could not walk any longer. They waited several days for him to recover but eventually had to continue their journey without him. Amazingly, he later made it to the refugee camp with the help of others.

Weary from a three-month walk and with no possessions or identification, six men crossed the border, traveled to a refugee camp, and joined approximately half a million other people in need of relief and assistance. Gorse and his friends stayed together for three more months, sharing two tents and daily rations of food. Relief workers and officials interviewed refugees, administered tests, and eventually made assignments based on the results.

Because Gorse spoke French, the official language of Djibouti, he received his first assignment, to attend school in a nearby city. Thus, he separated from his five remaining companions. Gorse moved to another refugee camp close to the city of Djibouti Ville and entered the ninth grade. He progressed well and graduated in 1981. During high school Gorse worked part-time for the United Nations High Commission for Refugees (UNHCR), serving as a translator because he spoke five Ethiopian dialects as well as French. After graduation, his part-time job became a full-time career.

During his first year in high school, Gorse also located his family. His parents had stayed in Dire Dawa, while several of his siblings relocated to Djibouti Ville. Because of these circumstances, when Gorse's father died, he was unable to attend his funeral. His mother joined his sister in Djibouti Ville and at least some of his family members were reunited.

Gradually, Gorse put his life back together through hard work and education. Four years after graduating from high school, Gorse received a scholarship to Ottawa University in Canada, left Djibouti Ville, and moved to Canada to study engineering. He applied for a work visa during his college years and struggled to support himself. Later, Gorse applied for asylum in Canada and became a citizen. Graduating with an engineering degree, Gorse renewed contact with a young woman he had met in the Djibouti refugee camp and married her in 1988. His spouse, who had immigrated to North Dakota due to the kindness of a Midwestern family, had become a U.S. citizen. After the marriage the couple moved to Minneapolis, Minnesota, in 1989 and started their life together. Gorse learned English after the move.

Educated but without experience, Gorse struggled to find an engineering position. While working as a custodian at night, Gorse volunteered to work *for free* to gain experience at Juno Enterprise. He did this for eight months, until they offered him a full-time position as a technician. Wishing to advance his career, Gorse enrolled in graduate school at the University of St. Thomas (UST) and earned a master of science degree in computer science in May 2003. He joined Medtronic, Inc., as an engineer in 2003, where he works today (2007). Seeking more education and credentials, Gorse applied to, was accepted by, and began a doctoral program in leadership at the UST in the summer of 2003. He plans to graduate in 2009.

Gorse became heavily involved in community work, family life, and education. When he first moved to Minneapolis there were approximately thirty or forty other Somali families there. Today, more than 25,000 Somali immigrants live in Minnesota, many of whom practice the Muslim faith (Brown, 2007, p. A1). It's not surprising that Minnesota elected the first Muslim member of the national House of Representatives, who took his oath of office using the Koran (January, 2007).

Describing the conditions for Somalis before and after 9/11, Gorse discusses the challenges of cultural survival, clashes, and adaptation. He said that many refugees may have fled for their lives and live in fear of returning to war-torn countries. Because of 9/11, obtaining employment is difficult and distrust separates people. People live in fear of being sent home. The obligations of family require that those living in the United States send money home to help their extended families. Conflicts over religious practices and customs increase distance between people, and dialogue is needed to overcome these barriers. Gorse's answer to the struggle between cultures is simple: We have to get to know each other so that we can hear and share our stories.

Regarding opportunity in America, Gorse said, "What can you get out of it? After all the work and education, can you get a job?" The opportunity exists for people to make it; however, they need others to give them a chance not based on racial or ethnic diversity but rather on economic need and life circumstances. Although we learn a lot from the past, Gorse says, "Looking back can send thoughts spinning in our minds; sometimes we need to disassociate, leave the past behind, and try to be happy."

Often immigrants find themselves at the borders of a country or living at the edge of their communities, not fully accepted in America. Challenged to preserve their cultures as well as assimilate, immigrants experience tensions within themselves, trying to live in their cultural communities as well as within the multiethnic cultures of the larger community. Cultural tensions and conflict cause people to retreat within their cultural communities and impose rigid boundaries on others. For example, some argue that immigrants must claim their American identity by ignoring or abandoning their cultural identity, effectively requiring them to choose one identity over another.

Those who frame the debate in this way may conveniently ignore the existence of their fraternal organizations and programs fostering intercultural exchange. Sarah Noonan lives across the street from the Swedish Institute in Minneapolis, Minnesota. Plenty of people explore Swedish culture and search for their cultural roots. American cities adopt "sister cities" in European and Scandinavian countries without considering it an unpatriotic act, yet disparage immigrants from other parts of the world for desiring to preserve their culture. We simply have to recognize the need to adapt to general aspects of culture, yet preserve the particular, local, and personal aspects of our family and cultural origins.

The tensions and complexity of the challenge call us to make inner changes to preserve identity as well as social unity. Takaki, author of *A Different Mirror: A History of Multicultural America*, offers Anzaldua's solution:

> Together, we have created what Gloria Anzaldua celebrated as a "borderland"—a place where "two or more cultures edge each other, where people of different races occupy the same territory." How can all of us meet on communal ground? "The struggle," Anzaldua responded, "is inner: Chicano, Indio, American Indian, Mojado, Mexicano, immigrant Latino, Anglo in power, working class Anglo, Black, Asian—our psyches resemble the border towns and are populated by the same people. . . . Awareness of our situation must come before inner changes, which in turn come before changes in society." (Takaki, 1993, p. 426)

The process begins within us but must also be adopted by members of the larger community who are willing to explore cultural difference through dialogue, sharing stories, and staying open to learning from each other. Inspiring a national passion for individual freedom as well as freedom found within communities (Greene, 1988), Gorse's story challenges us to see how those from a distant shore contribute to our national culture. "Meanings are made within contexts not only of private thought and event, but within the contexts of dialogue with those significant others who teach us, confirm us, challenge us and contradict us" (Carlsen, 1988, p. vii). Their stories continually renew and inspire the American dream—a dream that is sometimes myth, sometimes reality, but always an ideal *for those coming to the borders* and *those already here*.

The universal importance and communal nature of story and its relationship to survival of "the People" illustrate the way wisdom emerges through the exchange of story.

AN AFRICAN TALE

An African tale reveals the way one tribe struggled against the adversity found in nature. In this story the environment serves as a metaphor for the threats to their survival:

> But when People gathered once again around the fire telling the story of all that had happened, something new came to mind. "We have overcome the strength of Elephant," they said, "and our fear of Shark and Hawk. We have done this by sitting by the fire and telling stories of what has happened to us, and learning from them. Only we, among all the creatures, have the gift of story and the wisdom it brings. We do not need to be masters of the earth. We can share because it is wise to do so." From this day on the People held their heads high, never forgetting to sit by the fire and tell their stories. Never forgetting that in the stories could be found wisdom and in wisdom, strength. (Brown & Moffett, 1999, p. 103)

Linking history, present circumstances, and future visions, transformational leaders know how the exchange of cultural stories serves as a vehicle to explain the past, reveal the complexities and challenges of current conditions, and inspire us to consider new directions. Our past lives and evolving stories sometimes serve us by restraining us from ill-considered actions, while at other times stories may trap us by imposing unexamined, rigid ideas, routines, and roles. A close inspection of their influence offers insights about our motivations and goals as well as an opportunity to reflect on how the lived experience fundamentally changed us. The past, ever present in our daily decisions, frees or haunts us.

Personal, organizational, community, and global stories locate us in a place and time, chronologically establishing what happened, what it meant, and its significance to the way we live now. As people construct their present stories by sharing their daily experiences, they may lack the ability to see what is real and in front of them because of a limited horizon. Past stories serve as starting points to examine a novel problem in light of our experience as well as to compare these experiences to the current reality, whether through personal accounts or historical events.

Leaders manage the tensions inherent in preserving organizations and communities while simultaneously addressing dynamic changes within the environment, striking a balance between the two to ensure survival and growth. We can't ignore the past or stay in it too long. Leaders in diverse communities see the intimate connection between survivance and cultural story, facilitating the exchange of cultural stories as a central tool in the leadership they offer and share collectively with others. As the world in which we live becomes more complex, no ethical text exists to provide us with all the answers we need to life's situations:

> [P]aradoxically, the more complex things become the more personal the ethical judgments have to be. Cultural pluralism, diffusion of power and horizontalness of decision making require us to think of the public interest not as a code of ethics for the world, or for the nation, or even for a single organization, but as a nontransferable way of thinking. (Cleveland, 2002, p. 177)

Stories enrich and expand our culture, forge and maintain relationships, and "change minds" within diverse communities (Gardner, 2004). Whether individual or collective, leadership emanates from our membership, participation, and experience in cultural groups. "The underlying reason for the affinity between leadership and storytelling is simple: narrative—unlike abstractions and analysis—is inherently collaborative" (Denning, 2004, p. 149). Managing the tensions between individual and cultural distinctiveness as well as promoting social unity, leaders use story to invite members to use their gifts, such as authorship, love, power, and significance (Bolman & Deal, 2001), to fulfill both private and public dreams.

Called to engage in leadership with fellow travelers in a transglobal world, we take our place by the fire and breathe life into the community through the power of story, sharing knowledge about the ancient ways to live as well as learning from each other through the present interpretation of its meaning. The larger human story flows through the little stories of our lives in families, neighborhoods, and communities. Entering the river from our sacred places, we step into the water, traveling through time and space together, sharing our wisdom through story.

If we have been true to the "story ethic" in this book, the stories we offered you promoted the very changes we seek to make in the world: more ethical, collaborative, and intelligent leadership in the world. Let us know if we have succeeded by telling us what you think and sharing some of your stories with Sarah J. Noonan (sjnoonan@stthomas.edu) and Thomas L. Fish (tlfish@stthomas.edu).

REFERENCES

Ackerman, R., & Maslin-Ostrowski, P. (2002). *The wounded leader: How real leadership emerges in times of crisis.* San Francisco: Jossey-Bass.

Air Force Policy Directive. (2006, March 14). *Air Force instruction 11–2C-130, volume 3. Flying operations, C-130 operations procedures*, at www.e-publishing.af.mil

Alterman, E. (2004). *When presidents lie: A history of official deception and its consequences.* New York: Viking Adult.

All about Sunflower. (n.d.). Retrieved May 19, 2007, from www.sunflowernsa.com/all-about/default.asp?contentID=41

Allan, J., Fairtlough, G., & Heinzen, B. (2001). *The power of the tale.* West Sussex, England: John Wiley & Sons.

Allen, A. (2004). *The new ethics: A tour of the 21st-century moral landscape.* New York: Miramax Books.

Ambulance crew entranced by GPS navigation machine. (2006, December 7). Retrieved March 29, 2007, from www.npr.org/templates/story/story.php?storyId=6591629

Anasazi: More about kivas. (n.d.). Retrieved March 29, 2007, from www.cliffdwellingsmuseum.com/arch3.htm

Angelou, M. (2002). *A song flung up to heaven.* New York: Bantam Books.

Angus, L., & McLeod, J. (Eds.). (2004). *The handbook of narrative and psychotherapy: Practice, theory, and research.* Thousand Oaks, CA: Sage Publications.

Applebaum, A. (2006, December 17). Iran's president and others continue to ignore history by questioning the reality of the Holocaust. *StarTribune*, AA1, AA5.

Applebaum, B. (2005, September). In the name of morality: moral responsibility, whiteness and social justice education. *Journal of Moral Education*, 34(3), 277–290. Retrieved July 27, 2007, from Academic Search Premier database.

Argyris, C. (2004). *Reasons and rationalizations: The limits to organizational knowledge.* New York: Oxford University Press.

Armstrong, D. (1992). *Managing by storying around: A new method of leadership.* New York: Doubleday Currency.

Associated Press, MSNBC. (2006a, May 26). *Top NY heart surgeon scrubs out to save 8-year-old boy in El Salvador.* Retrieved March 10, 2007, from www.msnbc.msn.com/id/12995881/

Associated Press, MSNBC. (2006b, October 24). Man with amnesia reunited with family, friends. Retrieved May 24, 2007, from www.msnbc.msn.com/id/15373503/

Associated Press, MSNBC. (2006c, November 2). Amnesia sufferer struggling to recover. Retrieved May 24, 2007, from www.msnbc.msn.com/id/15538099/

Associated Press. (2007a, January 3). Cell phone saves man in garbage truck. *Star Tribune*, A7.

Associated Press, MSNBC. (2007, January 3). Hero saves teen who fell on NYC subway tracks. Retrieved January 16, 2007, from www.msnbc.msn.com/id/16444249/

Associated Press. (2007, March 6). Gay activists nationally praise lawmaker. *Billings Gazette.* Retrieved March 18, 2007, from www.billingsgazette.net/articles/2007/03/06/news/wyoming/20–zwonitzer.txt?CFID=6267&CFTOKEN=91935549

Awumey, E., & Harmon, M. (2004). What was the saddest moment of your life? StoryCorps. Retrieved March 19, 2007, from http://storycorps.net/listen/

Bakken, E. (1999). *One man's full life.* Minneapolis, MN: Medtronic, Inc.

Baldwin, B. (2005). *Storycatcher: Making sense of our lives through the power and practice of story.* Novato, CA: New World Library.

Banville, L. (2004, December 10). *Case study and the* USA Today. Retrieved March 29, 2007, from www.pbs.org/newshour/media/media_ethics/casestudy_usatoday.php

Bass, B. (1990). *Bass and Stogdill's handbook of leadership.* New York: The Free Press.

Bellah, R. (1985). *Habits of the heart: Individualism and commitment in American life.* Berkeley: University of California Press.

Benitez, S. (2006, May). My libraries. In *The Rake 17 Voices* [Supplement]. Minneapolis: Rake Publishing.

Bennett, J. (1998, September 11). Tearful Clinton tells group of clerics, "I have sinned." *New York Times*. Retrieved September 11, 2006, from http://partners.nytimes.com/library/politics/091298clinton.html

Bergman, R. (2002). Why be moral? A conceptual model from developmental psychology. *Human Development, 45*, 104–124.

Bettelheim, B. (1989). *The uses of enchantment: The meaning and importance of fairy tales*. New York: Vintage Books.

Blair, J. (2004). *Burning down my masters' house: My life at the New York Times*. Beverly Hills, CA: New Millennium Entertainment.

Bok, S. (1979). *Lying: Moral choice in public and private life*. New York: Vintage Books.

Bolman, L., & Deal, T. (2001). *Leading with soul*. San Francisco: Jossey-Bass.

Bolman, L., & Deal, T. (2003). *Reframing organizations: Artistry, choice and leadership*. San Francisco: Jossey-Bass.

Borey, V. (n.d.). *Kitchen stories* (film review). Retrieved December 21, 2006, from www.suite101.com/article.cfm/norwegian_culture/107546

Borg, Y., & King, L. (2007, January 24). Thousands mourn slain journalist. *Star-Tribune*, A4.

Bridges, W. (1980). *Transitions: Making sense of life's changes*. Reading, MA: Perseus Books.

Bridges, W. (1991). *Managing transitions: Making the most of change*. Reading, MA: Addison-Wesley Publishing.

Brown, C. (2007, March 25). Cultural clash. *StarTribune*, A1, A12.

Brown, J., & Moffett, C. (1999). *The hero's journey: How educators can transform schools and improve learning*. Alexandria, VA: Association for Supervision and Curriculum Development.

Bruner, J. (1990). *Acts of meaning*. Cambridge, MA: Harvard University Press.

Burbules, N. (1993). *Dialogue in teaching: Theory and practice*. New York: Teachers College Press.

Burns, J. (1978). *Leadership*. New York: Harper & Row.

Campbell, J. (1949). *The hero with a thousand masks*. Princeton, NJ: Princeton University Press.

Campbell, (with Moyers, B.) (1988). *The power of myth*. New York: Doubleday.

Candinin D., & Connelly, F. (2000). *Narrative inquiry: Experience and story in qualitative research*. San Francisco: Jossey-Bass.

Carlsen, M. (1988). *Meaning-making: Therapeutic processes in adult development*. New York: W. W. Norton.

Carr, D. (1985). Life and the narrator's art. In H. Silverman & D. Idhe (Eds.), *Hermeneutics and deconstruction* (pp. 108–21). Albany: State University of New York Press.

Carroll, J. (2007). *A Christian opportunity: The 50th anniversary of the Border-Hennepin Union* [pamphlet]. Available from Hennepin Avenue Methodist Church, 511 Groveland Avenue, Minneapolis, Minnesota 55403 (612-871-5303).

Chaleff, I. (2003). *The courageous follower: Standing up to and for our leaders* (2nd ed.). San Francisco: Barrett-Koehler.

Cheifetz, I. (2007, January 15). When an innovative ball doesn't enthrall. *Star-Tribune*, D8.

Chen, G., & Starosta, W. (2006). Intercultural awareness. In L. Samovar, R. Porter, & E. McDaniel (Eds.), *Intercultural communication: A reader* (11th ed.) (pp. 357–365). Belmont, CA: Thomson Wadsworth.

Ciulla, J. (1995). Leadership ethics: Mapping the territory. *Business Ethics Quarterly*, 5(1), 1–28. Retrieved August 9, 2006, from Business Source Premier.

Clayton, S., & Opotow, S. (2003). Justice and identity: Changing perspectives on what is fair. *Personality & Social Psychology Review*, 7(4), 298–310. Retrieved August 11, 2006, from Academic Search Premier database.

Cleveland, H. (2002). Nobody in charge. San Francisco: Jossey-Bass.

Coleman, N. (2006, September 20). A fragile witness for peace fasts, defying the rain. *StarTribune*, (B1, B3).

Coleman, N, (2007, January 26). My short scary career driving that bus. *Star-Tribune*, (B1, B7).

Coleman, N. (2007, January 26). My short scary career driving that bus. *Star-Tribune*, B1, B7.

Collins, J. (2001a). *Good to great: Why some companies make the leap . . . and others don't.* New York: HarperBusiness.

Collins, J. (2001b, September–October). *The misguided mix-up of celebrity and leadership.* Retrieved February 6, 2007, from www.jimcollins.com/lib/articles/10_01_a.html

Collins, J. (2003, December 30). Best New Year's resolution? A "stop doing" list. *USA Today*, 13A. Retrieved December 27, 2006, from Academic Search Premier.

Colby, A., & Damon, W. (1992). *Some do care: Contemporary lives of moral commitment.* New York: The Free Press.

Coles, R. (2000). *Lives of moral leadership.* New York: Random House.

Cooperrider, D., Sorensen, P., Whitney, D., & Yaeger T. (Eds.). (2000). *Appreciative inquiry: Rethinking human organization toward a positive theory of change.* Champaign, IL: Stipes Publishing.

Covey, S. (1989). *The seven habits of highly effective people: Restoring the character ethic.* New York: Simon & Schuster.

Csikszentmihalyi, M. (1990). *Flow: The psychology of optimal experience.* New York: HarperPerennial.

Daft, R., & Lengel, R. (1998). *Fusion leadership: Unlocking the subtle forces that change people and organizations.* San Francisco: Barrett-Kohler.

Davis, W. H. (2002). *Overcoming: The autobiography of W. H. Davis.* Afton, MN: Afton Historical Society Press.

Deggans, E. (2004, March 21). Jayson Blair and the fear factor. *St. Petersburg Times.* Retrieved January 12, 2007, from www.sptimes.com/2004/03/21/Columns/Jayson_Blair_and_the_.shtml

Delaney, F. (2005). *Ireland: A novel.* New York: HarperCollins.

Denning, S. (2004). *A fable of leadership through story telling.* New York: John Wiley & Sons.

Denzin, N. (2001). *Interpretive interactionism.* Thousand Oaks, CA: Sage Publications.

DePaul University. (1997). *Elie Wiesel: Learning and Respect.* Retrieved September 14, 2006, from www.humanity.org/voices/commencements/speeches/index.php?page=wiesel_at_depaul

DePree, M. (1989). *Leadership is an art.* New York: Doubleday.

DePree, M. (1992). *Leadership jazz.* New York: Doubleday Currency.

The Dergue (1974–1991). (n.d.). Retrieved March 27, 2007, from www.ethiopiantreasures.toucansurf.com/pages/dergue.htm

Didion, J. (2005). *A year of magical thinking.* New York: Alfred A. Knopf.

Ehrenreich, B. (2001). *Nickel and dimed: On (not) getting by in America.* New York: Metropolitan Books.

Ellison, R. (1995). *Invisible man.* New York: Vintage Books.

Emmert, D. (2006, December 17). [photograph] *StarTribune,* AA5.

Evans, R. (1996). *The human side of school change: Reform, resistance, and the real-life problems of innovation.* San Francisco: Jossey-Bass.

A failure of initiative: Final report of the Select Bipartisan Committee to investigate the preparation for and response to Hurricane Katrina. (2006, February 12). Retrieved March 19, 2007, from http://katrina.house.gov/full_katrina_report.htm

Featherstone, M. (1992). *Cultural theory and cultural change.* London, Sage Publications.

Fernandez, E. (1994). Salsa X 2. In R. Gonzalez (Ed.), *Currents from the dancing river: Contemporary latino fiction, nonfiction, and poetry* (pp. 1–10). San Diego: Harcourt Brace.

Fluker, W. (2005, October 6). Needed: Ethical leadership in the aftermath of Katrina. *Diverse Issues in Higher Education,* 77(35). Retrieved August 7, 2006, from Education Full Text database.

Forbes, H. (1985). *Nationalism, ethnocentrism, and personality: Social science and critical theory.* Chicago: University of Chicago Press.

Frank, A. (1995). *The wounded storyteller.* Chicago, IL: University of Chicago Press.

Frankel, M. (1995, April 16). McNamara's retreat. *New York Times.* Retrieved February 13, 2007, from www.nytimes.com/books/00/04/23/daily/mcnamara-frankel.html

Frankl, V. (1984). *Man's search for meaning: An introduction to logotherapy.* New York: Simon & Schuster.

From Ghana, with gratitude. (2005, November 8). *StarTribune*, A4.

Gardner, H. (2004). *Changing minds: The art and science of changing our own and other people's minds.* Boston: Harvard Business School Press.

Gardner, J. (2003). *Living, leading, and the American dream.* San Francisco: Jossey-Bass.

Gausman, P. (2006). *Leadership narrative.* Unpublished manuscript. University of St. Thomas, Minneapolis, Minn.

Gilligan, C. (1993). *In a different voice: Psychological theory and women's development.* Cambridge, MA: Harvard University Press.

Glasser, W. (1998). *Choice theory: A new psychology of personal freedom.* New York: HarperPerennial.

Goodpaster, K. (2007). *Conscience and corporate culture.* Malden, MA: Blackwell Publishing.

Gornick, V. (2001). *The situation and the story: The art of the personal narrative.* New York: Farrar, Straus & Giroux.

Greene, M. (1988). *The dialectic of freedom.* New York: Teachers College Press.

Griffin, J. (1960/1996). *Black like me.* New York: Signet.

Griffin, J. (2004). *Scattered shadows: A memoir of blindness and vision.* Maryknoll, NY: Orbis Books.

Grow, D. (2007, January 26). Doug Grow: Cindy Sheehan, nonstop antiwar activist. *StarTribune*, Retrieved March 21, 2007, from www.startribune.com/465/story/963208.html

Hagberg, J. (2003). *Real power: Stages of personal power in organizations* (3rd ed.). Salem, WI: Sheffield Publishing.

Halbwachs, M. (1950/1980). *Collective memory.* Trans. F. J. Ditter Jr. & V. Y. Ditter. New York: Harper & Row.

Hamer, B., Bergmark, J., & Hamer, B. (2003). *Kitchen Stories* [Motion picture]. USA: MGM Home Entertainment.

Handy, C. (1989). *The age of unreason.* Boston: Harvard Business School Press.

Harvey, E., Cottrell, D., & Lucia, A. (2003). *The leadership secrets of Santa Claus.* Dallas, TX: The Walk the Talk Company.

Heifetz, R. (1994). *Leadership without easy answers.* Cambridge, MA: Harvard University Press.

Heifetz, R., & Linsky, M. (2002). *Leadership on the line: Staying alive through the dangers of learning.* Boston: Harvard Business School Press.

Hendrickson, P. (1996). *The living and the dead: Robert McNamara and five lives of a lost war.* New York: Alfred A. Knopf.

Herring, G. (1995, May/June). The wrong kind of loyalty [Review of *In retrospect: The tragedy and lessons of Vietnam*]. *Foreign Affairs, 74*(3), 154–158.

History of landmines. (n.d.). Retrieved March 29, 2007, from www.icbl.org/problem/history

Hobgood, M. (2000). *Dismantling privilege: An ethics of accountability.* Cleveland, OH: Pilgrim Press.

hooks, b. (1996). *Killing rage: Ending racism.* New York: Henry Holt.

Hopkins school board accepts Superintendent Kremer's resignation. (2006, March 30). Retrieved February 17, 2007, from www.hopkins.k12.mn.us/pages/disrict/commun/olddistrict/05.06district.htm#MDEaudit

Horton, M. (with Kohl, J., & Kohl, H.) (1998). *The long haul: An autobiography.* New York: Teachers College Press.

Hoy, E. (2006). *Leadership platform.* Unpublished manuscript. University of St. Thomas, Minneapolis, MN.

Hsu, S. (2006, February 12). Katrina report spreads blame: Homeland Security, Chertoff Singled Out. *Washington Post.* Retrieved March 29, 2007, from www.washingtonpost.com/wp-dyn/content/article/2006/02/11/AR2006021101409_pf.html

Ignaz Phillip Semmelweis. (n.d.). Retrieved February 14, 2007, from http://upalumni.org/medschool/appendices/appendix-62a.html#fn735

Ignaz Semmelweis. (n.d.) Retrieved February 14, 2007, from http://en.wikipedia.org/wiki/Ignaz_Semmelweis

In La'kech. (2005, March 24). Retrieved January 23, 2007, from http://inlakech.tribe.net/

Ison, B. (2005). *Baby, baby we are going to war.* Unpublished manuscript. Morehead, KY.

The Jacob Wetterling Story. (n.d.). Retrieved March 20, 2007, from www.jwf.org/ReadArticle.asp?articleId=34

Jensen, I. (2006). The practice of intercultural communication: Reflections for professionals in cultural meetings. In L. Samovar, R. Porter, & E. McDaniel (Eds.), *Intercultural communication: A reader* (11th ed.) (pp. 39–48). Belmont, CA: Thomson Wadsworth.

JetBlue Attempts to Calm Passenger Furor. (2007, February 15). New York: CBS News. Retrieved February 20, 2007, from www5.cnn.com/2007/WORLD/europe/02/20/tuesday/index.html

JetBlue's customer bill of rights. (n.d.). Retrieved February 20, 2007, from www.jetblue.com/about/ourcompany/promise/index.html?&intcmp=imgHP-promise20070219&

JetBlue CEO pledges last week's meltdown won't happen again. (2007, February 20). Retrieved February 20, 2007, from www.cbsnews.com/stories/2007/02/15/national/main2480665.shtml

Jody Williams—The Long Biography. Retrieved January 24, 2007, from www.icbl.org/campaign/ambassadors/jody_williams/bio/

Johnson, D., & Johnson, F. (2000). *Joining together: Group theory and group skills* (7th ed.). Boston, MA: Allyn and Bacon.

Jorgensen-Earp, C. R., & Lanzilotti, L. (1998). Public memory and private grief: The construction of shrines at site of public tragedy. *Quarterly Journal of Speech, 84,* 150–170.

Kakesako. G. K. (2001, April 24). Waddle gets reprimand, but is allowed to retire. *Honolulu Star-Bulletin.* Retrieved August 16, 2007, http://www.starbulletin.com/2001/04/24/news/story4.html

Kegan, R. (1982). *The evolving self: Problem and process in human development.* Cambridge, MA: Harvard University Press.

Keillor, G. (2004). *Homegrown Democrat: A few plain thoughts from the heart of America.* New York: Viking.

Keshgegian, F. (2000). *Redeeming memories: A theology of healing and transformation.* Nashville, TN: Abingdon Press.

Kersten, K. (2007, February 12). Horrifying images are etched in his mind forever. *StarTribune,* B1, B3.

Kidder, R. (2006a, October 23). Hunt down a perpetrator or hold to a principle: A high school's dilemma. *Institute for Global Ethics, 9*(44). Retrieved May 21, 2007, from www.globalethics.org/newsline/members/issue.tmpl?articleid=10230619412067

Kidder, R. (2006b, October 30). Hunt down a perpetrator or hold to a principle: Part two. *Institute for Global Ethics, 9*(45). Retrieved January 2, 2007 from www.globalethics.org/newsline/members/issue.tmpl?articleid=10300619061465

Klein, M. (2007). *The cedar strip canoe.* Unpublished manuscript. University of St. Thomas, Minneapolis, MN.

Knox, A. (1977). *Adult development and learning.* San Francisco: Jossey-Bass.

Koestenbaum, P. (2002). *Leadership, the inner side of greatness.* San Francisco: Jossey-Bass.

Kottak, C., & Kozaitis, K. (2003). *On being different: Diversity and multiculturalism in the North American mainstream* (2nd ed.). Boston: McGraw-Hill Higher Education.

Kouzes, J., & Posner, B. (1987). *The leadership challenge.* San Francisco: Jossey-Bass.

Kremer, M. (2005). *December 2005—District prepares 2006–2007 budget, develops statutory operating debt plan.* Retrieved February 17, 2007, from www.hopkins.k12.mn.us/pages/district/commun/super.htm

Krishnamurti, J. (1994). *On conflict.* San Francisco: Harper San Francisco.

Krug, E., Dahlberg, L., Mercy, J., Zwi, A., & Lozano, R. (2002). *World report on violence and health.* Geneva, Switzerland: World Health Organization.

Kübler-Ross, E., & Kessler, D. (2000). *Life lessons: Two experts on death and dying teach us about the mysteries of life and living.* New York: Scribner.

Kusy, M., & Essex, L. (2005). *Breaking the code of silence: Prominent leaders reveal how they rebounded from seven critical mistakes.* Lanham, MD: Taylor Trade Publishing.

Langer, E. (1997). *The power of mindful learning.* Reading, MA: Perseus Books.

Langer, E. (2005). *On becoming an artist: Reinventing yourself through mindful creativity.* New York: Random House.

Lawrence-Lightfoot, S. (1999). *Respect: An exploration.* Reading, MA: Perseus Books.

Lerner, M. (2007, January 17). Deaths from hospital errors, mishaps still rise. *StarTribune*, B1, B5.

Lessons in crisis management. (2004, December 22). Retrieved December 22, 2006, from http://edition.cnn.com/2004/BUSINESS/12/22/giuliani.profile/index.html

Lindberg, A. (1955). *Gift from the sea.* New York: Pantheon Books.

Lonetree, A. (2006, October 4). St. Louis Park superintendent apologizes for lie on school closing. *StarTribune.* Retrieved January 2, 2007, from www.startribune.com/1592/story/718579.html

Lopate, P. (1995). *The art of the personal essay: An anthology from the classical era to the present.* New York: Anchor Books.

Maathai, W. (2004, December 10). *Nobel lecture.* Retrieved February 27, 2007, from http://nobelprize.org/nobel_prizes/peace/laureates/2004/maathai-lecture-text.html

MacGregor, R. (2006, October 7). Learning to read at 93. *The Globe and Mail*, A1, A4–5.

Maciejewski, P., Zang, B., Block, S., & Pirereson, H. (2007, February 21). An empirical examination of the stage theory of grief. *Journal of the American Medical Association*, 297, 716–723. Retrieved March 1, 2007, from EBSCO research database.

Mann, C. (2006, August 29). *The long, strange resurrection of New Orleans.* Retrieved March 19, 2007, from http://money.cnn.com/magazines/fortune/fortune_archive/2006/08/21/8383661/index.htm

Martin, K. (1999). *Women of courage: Inspiring stories from the women who lived them*. Novato, CA: New World Library.

Marx, D. (2005). Our inaugural issue—in recognition of a growing community. *The Just Culture Community*, 1,1–8.

Matthew Shepard Foundation. (n.d.). *Our story*. Retrieved March 5, 2007, from www.matthewshepard.org/site/PageServer?pagename=Our_Story_Mission

May, R. (1991). *The cry for myth*. New York: W. W. Norton.

McCallum, B. (2005, November 6). *Clinton says U.S. should improve damaged image*. Retrieved January 31, 2007, from http://news.minnesota.publicradio.org/features/2005/11/05_mccalluml_clinton/

McGaughey, B. (2004, November). Doctors must wash their hands: U.S. hospital have become an infection zone. *American Spectator* (pp. 22–25). Retrieved January 30, 2007, from Academic Search Premier database.

McNamara, R. (1995). *In retrospect: The tragedy and lessons of Vietnam*. New York: Vintage.

Mezirow, J. (1990). *Fostering critical reflection in adulthood: A guide to transformative and emancipatory learning/Jack Mezirow and Associates*. San Francisco: Jossey-Bass.

Mezirow, J., and Associates. (2000). *Learning as transformation: Critical perspectives on a theory in progress*. San Francisco: Jossey-Bass.

Miller, J. (n.d.). *Poverty among women*. Ohio State University Extension Fact Sheet. Retrieved January 31, 2007, from http://ohioline.osu.edu/hyg- fact/5000/5705.html

Moxley, R. (2000). *Leadership and spirit: Breathing new vitality and energy into individuals and organizations*. San Francisco: Jossey-Bass.

Nava, Y. (2000). Dichos. In Y. Nava (Ed.), *It's all in the frijoles: 100 famous Latinos share real-life stories, time-tested dichos, favorite folktales, and inspiring words of wisdom* (pp. 77–79). New York: Fireside.

Naranjo, A, & Lujan, M. (2000). The Ute creation story. In W. Worth (Ed.), *Ute Indians art and culture: From prehistory to the new millennium* (pp. 6–7). Colorado Springs, CO: Colorado Springs Fine Arts Center.

National Museum of American Indians. (2004). *Our lives: Contemporary life and identities*. Retrieved September 21, 2004, from www.nmai.si.edu/subpage.cfm?subpage=exhibitions&second=dc

Nelson, K., & Fivush, R. (2004). The emergency of autobiographical memory: A social cultural developmental theory. *Psychological Review, 111*(2), 486–511.

Network of Spiritual Progressives. (2006, November 1). *Basic tenets*. Retrieved January 20, 2007, from www.spiritualprogressives.org/article.php?story=tenets

Nobel Peace Prize 1997. (n.d.). Retrieved February 13, 2007, from http://nobelprize.org/nobel_prizes/peace/laureates/1997/press.html

Noonan, S. (2003). *The elements of leadership: What you should know.* Lanham, MD: Scarecrow Press.

Noonan, S. (2007, February). Culturally sensitivity pedagogy: Mandela's Way. *NCPEA Education Leadership Review, 8*(1), 1–12.

Noonan, S., & Fish, T. (2005). Understanding the role of metaphor in leadership: Gaining perspective, seeing new possibilities. In C. Fulmer & F. Dembowski (Eds.), *National Summit on School Leadership: Crediting the past, challenging the present, and changing the future* (pp. 53–63). Lanham, MD: Rowman & Littlefield.

Noonan, S., & Anderson-Sathe, L. (2006). *And the band played on: Developing ethical leadership through a case study of the AIDS crisis.* Unpublished manuscript. University of St. Thomas, Minneapolis, MN.

O'Connor, A. (1995, December 1). Minneapolis gas station in a "safe" community is site of 90th homicide. *StarTribune,* A1, A18.

Olson, D. (2006). *Leadership narrative.* Unpublished manuscript. University of St. Thomas, Minneapolis, MN.

Palmer, P. (1990). *The active life: A spirituality of work, creativity, and caring.* San Francisco: Jossey-Bass.

Peck, S. (1978). *The road less traveled: A new psychology of love, traditional values and spiritual growth.* New York: Simon and Schuster.

Pickett, J. (Ed.). (2000). *American heritage dictionary of the English language* (4th ed.). Boston, MA: Houghton Mifflin.

Piper, W. (1976). *The little engine that could.* New York: Platt & Munk.

Polkinghorne, D. (1988). *Narrative knowing and the human sciences.* Albany, NY: State University of New York Press.

Quinn, R. (1996). *Deep change: Discovering the leader within.* San Francisco: Jossey-Bass.

Quinn, R. (2004). *Building the bridge as you walk on it: A guide for leading change.* San Francisco: Jossey-Bass.

Quote DB. (n.d. a). Martin Luther King, Jr. Retrieved May 22, 2007, from www.quotedb.com/authors/martin-luther-king-jr/2

Quote DB. (n.d. b). Ralph Waldo Emerson. Retrieved May 22, 2007, from www.quotedb.com/authors/ralph-waldo-emerson

Quote DB. (n.d. c). Winston Churchill. Retrieved May 22, 2007, from www.quotedb.com/authors/winston-churchill/3

Quoteworld. (n.d.). Dominique de Meril. Retrieved May 22, 2007, from www.quoteworld.org/quotes/8968

Reason, J. (1992). *Human error.* Cambridge, UK: Cambridge University Press.

Reason, J., & Mycielska, K. (1982). *Absent-minded?: The psychology of mental lapses and everyday errors.* Englewood Cliffs, NJ: Prentice-Hall.

Remen, R. (1996). *Kitchen table wisdom.* New York: Berkley Publishing.

Rest, J. (1986). *Moral development: Advances in research and theory.* New York: Praeger.

Rest, J., & Narváez, D. (1994). *Moral development in the professions: Psychology and applied ethics.* Hillsdale, NJ: Lawrence Erlbaum Associates.

Richard Pryor. (n.d.). Retrieved February 1, 2007, from www.richardpryor.com/0/4113/0/1240D1271/

Ricoeur, P. (1991). Life in quest of narrative. In D. Wood (Ed.), *On Paul Ricoeur: Narrative and interpretation* (pp. 20–32). London: Routledge.

Riessman, C. (1993). *Narrative analysis.* (Qualitative Research Methods, Vol. 30). Newbury Park, CA: Sage Publications.

Robinson, J., & Hawpe, L. (1986). Narrative thinking as a heuristic process. In T. Sarbin (Ed.), *The storied nature of human conduct* (pp. 111–125). New York: Praeger.

Rochon, T. (1998). *Culture moves: Ideas, activism and changing values.* Princeton, NJ: Princeton University Press.

Said, E. (1993). *Culture and imperialism.* New York: Vantage Books.

Salka, J. (2004). *First in, last out: Leadership lessons from the New York Fire Department.* New York: Portfolio.

Samovar, L.A., & Porter, R. E. (2001). *Communication between cultures.* Belmont, CA: Wadsworth.

Second Hand Songs. (n.d.). *Artist: Bernard Ighner.* Retrieved February 22, 2007, from www.secondhandsongs.com/artist/2663

Selma to Montgomery March: National historical trail and all American route. (n.d.). Retrieved March 21, 2007, from www.cr.nps.gov/nr/travel/civilrights/al4.htm

Senge, P. (1990). *The fifth discipline: The art and practice of the learning organization.* New York: Doubleday Currency.

Shelton, G. (2005, November 10). Secret's out, demons gone for Demers. *St. Petersburg Times.* Retrieved March 21, 2007, from www.sptimes.com/2005/11/10/Columns/Secret_s_out__demons_.shtml

Shepard, J. (2006, April 6). *The Matthew Shepard Story.* Speech delivered at the University of St. Thomas, St. Paul, MN.

Silverman, L. (2006). *Wake me up when the data is over: How organizations use stories to drive results.* San Francisco: Jossey-Bass.

Spaulding, P. (2007, February 24). *You don't stand alone, Wyoming Rep. Zwonitzer.* Retrieved March 18, 2007, from http://pandagon.net/2007/02/24/you-dont-stand-alone-wyoming-rep-zwonitzer/

Spencer, P. (1983). *Who speaks for wolf: A Native American learning story as told to Turtle Woman Singing by her father, Sharp-eyed Hawk.* Austin, TX: Tribe of Two Press.

St. Louis Park Schools. (2006, October 2). Press release. Retrieved January 2, 2007, from www.slpschools.org/cancel.html

Sternberg, R. (2003). Smart people are not stupid, but they sure can be foolish: The in balance theory of foolishness. In R. Sternberg (Ed.), *Why smart people can be so stupid* (pp. 232–242). New Haven, CT: Yale University Press.

Sternberg, R. 2005. Understanding and combating hate. In R. Sternberg (Ed.), *The psychology of hate* (pp. 37–49). Washington, DC: American Psychological Association.

Strickler, A. (2007, January 3). Good Samaritan saves man on subway tracks. *Newsday.* Retrieved January 16, 2007, from www.newsday.com/news/local/new york/am-sub0103,0,5691223.story?coll=ny-top-headlines

StoryCorps. (2004). Retrieved March 20, 2007, from http://storycorps.net/about/

Sunflower: A native oilseed with growing markets. (n.d.). Retrieved January 23, 2007, from www.jeffersoninstitute.org/pubs/sunflower.shtml

Takaki, R. (1993). *A different mirror: A history of multicultural America.* Boston: Little, Brown and Company.

Tannen, D. (1998). *The argument culture: Moving from debate to dialogue.* New York: Random House.

Taylor, D. (1996). *The healing power of stories: Creating yourself through the stories of your life.* New York: Doubleday.

Tempesta, A. R. (2004, October). The right thing (book). *Army Lawyer,* 377, 24–29. Retrieved August 16, 2007, from EBSCO database.

Terry, R. (2001). *Seven zones for leadership.* Palo Alto, CA: Davies-Black Publishing.

This I believe—Jody Williams. Retrieved January 24, 2007, from www.prx.org/pieces/10918

Tournier, P. (1981). *Creative suffering.* San Francisco: Harper & Row.

Walker, B. (n.d.). *40 years of* Star Trek *and the real McCoy: The enduring legacy of DeForest Kelley.* Retrieved January 28, 2007, from www.startrek.com/startrek/view/features/specials/article/30875.html

The way of the spirit: Nature, myth, and magic in Native American Life. (1997). New York: Time-Life.

This I Believe—Jody Williams. (2006, January 9). Retrieved May 19, 2006, from www.npr.org/templates/story/story.php?storyId=5132997

Times reporter who resigned leaves a long trail of deception. (2003, May 11). *The New York Times.* Retrieved May 21, 2007, from www.nytimes.com/2003/05/11/national/11PAPE.html?pagewanted=1&ei=5007&en=d6f511319c259463&ex=1367985600&partner=USERLAND

Waddle, S. (with Abraham, K.) (2002). *The right thing.* Nashville, TN: Integrity.

Wenzel, M., & Edmond, M. (2001, March–April). *The impact of hospital-acquired bloodstream infections.* Centers for Disease Control. Retrieved January 30, 2007, from www.cdc.gov/ncidod/eid/vol7no2/wenzel.htm

Wheatley, M. (1999). *Leadership and the new science.* San Francisco: Berrett-Koehler.

Whelihan, T. (2006). *Leadership narrative.* Unpublished manuscript. University of St. Thomas, Minneapolis, MN.

White, M., & Epston, D. (1990). *Narrative means to therapeutic ends.* New York: W.W. Norton & Company.

Wiesel, E. (1960). *Night.* Trans. S. Rodway. New York: Bantam Books.

Witherell, C., & Noddings, N. (Eds.). (1991). *Stories lives tell: Narrative and dialogue in education.* New York: Teachers College Press.

Wroth, W., Bates, C., Ellis, R., Fowler, C., & Goss, J. (2000). *Ute Indians art and culture: From prehistory to the new millennium.* Albuquerque: University of New Mexico Press.

A young boy's stand on a New Orleans streetcar (2006, December 1). StoryCorps, National Public Radio. Retrieved August 15, 2007, http://www.npr.org/templates/story/story.php?storyId=6562915

Zerubavel, E. (2003). *Time maps: Collective memory and the social shape of the past.* Chicago: University of Chicago Press.

INDEX

Ackerman, R., 48, 167
Allan, J., 40
Allen, A., 203, 219
Alterman, E., 107
amnesia, 24
Anasazi, 232
Anderson-Sathe, L., 80
Angelou, M., 192
Angus, L., 46
Applebaum, A., 190–91
Applebaum, B., 203–04
appreciative inquiry, 148–49
Argyris, C., 147
Armenian genocide, 83–84
Armstrong, D., 41
Armstrong, L., 35, 39–41, 44
Auschwitz, 17, 19
Autrey, W., 77–82, 84
Awumey, E., 42–43

Bakken, E., 165–66
Baldwin, B., 37, 65–66, 234

Baltimore Sun, 112
Banville, L., 112–13
Bass, B., 93
Bellah, R., 9
Benitez, S., 47
Bennett, J., 107
Bergman, R., 86, 96
Bergmark, J., 26
Bettelheim, B., 36, 45
Big Grace, 60, 63
Bjørvik, 26–27
Blair, J., 107–114, 139
Blind, Inc., 181–83
Block, S., 175, 180
Bok, S., 98–99, 105–07
Bolman, L., 2, 10, 14, 58, 144, 224, 251
Border Avenue Methodist Episcopal Church, 162
Border-Hennepin Union, 163
Borey, V., 26
Borg, Y., 83–84

Bowers, D., 101–05
Brazier, C., 140–45
Brazier, F. M., 141
Brazier, G., 141
Bridges, W., 151, 155–56
Brooke Medicine Eagle, 170
Brown, C., 248
Brown, J., 250
Brown, R., viii
Bruner, J., 38
Burbules, N., 5, 148–49, 235
Burns, J., 31, 81
Bush, G. W., 84, 119, 187, 213–14

Campanella, R., 206
Campbell, J., 20, 22, 56, 74
Candinin, D., 46
Captain Kirk, 22
Carlsen, M., 15, 18–19, 173–74, 249
Carr, D., 44
Carroll, J., 161–63
Cedar Strip Canoe, 177–78
Chaleff, I., 31, 137, 231
change:
    adapt to, xiii, 35, 142, 144, 150,
        154–58, 161
    causes of, 17, 161
    effects of, 151, 154–55, 168
    mandated, 159–60
    myths, 158–60
    personal, vii, xiv, 2, 15, 39, 57–59,
        63–68
    phases of, 151, 156
    process of, 147–48, 150, 152
    promoting, 36, 249, 251
    resistance to, 142, 158
    social, xi, 86, 213, 216, 249
    story as catalyst for, 6, 150
    See also stories, change
Cheifetz, I., 157–58

Chen, G., 232
Chesner, C., 145
Chesner, S., 145
Churchill, W., 37, 98, 106, 150
Ciulla, J., 93
civil rights, 196, 201, 210–12, 217–18
Clayton, S., 79
Cleveland, H., 251
Clinton, W., 74–76, 103, 106–107
Colby, A., 93
Coleman, N., 71, 215
Coles, R., 94
Collins, J., 6–8, 138
colour-blindness, 203
Columbia disaster, 144
communication barriers, 231–32
Congress of Racial Equality (CORE),
    196
Connelly, F., 46
Cooperrider, D., 149
Corrine, S., 146
Coulter, A., 214
counterstories, 8–9, 202
cover story:
    defined, 99, 101–02
    engaging others in cover up, 102,
        105
    intent to deceive, 106
    loss of social trust, 105
Covey, S., 228
Coyote, 239–40
critical life event, 42, 50, 63, 68,
    71
Csikszentmihalyi, M., 16
cultural:
    adaptation, 30, 248–49
    barriers, 31, 228
    breakdowns, 239, 242–43
    change, 28, 94, 216, 238–39
    competence, 148, 232

conflict, 248
values, 216
cultural differences, 52, 68, 72–73,
    79–80, 201, 204, 208–09, 230,
    240–41, 249
cultural identity, 2, 30, 44–45, 63–64,
    218, 238, 240–42, 244, 249
cultural stories, 202
    collective consciousness and, 31
    defined, 4–5
    dialogue and, 5
    dominant, 4, 202, 240
    in diverse communities, 5, 54,
        240–42
    individual visibility, 31
    invisibility, 5
    purposes of, 2, 5, 33, 250–51
    social identity, 4
    social unity, 249
    traditional, 45
    wisdom, 29
culture:
    accountable, 106, 110, 114
    American, 144
    argument, 12–13
    as a gift, 28
    deceptive, 110
    defined, 2, 28, 158, 249
    dominant, 218, 239
    effects of, 218
    failing, 124
    fearful, 113
    healthy, 164, 239
    in organizations, 2
    Indian, 20, 240
    Just, 126–27
    Midwestern, xiv
    moral, 81, 114
    multiethnic, 248
    of resistance, 158, 163

personal, 30, 72
preserving, xiii, 1, 45, 239–40, 249
professional, 21, 139
purposes of, 2, 158, 237, 243, 251
survivance and, 237–38, 242, 248
Swedish, 249
tensions, 4, 248–49
Western, 13

Daft, R., 1
Damon, W., 93
Davis, H., 162–64
Davis, S., 89
de Menil, D., 195
Deal, T., 2, 10, 14, 58, 144, 224, 251
defining moments:
    character, 60
    core values and, 59, 63, 73, 194
    defined, 63
    development and, 55
    epiphany, 63
    importance of, 55, 59, 64
    in story, 7
    national, 76
    reflection and, 59
    self-story, 65
Deggans, E., 114
Delaney, F., 10
Demers, J., 142–45
Denning, S., 251
Denzin, N., 63
DePree, M., 28
dialogue, 148
    art of hosting, 232–34
    collective action, 4
    community meetings, 232
    core values and, 59
    cultural differences, 249
    cultural survivance, 236
    defined, 5, 148

dialectical tensions in, 174
facilitation of, 233
failure and breakdowns, 235
ground rules, 233
importance of story, 4, 56, 208
in diverse communities, 4–5, 208,
    220, 231, 233, 248, 249
internal, 174
meaning making, 4, 249
overcoming oppression, 208, 218
process of, 148–49
purposes of, xi, 148, 236
relationships and, 4–5
turning points in, 221, 236
use of talking stick and, 234
Dick, H., 83–84
Dick, R., 84
Didion, J., 172–74
diversity:
    cultural conflict and, 203
    cultural encounters and, 68, 203
    defined, 30, 231
    honoring, 4
    Star Trek myth, 21–22
    See also cultural differences,
        cultural identity

Ehrenreich, B., 204–05, 207
Einstein, A., 140, 160
Ellison, R., 44
Emerson, R., 195
Emmert, D., 190
Epston, D., 184
Essex, L., 123
ethnocentrism, 240
Evans, R., 157–58

Fairtlough, G., 40
Featherstone, M., 30
Fernandez, E., 96, 238
Fish, T., viii, 11, 252

Fivush, R, 23–24
Fluker, W., 207
followers, 2, 31, 58, 81, 97, 137–38
foolish mistakes, 114–17
foolishness, 121, 223, 239
Forbes, H., 241
Forest, L., 120
Frank, A., 41, 43, 58, 66, 92
Frankel, M., 92
Frankl, V., 17–18

Gardner, H., 8–9, 14–15, 33
Gardner, J., xiv, 3–4, 90–92, 251, 258
Gausman, P., 63
gay, lesbian, bi-sexual, and
    transgender people (GLBT), 210
gay rights, 209, 212
genocide, 84, 225, 245–46
Gilligan, C., 52–53
Giuliani, R., 37
Glasser, W., 224–25
Goodpaster, K., 78, 80
good Samaritan, 80, 82
    See also story: good Samaritan
Gornick, V., 35, 65–66
Gorse, I., 245–49
Greene, M., 45, 237, 249
grief:
    all-encompassing, 173
    bereavement and, 180
    complicated, 180
    effects of, 156, 179, 184
    private and public, 193
    stages of, 156, 175, 184
Griffin, J. H., 196–201, 205, 207
group dynamics, 228
groupthink, 226–27
Grow, D., 213–14

Hagberg, J., 65
Hailemariam, M., 244

Halbwachs, M., 28
Halloran, W., 19
Hamer, B., 26
Handy, C., 150
Hansen, P., 25
Harmon, M., 42–44
Harvey, E., 12
Harvey, P., 168
Hawkinson, M., 164–66
Hawkinson, R., vii
Hawpe, L., 15, 39
Heifetz, R., 110, 122–23, 213
Heinzen, B., 40
Henderson, R., 209
Hendrickson, P., 87, 89–90
Hennepin Avenue Union Church, 162
Hermundslie, P., 165
Herring, G., 88
Hobgood, M., 203, 205, 224
Hoffman, C., 31–32, 137
Hollopeter, C., 77–78, 80–82
hooks, b., 207
Horton, M., 196
Hoy, E., 229–30
Hsu, S., 206
human errors:
    accountability for, 128
    causes of, 129, 137
    effects of, 126, 130
    investigation of, 137
    preventing, 127, 130, 139
    responsibility of followers, 137
    sources of, 126, 129
    types of, 129–30
human needs, 121–22, 223–25
Hurricane Katrina, 83, 205–07

identity:
    as self-story, 43, 46
    authentic, 58
    belonging and, xiii

changes in, 15, 154
character and, 49, 52,
collective, 31
leadership role and, 48
    moral, 82, 86, 96
    multiethnic, 30
    preserve, 240, 249
    search for, 45–46, 48, 58–59
    threats to, 58, 157, 249
    See also cultural differences;
        cultural identity
illiteracy, 140, 143–44, 148
Ingram, J., 24–25
In La'kech, 79
Institute for Global Ethics, 103
International Campaign to Ban
    Landmines (ICBL), 85
Ison, B., 187, 189–90

The Jacob Wetterling Foundation,
    185
Jensen, I., 29, 32
JetBlue Airlines, 145–47
Jim Crow laws, 161, 196–98
Johnson, D., 224, 226–28
Johnson, F., 224, 226–28
Johnson, L., 88, 90–92, 217
Jorgensen-Earp, C. R., 193
Jungels, B., viii
Juno Enterprise, 247
Just Culture, 126–27

Kegan, R., 4
Keillor, G., xiv
Kelley, J., 107, 111–14, 139
Kersten, K., 19
Keshgegian, F., 191
Kidder, R., 103–04
Kimberly-Clark, 7–8
King, L., 84, 225
King, L. H., 89–90

King, M. L., 84, 89, 115, 217
Kitchen Stories, 26–27
kiva, 232, 234
Klein, M., 177, 179, 215
knock it off, 130–31
    See also human errors
Knox, A., 57
Koerner, T., viii
Kolletschka, J., 125
Kottak, C., 20–21, 23
Kottak, K., 20–21, 23
Kouzes, J., 31
Kremer, M., 100
Krishnamurti, J., 219
Kübler-Ross, E., 175, 177
Kusy, M., 123

Laney, F., 10
Laney, R., 101–02
Langer, E., 121, 150
Lanzilotti, L., 193
Lawrence-Lightfoot, S., 180
leaders:
    authentic, 48, 53–54, 74, 96, 161
    compassionate, 168, 180, 184, 193
    courageous, 7, 65, 84, 166, 176,
        194, 205, 211, 217, 219, 238, 243
    credible, 8, 48, 74, 97
    cultural, 5, 203, 231–32, 235, 250
    democratic, xiii–iv, 5, 238
    effective, 2, 15, 137, 142, 147, 150
    ethical, 2, 91, 93, 97, 118, 225, 251
    ethical failure of, 124, 206–07
    failures of, 121, 123, 139, 143, 204
    in crisis, 147, 217
    learning from mistakes, 138–39, 147
    moral, 78–82, 84, 92–94, 97,
        203–05, 218–19, 234, 241
    reflective, 15, 59, 64, 73, 139, 149
    transformational, 84, 250
    wise, 59, 73, 121, 123, 138, 168

leadership:
    accountability, 106, 124, 138
    achieving goals and, 6, 8, 35, 54
    as a learning process, 149
    as a way of being, 67
    authenticity and, 37, 47, 54
    challenges of, 62, 149–150
    change and, 150, 160, 213, 217, 251
    context for, 2–3, 25–26, 28, 149, 251
    courageous, 78, 195, 207, 213, 218
    defined, 31, 93, 147, 149–50
    democratic, xiii, xiv, 5
    developmental model of, 65
    earning trust and, 54
    ethical, 91–93, 118, 207
    failures in performance, 106, 113,
        123, 205–07
    futuristic work of, xii, 150
    global activism and, 85
    in diverse communities, 5, 27, 31,
        44, 54, 212, 228–29, 230–31,
        239, 241, 250–51
    learning and, xii, 63, 149
    listening and, 223, 228
    moral, xiii, 69, 74, 76–85, 93, 96,
        207, 219, 230–31
    organizational culture and, 2,
        160
    participatory, xii, 5, 16, 31, 38, 71,
        93
    persuasion and, 33
    power and, 138, 225
    process of, 28
    purposes of, xiii, 2, 6, 8–9, 93–94,
        148
    relational, 31
    serving members and, 31, 44
    social justice and, 164, 195, 210,
        203, 210, 216, 218, 223, 226,
        230
    team, 63

INDEX

273

visionary, 164, 166
leadership and story:
purposes, xii–xiii, 2–3, 6, 9, 32, 37, 46, 98, 251
learning:
accepting challenges, 58
adult, 57
defined, 15
double-loop, 147
exchange of stories and, 116, 117
from mistakes, 137
from others, 225, 249–51
life experience and, 58
life-long, 121, 145
literacy and, 142
mental models, 145
organizations, 144–45, 147
reflective, 64
strategies, 144
systems thinking, 144
transformation, 142
Lengel, R., 1
Lerner, M., 126, 128
lie(s):
defined, 98
noble, 99
public, 105
well-placed, 104
Lindberg, A., 56, 74
listening
adapting to change and, xiii
defined, 4
dialogue and, 234
diverse voices, 5, 131, 220–21, 223–25, 231, 236, 249–51
innovation, 138
overcoming barriers, 230
process, xii
See also dialogue

literacy:
defined, 139
types of, 147–48
logotherapy, 18
Londoners, 36
Lonetree, A., 104
Lopate, P., 64–65
love, 18, 22, 82, 169, 179, 181, 194, 208, 210, 224, 240, 251
Lujan, M., 239
lying:
culture of deception, 111
dangers of, 107
deceptions and, 99, 106–07
defined, 98–99
impact on others, 113
presidential, 107
public trust, 103, 105
unethical environments, 111

Maathai, W., 234
MacGregor, R., 140–43
Maciejewski, P., 175, 180
Magnus, J., 186
Mandela, N., 84, 216–20
Mann, C., 206
Manuel, J., 228–29
Martin, K., 170–71, 208
Marx, D., 127
Maslin-Ostrowski, P., 48, 167
Maslow, A., 224
Matthew Shepard Foundation, 211
McCallum, B., 75
McCaughey, B., 126
McCoy, L., 22
McDonald, B., 214
McGaughey, B., 125
McKinney, A., 209
McLeod, J., 46
McMurdo Station Antarctica, 132–36
McNamara, R., 87–92

meaning:
  breakdowns in will to live, 17
  creating, xi, 18, 34, 149, 231, 233,
    237
  exchange of stories and, 2–3, 38
  interpretation of story and, xii, 27,
    32, 34, 39, 59, 64–66, 98
  life purpose, 16, 18, 33, 45–46,
    59–60, 74, 191
  of life, 4–5, 9, 16–18, 27, 57
  process of making, xii, 5, 14–5, 19,
    27–28, 33, 38–40, 54, 249
  purposes of meaning-making,
    15–17, 174, 237
  shared, xi, 45, 53, 251
  state of meaninglessness, 18–19, 48
Medtronic, Inc., 164–66, 247
memoir, 65–66
memory, 10
  autobiographical, 23–24
  cultural, xi, 25, 46
  disorders, 25
  nostalgic, 18
  protective layers of, 61
  public, 23, 93, 106, 190–93
  purposes of, 23, 25
  social, xi, 3, 10, 19, 23, 192
  typology of, 191
Mengistu, H., 245
mental schemata, 32
metaphor(s), 10, 250
  cultural, 14
  defined, 11
  experience, 11
  in leadership, 12, 263
  limiting, 13–15
  military, 12
  power of, 12–13
  role, 11
  sports, 14
  sunflower, 94

  use in story, xi, 10–11, 13, 250
  vocational, 11
Mezirow, J., 63–64, 144
Miller, J., 205
mindlessness, 115–17, 205
Moffett, C., 250
Moore, B., 126
Moore, P., 126
moral:
  action, xiii, 81, 93, 219
  agency, 83
  authority, 43, 54, 69, 92
  behavior, 81
  capacity, 81
  character, 81–82, 208, 231
  commitments, 94
  community, 79–80
  consciousness, 234
  core, 74, 82–84, 96
  courage, 94
  duty, 66
  endeavor, 79–80
  identity, 59, 82
  imagination, xi, 22
  insight, 78
  judgment, 81
  leaders, 81
  leadership defined, 79
  motivations for action, 96
  of the story, 8
  perspective, 24
  purpose, 66, 79
  responsibility, 210
  sensitivity, 81
  tales, 45
  values, 82
See also identity; moral; leaders,
    courageous; leaders, moral;
    leadership, ethical; leadership,
    moral
Moshe the Beadle, 225–27

Mother Theresa, 36, 84
Mothers Against Drunk Drivers
 (MADD), 185
Moxley, R., 4–5, 54
Mycielska, K., 129
myth:
 American dream, 204, 249
 as "truth," 10
 change, 158–60
 cultural values, 23
 defined, 20, 23
 dominant, 20
 enduring power, xi, 23
 functions of, 20
 healthy communities, 23
 purposes of, 19–23
 Star Trek, 21
 Thanksgiving, 20
 unity, 21

Naranjo, A., 239
narrative repair, 39
narrative themes:
 change, 35, 42
 defined, vii, 8, 35, 38, 41
 identity, 42
 illness, 41
 leadership, 35–36
 learning, 42
 progression of, 15, 43
 quest, 55
 restitution, 41
 survival, 35, 42
National Aeronautics and Space
 Administration (NASA), 144–45
National Basketball Association
 (NBA), 157–58
National Museum of American
 Indians, 30
native identity, 30, 140
 See also cultural differences

Nava, Y., 29
Neeleman, D., 146–47
Nelson, K., 23–24
Network of Spiritual Progressives, 82
never events, 126
New York Times, 89, 107–08, 110,
 113, 163
Nicholas, D, viii
Nilsson, 26–27
Nobel Peace Prize, 85
Noddings, N., 31
Noonan, M., viii
Noonan, P., 33–34
Noonan, S., 11, 30, 53, 59, 67–68, 80,
 101, 219, 235, 252
Northwestern Hospital, 164–65
nosocomial infections, 125

O'Connor, A., 186
official story, 99
Olson, C., 165
Olson, D., 61
Opotow, S., 79
oppression, 225
 acts of, 201, 203, 208
 causes of, 201, 203–05, 207–08,
  225
 counterstories and, 202
 effects of, 217, 224
 fighting against, 84, 194–95,
  218–19
 racism and, 196
 survivor stories and, 191
 witness to, 191

pacemaker, 164, 166
Page, A., 126
Paideia School, 167
Palmer, P., 147, 165
Parks, R., 195
peace workers, 85, 214–16

Peck, S., 181
Pennington, C., 163
personal story:
    composing a, 67
    critical life events and, 68, 71
    cultural identity and, 72
    family and relationships and, 52, 67
    milestones and achievements, 67,
        70
    process of transformation, 15
    stages of change, 66
Phyllis Wheatley Settlement House,
    162
Pickett, J., 30, 148, 238
Piper, W., 7
Pirereson, H., 175, 180
plagiarism, 108–14
Polkinghorne, D., 16
poor decisions, 120, 122
Porter, R. E., 2
Posner, B., 31
Post Traumatic Stress Disorder
    (PTSD), 183, 188
poverty, 204–07
Premiere Speakers Bureau, 33
privilege, 14, 196, 203–04, 214,
    224–25, 259
Pryor, R., 170–71
psychology of hate, 201
public trust, 91, 107, 113
    See also lying, public trust

quest narrative:
    adult personality, 57
    defined, 41, 55–56, 59, 65, 74
    hero's journey, 56
    identity, 58
    stage theory, 56
    universal story, 59
Quinn, R., 160–61

racism, 43–44, 110, 163, 196–99, 200,
    203–04, 218, 228
    See also oppression
Reagan, R., 34
Reason, J., 129–30
reckless conduct:
    causes of, 114
    changes caused by, 48, 53, 61, 94
    cognitive and psychological traps,
        122
    combined with lax environment,
        111
    defined, 111–12
    effects of, 114
    egocentrism, 122
    honest, 64
    internal critic, 53
    interpretation of life meaning, 48,
        53, 63
    interpretation of story, 15
    learning and, 15, 64, 117
    reinterpretation of story and, 61, 64
    re-lived memory, 64
refugees, 246–48
Remen, R., 53, 64, 169, 171
Rest, J., 81, 82
Richardson, B., 101
Ricoeur, P., 38
Riessman, C., 36, 38–39, 41, 44
Roberts, J., 109
Robinson, J., 15
Rochon, T., 216–17

Said, E., 242
Salka, J., 12
Samovar, L. A., 2
self-story, xii, 43, 46, 65–66
    See also memory, autobiographical
Semmelweis, I., 124–25
Senge, P., 145, 147

Sexton, C., 162, 164
Shea, P., 167
Sheehan, C., 213–14
Shelton, G., 143
Shepard, J., 209–11
Shepard, M., 209–11
Silverman, L., 97
Sinawav, 239
Smith, D., 7–8
Smith, E., 50–52
Smith, J., 195–96, 207
Smith, J. M., 181, 184
social change, 86, 161, 213, 216, 217
   See also change, social
Sorensen, P., 149
Spaulding, P., 212
Spencer, P., 221–23
Spock, Dr., 22
St. Louis Park Schools, 102
Starosta, W., 232
Stensby, M., ix
Sternberg, R., 120–21, 201–02
stories:
   achievement, 70
   chaos, 41
   collective, 27, 32
   community, 3–4, 32
   creation, 239–40
   cultural, 2, 4–5, 23, 31, 45, 202,
      241
   empowerment, 8
   euology, 46
   exchange of, 2, 8, 27, 251
   family, 45
   future, 54
   global, 32, 250
   good Samaritan, 14, 37
   hatred, 202
   healing, 45
   heroic, 20

identity, 4, 29, 45, 50, 73
illness, 41
immigrant, 243–44
inspirational, 6
life, 56, 60, 68
memorable, 8
mini, 41
Native American, 223
of exclusion, 72
official, 32
parables, 36
personal, 44, 49
persuasive, 36
pioneer, 240
privilege, 14
propaganda, 201
quest, 41
resistance and protest, 187
restitution, 41
species, 32
spiritual, 36
survival, 35, 142
survivor, 191
Thanksgiving, 20
traditional, 45
transformational, 65
   See also counterstories; cover story
story:
   acquiring wisdom through, 23, 32,
      34–35, 46, 59, 73, 149–50, 234,
      250
   core values, 5, 41, 49, 54, 59,
      67–68, 81, 124, 155
   credibility, 8, 48, 97
   elements of, 10, 36, 39–40
   ethics, 74, 98
   evaluation criteria for, 46
   exchange of, 10, 46, 48, 54–55
   fairy tales, 45
   gifts of, 37

interactive and transformational
  aspects, 37–39
interpretation of experience, 2, 10
moral of the, 34–37
power of, xiv, 4, 43, 150, 234, 251
purposes of, 2–3, 27, 34, 48, 54,
  250, 251
resolution of, 39
therapeutic nature of, 169, 174
StoryCorps, 41, 206
storyline, 34, 40
  See also narrative themes
storytelling:
  co-reminisce, 32
  purpose of, 1, 10, 45, 55, 239, 251
Strickler, A., 77
suffering:
  bereavement and, 180
  causes of, 219, 220
  creative response to, 171, 216
  effects of, 184
  externalizing events, 174
  fighting against loss, 184
  healing through story, 171
  importance of agency, 184
  indifference to, 214
  internal dialogue, 174
  living with courage, 176
  personal violence and, 186
  survivors and, 171
  using story to heal, 184
  with courage, 177
  wounds of war, 187, 213, 216, 246
Sumner, W., 240
Survivance, xi, 236, 238, 242

table creep, 152–55
Takaki, R., 249
Tannen, D., 12–13

Taylor, D., 48
Terry, R., 48
Teul, C., viii
time out, 130–31
  See also human errors
Tournier, P., 176, 180
trust, 228
truth:
  accountability in leadership and,
    119
  constructions of, 202
  continuum of, 99
  damaged, 91
  half-truths and, 99
  loss of, 103
  narrative, 48
  principle of veracity and, 107
  public trust and, 91, 100, 106–07,
    113,
  telling standards, 101

United Nations High Commission for
  Refugees (UNHCR), 247
University of St. Thomas (UST), 209,
  247
USA Today, 112–13
USS *Greeneville*, 118–19
Utes, 239–40

visual impairment, 181, 183, 198–99
vortex effect, 173

Waddle, S., 117–20
Walker, B., 22
Weaver, D., viii
Weinstein, S., 96–97
Wellstone, P., 214
Wetterling, J., 185–86
Wheatley, M., 147, 234

Whelihan, T., 230, 231
White, M., 184
white privilege, 204
Whitney, D., 149
Wiesel, E., 225–27
Williams, J., 84–86
Williams, S., 197
Witherall, C., 31

World Trade Center attack, 36
Wroth, W., 239–40

Yaeger, T., 149

Zang, B., 175, 180
Zerubavel, E., 23, 32
Zwonitzer, D., 211–12

ABOUT THE AUTHORS

Dr. Sarah J. Noonan, an associate professor in the Leadership, Policy and Administration Department at the University of St. Thomas in Minneapolis, Minnesota, teaches doctoral and masters courses in leadership and organizational theory, intercultural communication, and issues and challenges in executive leadership. Noonan previously served as a superintendent and assistant superintendent of schools, director of teaching and learning, and state director of gifted education before receiving an appointment to associate professor at the University of St. Thomas in 2000 (sjnoonan@stthomas.edu).

Noonan has written *The Elements of Leadership: What You Should Know* (2003) to help novice leaders understand theories of leadership and their practical application to education and business environments. Responsible for the superintendent licensure program as well as doctoral teaching and advising, Dr. Noonan draws from her 30+ years of teaching and administrative experience in rural and urban K–12 school systems to prepare future leaders. She also serves as a consultant in leadership and professional development, human resource management, team building, intercultural communication, and culturally sensitive pedagogy.

Noonan earned a Bachelor of Arts from the University of Minnesota, a Master of Art in Teaching and Education Specialist degree in Administration from the University of St. Thomas, and Doctor of Education in Educational Leadership from the University of Wyoming.

Dr. Thomas L. Fish, an associate professor in the Leadership, Policy and Administration Department at the University of St. Thomas in Minneapolis, Minnesota, for 35 years, teaches masters and doctoral courses in higher-education administration, leadership and organizational theory, and survey research. Named as a charter member of the National Community Education Hall of Fame, Fish also served as past president of the Minnesota and National Community Education Association. Fish earned a Bachelor of Science degree from Lock Haven University, a Master of Education from the University of Delaware, and a Doctor of Education from Western Michigan University.